THE NONPROFIT DILEMMA

THE NONPROFIT DILEMMA

Insights & Strategies for
Purpose-Driven Leaders

DC Armijo

MILFORD BOOKS

Credits & Contact Information
Published by Milford Books LLC (milfordbooks.com).

Cover design: James Jones
Interior design: Phillip Gessert
Editing: Sarah Busby, Lisa MacDonald
Indexing: Sandy Blood

For inquiries, please visit: http://nonprofitdilemma.com

Names:	Armijo, D. C., author.
Title:	The nonprofit dilemma : insights and strategies for purpose-driven leaders / DC Armijo.
Description:	[Milford, Michigan] : Milford Books LLC, [2024]	Includes bibliographical references and index.
Identifiers:	ISBN: 979-8-9898584-0-8 (trade paperback)	979-8-9898584-2-2 (hardcover)	979-8-9898584-1-5 (kindle)	979-8-9898584-3-9 (ebook)	979-8-9898584-4-6 (audiobook)	LCCN: 2024901646
Subjects:	LCSH: Nonprofit organizations--Management.	Nonprofit organizations--Finance.	Charities--Management.	Associations, institutions, etc.--Management.	Leadership.	BISAC: BUSINESS & ECONOMICS / Nonprofit Organizations & Charities / Management & Leadership.
Classification:	LCC: HD62.6 .A76 2024	DDC: 658/.048--dc23

To the many people working in nonprofit organizations who have dedicated their lives to meaningful work. Thank you for all the amazing things you do. You are an inspiration to me and many others who are driven to make the world a better place.

To the love of my life, Shannon, and our phenomenal daughter, Norah. Thank you both for tolerating me. You make *my* world a better place.

We live in a world in which we need to share responsibility. It's easy to say, "It's not my child, not my community, not my world, not my problem." Then there are those who see the need and respond. I consider those people my heroes.

—*Beloved educator and television host* FRED ROGERS

TABLE OF
CONTENTS

FOREWORD

I ABSOLUTELY ADORE the title DC Armijo selected for this book. The word "dilemma" is so freeing. It allows us to be transparent with the truth that nonprofit organizations are fraught with perplexing situations and hard choices. Amazingly, at the same time, DC takes us on a journey of learning and skill-building that leaves us thinking, "I can do this."

I could have really used this book a decade ago when I first entered the nonprofit space as a senior leader. Before that, I spent my career in governmental spaces: local government, state government, and public universities, which are quasi-governmental. While government and nonprofits strive to benefit the public, governmental spaces are distinct in that they are much more hierarchical, more regulated, and, in many ways, more political. The rules are ever-present, and the cultures are inarguably different from those desired in nonprofits. In these governmental spaces, I first learned how to lead. And many of those skills did not easily transfer to the nonprofit space.

I have a clear memory of sitting in my new office that had been refreshed to my liking (they had let me choose my own carpet, wallpaper, and furniture! No standard issue gray filing cabinets? I was definitely not in Kansas anymore). I sat idly, resisting the temptation to twiddle my thumbs or drum my fingers, as I wrestled with the thought, "What exactly *is* my job?!" *The Nonprofit Dilemma* guides leaders at various stages of leadership on a journeyed response to that very question.

Nonprofit organizations are vital to addressing community needs, promoting civic engagement, and advancing social justice. However, nonprofit leaders face complex and interrelated challenges due to limited resources, accountability pressures, diversity gaps, and power dynamics. How can nonprofit leaders navigate these challenges while leading with equity, integrity, and effectiveness? The book you are holding offers new insights into these challenges and the dilemmas we leaders seek to untangle.

Leadership, especially in the nonprofit space, is about people, purpose, power, and passion. As a relationship-driven leader, I have found that success in any nonprofit rests on the foundation of its people. Those people are inspired by a connection to the organization's purpose. Centering purpose and building purpose-driven teams have been essential to my career success. Power for good and power for ill both exist inside organizations. Effective leadership requires understanding and accepting both the affirming and problematic roles that power plays in your organization. Lastly, passion is the fuel that keeps leaders moving forward. On my most weary days, my passion for the purpose of my nonprofit keeps me going. Just as it is easy to embrace someone for whom we feel passion, we must embrace our roles and organizations to lead successfully.

With a fresh take on nonprofit leadership, *The Nonprofit Dilemma* provides actionable advice for anyone looking to improve their leadership game. It explores many people, purpose, power, and passion topics; and provides a practical framework for effective leadership. As an equity leader, I also believe it is subtly and directly grounded in the principles of equity, inclusion, and social change; values that I hold dear.

Whether you are a new or experienced nonprofit leader, this book will expand your leadership skills, enhance your organizational effectiveness, and advance your social impact. *The Nonprofit Dilemma* is more than just a book; it is a call to action. In this regard, DC is a kindred spirit seeking to catalyze change. This book affirms our shared desires and values. Interestingly, these are only strengthened across our differences; differences in our careers, genders, races/ethnicities, and cultures—the beautiful tapestry of who we are and what each of us brings to our perspective on leadership.

DC and I invite you to join this community of practice—a movement of leaders committed to creating a more equitable and just world. I hope this book inspires you, challenges you, and supports you on your leadership journey.

RENÉE BRANCH CANADY, PhD MPA

Author of *Room at the Table: A Leader's Guide to Advancing Health Equity and Justice*

CEO, Michigan Public Health Institute

PREFACE

As I write this, I am sitting in the gazebo in our backyard amid the buzzing of bumblebees in the morning sun. After a long career working in the nonprofit sector, I decided to take a few years off to write down all I have learned about nonprofit leadership (including the lessons I learned the hard way). I didn't come to this decision out of vanity, to launch a consulting business, or even with a desire for the book to be a profitable venture (few are). I started this journey with one simple aim—to help *you* succeed as a nonprofit leader.

Maximizing mission impact while being a good organizational steward isn't easy. Nonprofit leaders are motivated by personal meaning in their work and are deeply committed to their organization's mission and its health. They must continually strike the right balance between these competing aims. The nonprofit sector needs leaders who strategically use their limited resources to create organizational leverage. Passionate leaders who thoughtfully motivate their employees and effectively partner to advance their organization and its cause. Leaders who are catalysts for change. *Better leaders build better nonprofits.* And this offers a brighter future for us all: one that is kinder, healthier, more equitable, and more sustainable.

Helping nonprofit leaders and their organizations flourish is about the only thing that could inspire me to write a "business" book. While I've read dozens of them over my career, I find the genre tedious. They promise paradigm-shifting insights, novel management techniques, and business acumen targeting every topic imaginable. The payoff seldom lives up to the hype. Even the best books have been only superficially helpful in solving the challenges I faced as a nonprofit leader. I've done my best to make this one different.

—DC Armijo, in a quaint Michigan village

INTRODUCTION

I N THE EARLY 1900s, the following advertisement may have appeared in the *London Times*:

Men wanted for hazardous journey. Small wages. Bitter cold. Long months of complete darkness. Constant danger. Safe return doubtful. Honour and recognition in case of success.

Ernest Shackleton had reportedly posted it to recruit a crew for his 1914 exploration of Antarctica. Historians have struggled to verify this account and have yet to prove that the ad ever appeared in the newspapers of the day. The anecdote may be nothing more than the fanciful creation of an early Shackleton biographer. Even so, the blunt, crisp description of the dire odds facing the recruits remains captivating over one hundred years later.

Why would someone sign up for such a perilous job? Low self-esteem? ("Can't do anything else; I might as well do this.") Perhaps it was desperation to get away by any means necessary, especially with the added allure of adventure. Or maybe it was the chance to be part of something important? Even if a biographer created the ad *after* the harrowing journey, I imagine motivations varied widely among the men boarding that ship in 1914.

Few nonprofit organizations engage in activities as hazardous as Shackleton's. However, most nonprofits have missions that require shared sacrifice, and many face discouraging odds of success. Also discouraging are the "small wages" common in the sector. Yet, many nonprofits offer the chance to be part of something meaningful, and the possibility of "honour and recognition in case of success." Wouldn't you want to be part of the team that solved one of society's toughest challenges? Whatever your motivation for wanting to be a nonprofit leader, recognize that it will be challenging, will require sacrifice—and, at times, it will be up to you to inspire your colleagues to soldier on.

Wherever you are on your leadership journey, this book was written with the express intent to provide the ideas, tools, and advice needed to help you succeed. I am by no means an expert in *all* of the challenges that confront nonprofit organizations; however, I have spent much of the past thirty years contemplating and working on many of them.

I grew up in a household marked by chronic illness and poverty.[1] Clothing, meals, healthcare, and holidays were provided by nonprofits, government programs, and Good Samaritans. By the age of sixteen, I was living on my own and working nights as a cook in an all-night diner. By twenty-four, however, I had earned two degrees, including a master's degree from the top hospital administration program in the country. Education was my ladder out of poverty, and I was eager to use what I had learned to help others. I spent the next twenty-five years working for nonprofit organizations and have had a meaningful and impactful career. In those organizations, I've served a variety of executive and governance functions including fellow, director, SVP, COO, CEO, trustee, and board member.

I started this writing journey because I felt I must have learned valuable lessons in the nearly fifty thousand hours I've spent working, partnering, and volunteering with nonprofits—lessons that strengthened my skills as a nonprofit leader. In my desire to create something of value for you, I spent the last two years contemplating which leadership issues are most prevalent across the nonprofit sector. I also sought the input of many nonprofit leaders I had worked with.

Books meant to advance organizational leadership generally fall into two groups. First, there are academic books written by university professors that are heavily researched, highly theoretical, and usually difficult to read and apply. This literature offers valuable ideas, grand designs, and novel strategies. However, much of it is delivered in a form that will chal-

---

1. My dad was unable to work during most of my childhood. He was severely ill with complications from Crohn's disease, was often hospitalized, and later died of leukemia. My mom, a licensed practical nurse, raised my brother and me, prayed for and tended to my father as he recovered from more surgeries than anyone should endure, and worked at the local hospital when she could.

lenge the attention span of the busy practitioner (i.e., someone who works in the nonprofit sector rather than studies it).

There are also leadership-focused business books written by consultants or retired executives that attempt to deliver practical advice about a specific topic (e.g., strategic planning, finance, how to talk with your employees, how to lead meetings, etc.). They are usually written in more accessible language, with some offering provocative ideas that start management fads (e.g., *Radical Candor*, *Good to Great*, *The Seven Habits of Highly Effective People*, *The Five Dysfunctions of a Team*, etc.). These books employ simple and efficient principles and mental shortcuts to common problems, promising pragmatic value to the reader. They are usually also chock-full of case studies meant to entertain and convince us of the accuracy of the author's worldview and the utility of their ideas and methods.

This book falls into the latter category, offering practical advice to help those working in nonprofit organizations. While it offers plenty of ideas, tools, and methods, I skipped the case studies in favor of providing useful advice across a broader range of issues. I trust the reader to judge the value of the advice based on their own knowledge, experience, and gut instincts. While the material is well-researched, I've resisted the urge to treat topics academically. I wanted to keep the lessons of *The Nonprofit Dilemma* accessible, although complex topics are sometimes nuanced and, well, complex.

As the title suggests, this book introduces the idea that nonprofit leaders face a recurring dilemma. Although we'll explore strategies to navigate many leadership dilemmas, there is one challenge common to all nonprofits that I'm referring to here. It's something that arises because of their very nature. That challenge is the relative priority between two competing aims: executing the organization's mission and improving its financial health. These aims are intertwined, of course, because financial health is necessary to produce mission impact in the future. While not always mutually exclusive, most leadership decisions favor one objective over the other. This dilemma is present regardless of industry or mission and is in the background of nearly every decision a nonprofit leader makes.

For example, spending to deliver impact *today* negatively impacts financial health, but saving to ensure the organization survives to deliver impact *tomorrow* reduces what you can accomplish today. This is what makes nonprofit management uniquely challenging. Unlike for-profit organizations, where financial health is *always* the goal, in nonprofit organizations, leaders are confronted with the same dilemma every day—which aim to prioritize? While this book delivers many practical management techniques, I hope it also fosters a candid discussion about this dilemma and its many implications.

Of course, the ultimate goal of any nonprofit should be impact. But achieving that goal over time (and at scale) requires financial health. When we prioritize financial health, what we are implicitly saying is that we value the organization's future potential over the impact it can make today. The trade-offs and sacrifices implicit in these kinds of decisions can be complex and convoluted. So, throughout this book, we'll examine them with the goal of making you the best steward of the nonprofit organization you love and lead (or hope to lead one day).

Who should read *The Nonprofit Dilemma?*

This book is written for three audiences: aspiring nonprofit leaders, nonprofit executives and managers, and nonprofit board members. Each chapter begins with a section centered on the needs of *Future Leaders*, followed by one targeting the needs of current *Executives and Managers*, and ends with a section focused on helping nonprofit *Trustees.*[2] If you are a student or work in a nonprofit and aren't yet a manager or executive, then you are a future leader! Thank you for choosing a purpose-driven career (one motivated by personal meaning and commitment to a cause). I hope the many insights and strategies in this book help you achieve your career aspirations.

Constructing the book in this way helps ensure that the content is tailored to the needs of each audience. It also helps me, as an author, to be concise and worry less about the experience and knowledge each reader is likely to have or what challenges they are likely to encounter. Below, I've

---

2. While not legally accurate, I use the terms trustee, board member, and director interchangeably. In all cases, I am referring to a person serving on a nonprofit board who is charged with providing oversight of the organization's operations, making strategic decisions like selecting a CEO, and ensuring that the nonprofit complies with legal and ethical standards. In some cases, this person may also hold fiduciary duties related to a charitable trust, foundation, or endowment.

outlined what I see as the defining attributes of each of these audiences. Not every attribute will apply to you, but I'll share them for context.

Audience	*Defining Attributes*
Future Leaders	• Students and those who are early–to–mid career • Still have directional career choices • Likely passionate and hopeful about the future • Naïve about some aspects of leadership • Hungry for knowledge, coaching, and development
Executives & Managers	• Mid–to–late career • Focused on finances, strategy, or operations • Decisive and confident (perhaps overly so) • Busy and pragmatic (looking for solutions) • Potentially jaded about future possibilities
Trustees	• Late career • Governance and mission focused • May not have had the experience of being a nonprofit executive • May feel ill-equipped for some topics and thus reliant on the perspectives of the CEO or other board members • Have a higher tolerance for theoretical and abstract conversation

Table 0.1 Defining Attributes of Reader Segments

View each section heading as a signal that the content will be particularly relevant for that audience. That said, you won't get much out of this book if you just read the sections that target your current role. The sections for *Executives and Managers* and those for *Trustees* build upon the concepts introduced in the *Future Leaders* sections. There are benefits to this approach. For example, many trustees have not served as nonprofit executives. Developing a deeper understanding of the strategic and operational challenges facing executives will help these trustees provide more valuable input to their executive team. Another benefit is specific to aspiring leaders. The sections focused on managers, executives, and trustees provide future leaders with a sneak peek into the likely challenges, considerations, and motivations of the current leaders in their organization.

By allowing the reader to explore the concerns and perspectives of different roles, I hope to help these different audiences better understand and communicate with one another. Improving cross-functional communication is essential to creating a more efficient and effective nonprofit sector. It's also important to remember that roles change. Today you may be an aspiring nonprofit employee, but next year you may find yourself in a boardroom presenting to your trustees. Or perhaps you've just become a manager. Something in a *Future Leaders* section may help you better connect with and mentor the team that now reports to you.

Two other audiences may find value in these pages. One is employees of nonprofits without current management duties or aspirations. These are usually technically focused employees most interested in honing their skills and delivering the unique value they provide. Even if you have no desire for a formal leadership position, these pages have concepts and ideas that will help you better translate the organization's strategy into success and improve your value to the team. The other audience for *The Nonprofit Dilemma* is philanthropic or government leaders who partner extensively with nonprofits and are looking for ways to help them be more efficient and effective.

It's been my experience that well-meaning philanthropic or government funders can (at times) constrain the solutions to tough problems. I'm talking about things like overly specific funder priorities, favoritism for individual organizations or certain thought leaders, or restrictive beliefs (sometimes ill-informed) about what works and what doesn't. Instead of encouraging creativity and innovation in the nonprofit sector, these constraints have the unfortunate effect of limiting progress on the very things funders care about. Perhaps the ideas in this book will help some in the funder community think differently about their relationship with nonprofits.

If you're reading *The Nonprofit Dilemma* after a long career, some of what is offered may seem self-evident—things you learned long ago. However, future leaders may not yet have learned these simple truths, and we should do all we can to equip them for success. There is real value in describing concepts and frameworks more clearly—even those we *believe* are widely understood. This book's foundational content may be helpful when explaining your own decision-making or mentoring promising employees.

Identifying leadership challenges

This book is full of ideas, lessons learned, and opinions. You can expect to learn why everything starts with clarity of purpose; how there's tension between mission and fiduciary goals in the background of most decisions; and why the best business development strategies create leverage.

You can also expect advice and tools to help with a myriad of leadership challenges:

- Selecting the right strategy and executing it.
- How to build a purpose-driven team and empower them to be successful.
- Where to focus your team, your board, and your own energies.
- The best ways to tackle common governance issues.
- How to write winning grants and attract donors.
- What to focus on when measuring and communicating impact.
- Finding and embracing values that differentiate your nonprofit.
- How to deal with the inevitable "brilliant jerk" (and the not-so-brilliant ones).
- How to build effective partnerships and motivate your collaborators.

In my eagerness to deliver value to you, I'll relay my opinion on lots of issues in a frank manner. On some particularly complicated topics, I may argue both sides of an issue and leave it to you to decide which is most compelling. But in most cases, I'll take a position. At times, you may disagree with my perspective. That's fine. My carefully considered opinion may very well be wrong. As a leader (or aspiring one), you should also remain open to the possibility that your opinion might be due for a refresh.

Our experiences, belief systems, and biases shape our attitudes and opinions. How strongly we cling to those in the face of evidence that clashes with them is a direct reflection of our leadership potential. As leaders of purpose-driven organizations, we must have the courage to periodically (and honestly) assess our convictions and the soundness of their logic. We all know it takes confidence to express an opinion. But "kicking the tires" on that opinion and seeking to better understand opposing viewpoints is a fundamental aspect of leadership maturity. It takes *introspection* to recognize confirmation bias (the tendency to favor information that confirms your existing beliefs). It takes *humility* to question what you "know" to be true. And it takes real *courage* to actively seek out evidence and perspectives that might lead you to different conclusions. My job as an author is relatively easy—to share what I have learned and my perspective on the challenges facing nonprofit leaders. Your job as a leader—deciding on and owning a particular course of action—is much more difficult.

Throughout *The Nonprofit Dilemma*, I'll ask questions to encourage introspection. While writing, I imagined discussing these topics with a trusted colleague. I've always found that asking questions was a useful way to encourage introspection and foster a mutual understanding. As we embark on this journey together, let me start by asking some big picture questions:

- *What is preventing you from changing the world for the better? Is it a person? Is it resources? Is it fear?*
- *Maybe you feel you are already changing the world for the better. If so, what's preventing you from doing more?*
- *Is there some aspect of your organization that is distracting or constraining you? Are you struggling to attract the right talent? Or motivate the right stakeholder?*

Whatever the barrier is, be honest with yourself about it. As you read this book, look for ideas and tools that will help you overcome that barrier. I'm rooting for you.

I hope you enjoy *The Nonprofit Dilemma* and that it ignites (or reignites) your passion for nonprofit leadership. I also hope it comes in handy on your journey to better the world (or at least your little corner of it)!

1
A MEANS TO AN END

Money often costs too much.

—Essayist Ralph Waldo Emerson

My first job after grad school was in a mid-sized community hospital. As an administrative fellow, I reported directly to the CEO (Tom) and shadowed him. This meant I tagged along to meetings of the medical staff committee, meetings to review hospital finances, meetings to review quality improvement initiatives, meetings with the vice president of medical affairs (whom I usually found inspiring), meetings with subsidiary boards, and the hospital board, and the health system board—basically, a *lot* of meetings.

At the end of each week, Tom would sit with me in his cherry-paneled office, and we would discuss what I'd learned, the progress I'd made on my various projects, and what challenges he was facing. He was a good man, and I recall feeling that perhaps our talks were therapeutic for him. He was under tremendous stress at the time, and it was clear to me that he cared deeply about the organization and its commitment to the city and its residents.

The most important thing Tom taught me was how vital it is for leaders to actively demonstrate that they recognize and value the contributions of the organization's employees. He did this in many ways. One simple technique has always stayed with me. At the end of each day, he would do a random check-in on a hospital department. He would ask how things were going, what challenges they faced, and what could be improved. Before leaving, he would always thank whoever he was talking to for their service to the organization, the care they showed patients, or their dedication to the community.

I looked forward to these end-of-day walkabouts. The conversations were genuine and enlightening, and I usually came away with tasks that directly responded to organizational needs. My admiration for him grew, and I felt empowered to help make the hospital work better for its employees and community.

Flash forward twenty years. I was working as the COO of a large nonprofit government contractor. At the end of most days, I made a point of wandering one of the floors of the building to see who was still working. Sometimes, I found no one (executives tend to work long days). But usually, I would encounter someone quietly working at their computer. I would chat briefly with them about whatever they were working on, ask them if they needed anything, thank them for their dedication, and encourage them to head home soon.

This nonprofit did lots of amazing things. One project I was particularly proud of was focused on improving oral health among poor and vulnerable children. We trained pediatricians to do oral health screenings and deliver preventative care, built software to support dental referrals, conducted dental health fairs, and created mechanisms to get oral health supplies in the hands of new moms, teachers, and others who needed them.

After a particularly challenging day, on one of my walkabouts, I had a conversation with an older software developer who was a bit rough around the edges. It had been dark outside for a while, so I didn't want to make his day even longer, but I was curious. Based on the little I knew about him and his role, I wrongly assumed this was more of a job than a passion for him. I assumed he was working late because of some technical issue or a software release deadline that he was up against.

As we talked, his computer screensaver kicked in. The pictures that flashed across his screen were of smiling children holding bags of oral health supplies, kids reclined in chairs being screened for cavities, and families embracing young dentists in disposable gowns. I recognized the images immediately from a recent event we did for Syrian refugees who were relocated to the U.S. I asked about the images, and he replied that they were for inspiration. He said he could easily get a job that paid more but wouldn't find it as fulfilling. He enjoyed working with the team on something so important. He felt like his work really mattered, and that's why he was here working late.

I thanked him for his dedication and walked back to my office. I could barely hold back the tears until I got to the privacy of my office. I was embarrassed that I had misjudged his motivations, and I was moved by his humble dedication to our work. It had been a long day. Though, at the end of it, I was reminded that the entire team was doing something *meaningful*. Something we were *all* dedicated to and proud of.

L EADING A NONPROFIT organization can be very gratifying. It can also be stressful and overwhelming. I believe nonprofit leadership is more challenging than leading a for-profit company of similar size and complexity. The primary reason for this is differences in the clarity of organizational objectives. For-profit organizations are easier to lead simply because the profit motive should ultimately guide *all* decisions. The organization *exists* to make a profit. Regardless of the firm's market or statements about vision and purpose, every decision in a for-profit can be (and usually is) assessed through the lens of whether it will increase or decrease profits. This is not true for nonprofits.

The nonprofit organization exists for some reason *other* than making a profit. A nonprofit leader doesn't have the luxury of boiling every decision down to whether something would positively or negatively impact future profits. Nonprofit leaders face two equally important objectives: a fiduciary responsibility[1] to ensure that decisions advance the organization's financial health, and a mission responsibility to maximize the organization's impact (the reason the organization *exists*). Since these goals can conflict with one another (maximizing impact usually costs money), nonprofit leaders regularly face the dilemma of which goal to prioritize in any decision. That is what the title of this book refers to—that is *the nonprofit dilemma*.

Of course, entrepreneurs are sometimes intrinsically motivated to "make a difference" and for-profit firms also have missions, many of which are compelling. Their existence, however, is predicated on the primary goal of earning a profit. When conflict arises between mission and profit, which do you think usually comes out on top? Even when mission appears to be prioritized, the consideration of things like public relations and brand equity on future profits tends to be the justification. In the long

---

1. A fiduciary is someone who is legally and ethically bound to act in the best interests of another person or organization.

run, giving the impression that you are putting mission over profit ends up being a pretty good profit-maximizing strategy.

Such clarity is lacking in nonprofit organizations. The tension between mission and fiduciary objectives is ever-present and neither should be consistently favored. Balancing these objectives presents a dilemma for even the most capable nonprofit leader. To make matters worse, the aims aren't always easily separated from one another. For example, imagine a nonprofit leader facing the decision to reduce headcount. On the surface, what that leader is trading is mission impact *today* in return for financial health and the possibility of greater impact *tomorrow*. However, when making cuts isn't really a question of organizational survival, the waters get a little murkier. How about when a reduction in workforce is really to do with meeting an arbitrary financial target agreed to with the board? Or when it's based on an executive's own belief that the organization has grown inefficient? Or when a nonprofit's new priorities demand a different mix of labor? Each rationale carries its own distinct set of mission and fiduciary implications. Choosing the best course of action comes down to weighing the impact on both financial health and mission.

Another example is deciding how much time and resources to divert from mission pursuits to development or fundraising activities. Pulling resources from the mission to invest in financial health may improve your ability to carry out your mission in the future. It is easy to imagine how winning the support of a significant funder could expand or even alter your mission. Delaying mission gratification today to focus on financial health is usually done with the intent of ultimately advancing the organization's mission. Nevertheless, it really depends on what you do with that improved financial health in the future, doesn't it?

We will discuss many challenges confronting nonprofit leaders, but the foundational dilemma of choosing between financial health or mission advancement underpins most of them. To help you recall the specifics of the "nonprofit dilemma," at times, I'll refer to it as the fiduciary/impact dilemma. Figure 1.1 provides some examples of the interplay between decisions that advance mission impact and those that advance financial health.

COSTS FINANCIAL HEALTH ADVANCES MISSION	ADVANCES FINANCIAL HEALTH & MISSION
Examples: • Spending resources to *effectively* carry out mission-aligned activities • Adding leadership capacity to plan for the future • Developing workforce • Investing in strategic planning	Examples: • Pursuing and winning mission-aligned grants • Partnering with others that can more efficiently carry out mission-aligned activities • Reducing waste by embracing mission priorities and focusing organization
COSTS FINANCIAL HEALTH DOES NOT ADVANCE MISSION	IMPROVES FINANCIAL HEALTH DOES NOT ADVANCE MISSION
Examples: • Spending on ineffective projects or efforts that aren't mission-aligned • Hiring or retaining ineffective or unnecessary team members • Paying excessive compensation (e.g., board, executive, manager)	Examples: • Rightsizing workforce and other cost-cutting initiatives • Investing organizational resources (instead of using them) • Generic fundraising or pursuing revenue for efforts that are not mission-aligned

Advancing Mission Impact →

Advancing Financial Health →

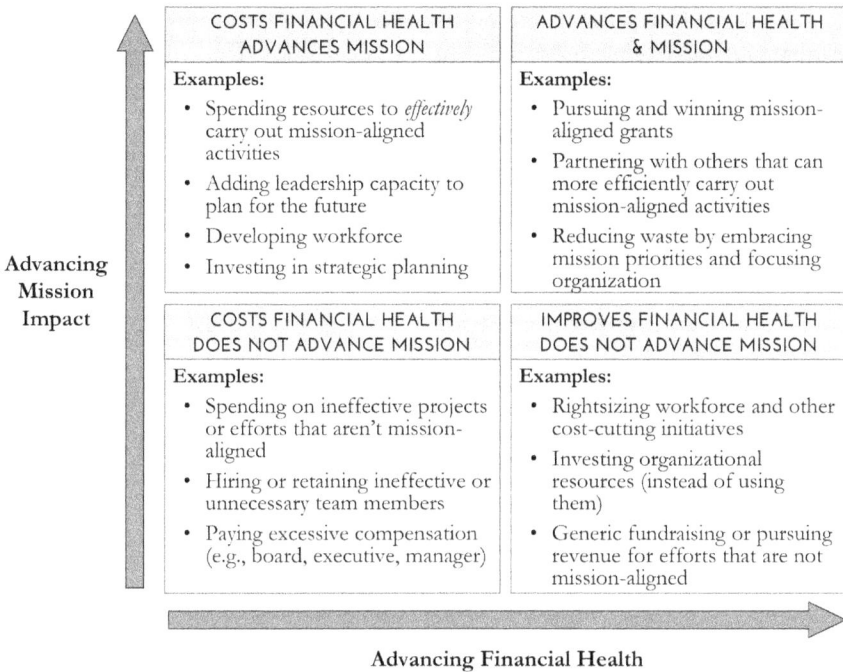

Figure 1.1 Mission Impact vs. Financial Health

Only a handful of decisions advance both an organization's mission impact *and* its financial health simultaneously. Partnering with other nonprofits is a notable example of a decision that offers the promise of advancing both (we'll explore how in Chapter 9). Whether done explicitly or implicitly, most decisions you make as a nonprofit leader further one objective or the other. Determining and maintaining the right balance for your organization is the key to being a successful nonprofit leader.

The nonprofit starvation cycle

Closely related to the fiduciary/impact dilemma is the "nonprofit starvation cycle." The starvation cycle is common among small nonprofits that face multiple challenges raising funds and using them effectively to achieve their mission. They rely on donations and grants to fund all aspects of their operations. As a result, they have limited capacity to execute their mission over longer time horizons. The unpredictable nature of their funding constrains their ability to adequately plan for the future.

Like everyone else, these nonprofits face pressure to show tangible results, but they get stuck treading water to keep from drowning. Since funders are more interested in funding mission activities than organizational development, these nonprofits can end up in a cycle of constantly seeking additional funding just to stay afloat. When your nonprofit spends most of its time and resources looking for more resources, you have a serious problem.

Your job as a purpose-driven leader is to maximize your organization's mission impact now *and* in the future. To do so, you must balance mission and fiduciary objectives that, at times, can conflict with one another. Effectively doing that requires you to be *explicit* about trade-offs, objectives, and appropriateness. In a nonprofit organization, money is truly just a means to an end. It is something that should not hold value beyond its usefulness in advancing your organization's mission now and in the future. How far into the future is a matter of debate.

FUTURE LEADERS

Being a nonprofit leader can be tremendously rewarding. We derive a sense of purpose from our work that, for many of us, guides our entire careers. Whether you are delivering care to patients in a nonprofit hospital, providing access to clean water in an indigenous community, or sitting behind a computer shaping public opinion about climate change, part of your self-identity is wrapped up in your work and its impact.

But nonprofit leadership can also be challenging. Nonprofits are not only difficult organizations to lead; they can also be tough places to work. Resource constraints, political infighting, competition for talent, and long hours are commonplace. As someone with leadership aspirations, you must embrace your drive for a purpose-driven career to see beyond those challenges. Your passion for meaningful work may have been sparked by life experiences, a book you read, or a documentary you saw. Your empathy for others may have come from personal suffering, or your drive may be based on religious beliefs. Whatever got you to this place matters only to the extent it continues to feed your drive for purpose and impact. That drive is what gives you the energy, resilience, and optimism necessary to be a successful nonprofit leader.

An overview of the nonprofit sector

The nonprofit sector is large and extremely broad. A summary of the different types of nonprofits in the U.S. and the rules and regulations that define them can be found in an Appendix at the end of this book. There are over one and a half million nonprofits in the U.S. and the sector contributes a little under 6% of U.S. gross domestic product (GDP).[2] Nonprofits employ over 10% of the total private (i.e., non-governmental) workforce with over 80% of the jobs concentrated among healthcare, education, and social assistance nonprofits.[3] Interestingly, while there are far fewer nonprofits in Canada, the sector makes up a larger share of the Canadian economy, comprising around 8.5% of GDP and over 11% of the private workforce.[4]

Small organizations dominate the nonprofit sector in the U.S. with 92% of nonprofits having an annual budget of less than $1 million.[5] Many of these organizations struggle to stay afloat, and the dilemma of whether to prioritize mission impact or financial health is a daily reality. Even so, remarkable things are accomplished by the sheer willpower of dedicated employees in these small, resource-constrained organizations.

There are nonprofits working to provide access to clean and safe water to every person on the planet. There are organizations that provide yoga classes for prison inmates, and there are those seeking to end world hunger by giving impoverished families goats, sheep, cows, and chickens. There are even nonprofit organizations focused on administering college entrance exams. There are over one hundred thousand nonprofits focused on health research or healthcare delivery;[6] over sixty thousand trade and professional associations;[7] around four thousand nonprofit chambers of

2. NCCS Project Team. "The Nonprofit Sector in Brief 2019." National Center for Charitable Statistics. June 2020. https://nccs.urban.org/publication/nonprofit-sector-brief-2019#the-nonprofit-sector-in-brief-2019

3. Salaman, L.M. & Newhouse, Chelsea L. (Jan 2019). "The 2019 Nonprofit Employment Report." Nonprofit Economic Data Bulletin no. 47. Johns Hopkins Center for Civil Society Studies. http://ccss.jhu.edu/

4. Statistics Canada. Data available at https://www.statcan.gc.ca/eng/start

5. National Council of Nonprofits. Data available at https://www.councilofnonprofits.org/about-us

6. Candid.org. Data available at https://www.guidestar.org/NonprofitDirectory.aspx?cat=4

commerce;[8] over eighty-six thousand grant-making foundations, including around nine hundred community foundations;[9] and thousands more that support colleges, universities, churches, museums, and libraries. As you might imagine, authoring a book that delivers value to the leaders of such a broad range of organizations is a considerable challenge!

Not only is the nonprofit sector made up of organizations with little in common other than their nonprofit designation; the label itself is also misleading. A more appropriate name might be "non-owner organizations" as the primary difference between nonprofits and for-profits is that *all* nonprofits lack owners or shareholders. Because there are no owners, it is the responsibility of the nonprofit governance board to ensure the organization complies with the law and operates for the purposes outlined in the organization's governing documents. Another interesting fact that results from not having any owners is that nonprofit organizations cannot be sold. They can be merged, or operations can be wound down and assets distributed to another nonprofit, but they can't be sold.

Many nonprofit organizations do, in fact, generate a "profit" as a result of their activities (they may call it something else, but it's there). Those profits, though, must be reinvested into the organization or saved for the future on the organization's balance sheet. Without owners, there is no one to benefit from the profits except the mission itself. Throughout this book, I will use the term *purpose-driven organization* interchangeably with nonprofit. I find it a more meaningful designation because the organization exists for some purpose other than to make a profit. That is, all nonprofit organizations should be driven by their purpose.

Nonprofit missions range from the relatively simple (i.e., professional associations deliver value to members) to the highly complex missions of organizations trying to solve stubborn societal problems (e.g., to solve poverty and homelessness, reduce plastic waste in the ocean, or cure cancer). Nonprofit balance sheets also range from the weak and meager finances of small community organizations to the robust resources of

---

7. American Society of Association Executives. Data available at
   https://www.asaecenter.org/
8. Association of Chamber of Commerce Executives. Data available at
   https://secure.acce.org/pages/chambers/
9. Candid.org. Data available at http://data.foundationcenter.org/#/foundations/all/
   nationwide/total/list/2015

huge organizations like *United Way, Feeding America, St. Jude Children's Research Hospital,* and *The Salvation Army*. Even in organizations where balance sheet assets are in the billions, the fiduciary/impact dilemma is still present. Complex organizations come with complex questions.

- How much of those extensive assets should be deployed today?
- Are there upstream opportunities to deploy resources now that offer lasting impacts long into the future?
- How fleeting are the impacts that can be achieved?
- What is the likelihood that technological or scientific advancements will create new opportunities to deploy assets in more impactful ways in the future?
- What is the likelihood that the societal need will be greater in the future?
- What is the likelihood that someone else (like the government) will address the societal need?
- How does the current investment environment compare to the risks/returns of expending resources?

Spending resources is inherently riskier than saving and investing them for the future. This simple truth drives the behavior of many nonprofit executives and trustees. I felt compelled to write this book partly because the nonprofit sector needs more leaders who can better justify resource use. More capable leaders develop more compelling ideas, strategies, and teams. This instills confidence and strengthens the case for investment in mission impact *today*. Leaders that are particularly insightful and collaborative can build multi-organizational strategies that benefit from economies of scale, offering the potential to solve problems bigger than any one organization's reach. These more effective teams, led by more capable leaders, can dream bigger. Those big dreams inspire the workforce, the board, potential partners, and the funding community.

While a nonprofit leader's primary responsibility is to maximize the organization's impact now and in the future, we sometimes get distracted by secondary goals. These goals are things like becoming an employer of choice, dealing with internal competition, drafting employee newsletters, conducting competitive research, fighting legal battles, or any number of administrative duties. These pursuits are valuable to the extent that they further our primary aim, but there's a problem. Nonprofits tend to be short on leadership capacity. That scarcity of leadership talent means distractions can be costly. The opportunity cost is high when leaders engage in urgent but less important activities that someone else could have effectively accomplished.

The concept of "opportunity cost" is about scarcity and choice. There is a scarcity of leadership time available. When the choice is made to spend time on one thing, the result is to forgo spending time on something else. That lost opportunity to do something else is the opportunity cost. You've undoubtedly experienced this countless times in your life. When you were young, with a dollar in your hand, you felt the pain of opportunity cost when deciding whether to spend your scarce resources on candy or a toy. Last night, when you decided to stream that show, you missed the opportunity to spend that time reading this book or learning to bake (it's okay, you probably made the right decision). When you chose to marry someone, you gave up the opportunity to marry anyone else (well, not without a lot of hassle). You get the idea. Time is valuable and choices come with consequences.

Acting like a leader

If your nonprofit is short on leadership talent, and the opportunity cost associated with their time is fairly high, that's where you come in. Opportunities to contribute in new ways to advance the organization's financial health or mission impact are likely all around you. Offer to take some small thing off your manager's plate. Propose an idea to save money on supplies. Help a struggling coworker with their community outreach. Offer to lead an employee diversity, equity, and inclusion (DEI) committee. Help with the fundraising campaign or train the new intern so they'll be more productive. Offer to facilitate a process improvement brainstorming session over lunch. Conduct research online to identify potential partners or offer to proofread the membership newsletter. Whatever your role and organization, I am sure there are new ways for you to shine.

The people who ultimately become leaders usually *acted like leaders* long before they were given a formal title and new role. Don't worry about being recognized for going above and beyond; just stay at it. Every organization has some level of dysfunction. Ineffective managers and untapped potential are common. It may take a while to break through the noise, but if you believe the organization has potential, then challenge yourself to help lead it to greatness. Your contributions will eventually be noticed and appreciated. The mere fact that you're reading a book about nonprofit leadership bodes well for your future potential. You are already acting like a conscientious leader!

I am fond of using the term *self-directed* to describe people who organize their own work, show initiative, and demonstrate leadership traits like those mentioned above. To me, it signifies that a person needs minimal supervision and that they are resourceful, reliable, and a team player. Being self-directed means being the person who is always stretching to contribute the most value they can. No matter what role you are currently in, you should see yourself as a leader. Whether you're a board member, executive, project manager, or intern matters less than how you conduct yourself and inspire those around you. By seeking to better understand the challenges facing your organization and its mission, you are alerting others to your leadership potential. By starting out each day with purpose-driven intentions, you are building the self-discipline necessary to be an effective leader. By bringing out the best in your colleagues, you are declaring your intention to lead.

Something interesting and exciting happens when you begin contributing as a leader. You move from working *in* an organization to working *on* it. Regardless of your role, part of being a leader is caring about the health of the organization, its people, and its impact. That concern means that you start to look for ways to improve the organization and for ways to broaden your own impact on the organization. Whether you have a leadership title or not, when you begin working *on* your organization, you begin your journey as a leader.

Leadership Questions

1. *How self-directed are you in your work?*
2. *Are you inspired enough by your organization's potential to live up to your own?*

3. *What are the top fiduciary/impact challenges facing the nonprofit you work for? How can you raise awareness of these and help to address them?*

EXECUTIVES & MANAGERS

In some ways, the nonprofit dilemma is about whether an organization's leaders (i.e., you) value its impact more or less than the organization itself. Are you primarily interested in ensuring the organization positively impacts the world? Or are you more interested in ensuring it delivers value to its employees and exists far into the future? How concerned are you that the organization is financially healthy enough to provide stable employment and growth opportunities for your people? Or that it is healthy enough to provide an appropriate level of executive compensation for you and your leadership team? How concerned are you that the organization is living up to its potential and delivering on its mission *right now*?

This is a safe place for introspection. Responses will not be posted on the lunchroom wall for your employees to read or on the company's website for scrutiny by your peers, board chair, funders, and other stakeholders. Take a few minutes to honestly assess your feelings about the organization you work for and whether any aspect of the fiduciary/impact balance feels off.

Some may think that the fiduciary/impact dilemma is based on an inaccurate premise, a false dichotomy, or that my reasoning has been reductive. As an executive or manager, you probably have a fair amount of confidence in your abilities and worldview. There's nothing wrong with that. Confidence is essential to risk-taking, and risk-taking is essential to success. You are already in a leadership role, largely because of that confidence. What I am encouraging is introspection and an open-minded assessment of what drives the behaviors within your organization. I want to help you become a better leader. Because the better you are, the better the world is for all of us.

Let's explore the false dichotomy concern. In the Introduction, I framed the nonprofit dilemma as the relative priority of two *competing* objectives. For you to believe that representation is accurate, we first need to agree that the two most important objectives of any nonprofit are to: 1) deliver mission impact and, 2) protect the organization's health so that it may deliver impact long into the future. I suspect we agree on these points. Every nonprofit organization was created to serve a specific purpose or mission, and as a leader, you have a fiduciary responsibility to protect that organization's financial health. We also need to agree that these objectives are roughly equal in importance and often in competition with one another. It's that last bit about competition that may have you hung up. Surely, financial health is just the means to produce future mission impact, isn't it?

As a nonprofit leader, you've made decisions that don't really further either objective (let's call those mistakes or inefficient use of your time). You've also made decisions that benefit one objective or the other. And occasionally, you've lucked into making a decision that advances both objectives at the same time. An example of this is pursuing and winning a large grant that is tightly aligned with your mission. However, not all mission-aligned grants contribute to financial health. Grantees actually end up subsidizing lots of grants because the grantor doesn't fully cover the cost of the activity. When your overhead costs are higher than the grantor's cap on such costs, you are partially supporting the activity. In that case, winning the grant advances mission impact but also reduces the nonprofit's financial health to some degree. We'll dig more into this topic later.

Another aspect of the fiduciary/impact dilemma we haven't yet touched on is when tension arises between the organization's mission and the objectives of funders or other stakeholders. For example, a policy-focused nonprofit may refrain from publishing certain results in case they offend funders, politicians, or other stakeholders (and could negatively impact future funding). Another example would be accepting resources from a funder that creates the appearance of a conflict of interest, or from a funder who unduly influences the work. These and other examples underscore the complexity of the fiduciary/impact dilemma. At times, every nonprofit executive is faced with judgment calls that reveal the strength of their financial and mission convictions. Making the right call for your organization is about weighing competing risks, seeking clarity of mission, and acting with integrity.

Financial health can be the means to produce future mission impact, but it can also be an excuse for inaction. Some nonprofits continue to prioritize financial health long beyond the levels necessary to guarantee survival many decades into the future. Forgoing mission impact today for the potential of mission impact in the future raises several questions.

- Do you believe the problem you are focused on is growing in complexity or urgency?
- Is your conservatism based on a concern you have about the merits of the current team or the quality of their ideas?
- Will future leaders of your organization expend more resources on the mission, or will they also be inclined to conservatively save for the future?

Prioritizing long-term financial health over mission impact today is considered a safe bet by many nonprofit executives and boards. However, the reality is they are just trading one set of risks for another. We are all familiar with the phrase, "You have to spend money to make money." In nonprofits, this virtuous cycle is tied to your impact story. Spending money to accelerate mission achievement improves your impact story, and *that* improves your nonprofit's attractiveness to funders. The nonprofit phrase to remember is, "More impact attracts more funding."

You're probably already keenly aware of the ever-present tension between mission and fiduciary objectives. We will explore the ways in which your actions can be more consistent with the needs of your organization. My goal is to ensure that your actions don't ebb and flow without clear evidence of forethought. I want you to know which fiduciary or impact objective you are implicitly prioritizing in every decision you make.

Before trying to negotiate a salary increase based on the argument that "leading a nonprofit is more challenging than leading a for-profit," consider *why* you work in the nonprofit sector. Was it a conscious choice or something that just happened?

Leadership Questions

1. *Does the organization's mission bring fulfillment and purpose to your life? How meaningful is that to you?*

24   A MEANS TO AN END

2. *Are the leaders in the organization (including you) capable of advancing its financial health and accomplishing its mission? Where are the weak spots?*
3. *What will be your legacy as a nonprofit leader?*

TRUSTEES

In the Preface, I stated that *better leaders build better nonprofits.* The need for better leaders in the nonprofit sector includes trustees.

Today's nonprofit organizations are rife with challenges, many stemming from the tension between mission and fiduciary objectives. Some nonprofits suffer from poor executive leadership, others from well-meaning but ill-equipped boards. Many nonprofits struggle with employees who are engaged with the mission but believe the organization's leadership is misguided. These employees never fully embrace strategic direction. The fiduciary/impact dilemma presents itself in ways large and small across all organizations in the sector. The boards, executives, and managers in these organizations need to better equip themselves to handle these issues with confidence and transparency. This book will help you do just that.

The dilemma that faces trustees is real, persistent, and not always obvious. Sometimes nonprofit executives (and, yes, even trustees) lose sight of the fact that money is just a means to an end for nonprofits. Financial health shouldn't really hold much value beyond its usefulness in achieving our aim—maximizing the organization's mission impact now and in the future.

Early in my career, I worked for a nonprofit Catholic health system. The nuns were partial to the saying, "No margin, no mission!" as a justification for decisions that prioritized fiduciary objectives over mission ones. I've heard this phrase repeated at many nonprofit board meetings in different organizations over the years. It is shorthand for the idea that nonprofit leaders must be good stewards of an organization's resources so that it will continue to exist and provide mission benefits in the future. Said another way, if a hospital doesn't make enough money to stay in business, it doesn't really matter what its mission is (or was).

As you may have guessed by now, I wholeheartedly support the idea that better business practices are an important means to advance organizational impact among nonprofits. However, the phrase "No margin, no mission" is an oversimplification, and sometimes, it can simply be a cop-out. Over my career, I've met plenty of people in the nonprofit sector whose behavior could be better described as "*all* margin, no mission." And I'm not just referring to chief financial officers!

But what does it mean to be a good steward of an organization's resources? We can probably agree that private jets for executives and board meetings held in lush, tropical settings are not evidence of good stewardship. But what is? A strong balance sheet? How strong? Market-aligned executive compensation? Which market? Year-over-year growth? At what rate?

If an organization *exists* to further its mission, then how should board members value mission impact today versus impact tomorrow? Should tomorrow's impact be discounted in some way? Should we assume the costs of achieving a certain level of impact will typically grow over time because of inflation or decrease because of technology? Should we assume that as a nonprofit grows in scale, its size and leverage create efficiency gains or even the ability to generate wholly new types of mission impacts? These are all complex questions that conscientious board members need to ponder as they consider their role in governance.

I expect that, as a trustee of a nonprofit organization, you've reviewed and reflected upon your organization's mission effectiveness and fiduciary goals. Most likely, you've thought about and discussed these things independently of one another. In the back of your mind, you know they are interrelated, but how, exactly? Think about your last year of engagement on the board. Which topic (organizational impact or financial health) does the organization spend more time on? Which one keeps you up at night? How balanced are the skills of the organization's leaders across these two vital objectives?

We are going to talk a lot about your role as a trustee in this book. At the outset, let's start with three deceptively simple questions:

Leadership Questions

1. *How well do you understand the organization's mission and its mechanism of impact?*

2. *How well do you understand the organization's financial health and fiduciary needs?*
3. *Given your background, knowledge, and experience, are you more equipped to help advance the organization's financial health or help it accomplish its mission?*

SUMMARY

- Leading a tax-exempt nonprofit organization can be very gratifying. It can also be stressful and overwhelming.
- Nonprofit leadership is more challenging than leading a for-profit company of similar size and complexity because of differences in the clarity of organizational objectives.
- Two aims are common to all nonprofits: advancing the organization's mission and advancing its financial health. These aims can be in conflict with one another. The tension between mission and fiduciary goals lurks in the background of every decision a nonprofit leader makes. Effectively navigating that tension is the "nonprofit dilemma."
- Chronic underinvestment in organizational infrastructure leads to the "nonprofit starvation cycle." This is when nonprofits are stuck in a cycle of constantly seeking new funding sources to stay afloat. They grow distracted from their mission and struggle to improve organizational effectiveness. This describes many small nonprofits in the U.S.
- Small organizations dominate the nonprofit sector in the U.S., with 92% of nonprofits having an annual budget of less than $1 million.
- Spending organizational time on one thing means forgoing time on something else. That lost opportunity to do something else is the opportunity cost associated with a decision.
- When you move from working *in* an organization to working *on* it, you've started your leadership journey.
- Spending money to accelerate mission achievement improves your impact story, and that improves your nonprofit's attractiveness to funders. Remember the phrase, "More impact attracts more funding."
- Sometimes, nonprofit executives and even trustees lose sight of the fact that money is truly just a means to an end for nonprofit organizations.

2

CLARIFYING PURPOSE

To understand the heart and mind of a person, look not at what he has already achieved, but at what he aspires to.

—Poet and artist KAHLIL GIBRAN

A NONPROFIT'S MISSION is its reason for existence—its purpose. The tension between mission and fiduciary aims in a nonprofit is influenced by how clear and widely understood the mission is. Employees, board members, donors, and other stakeholders need clarity about why an organization exists and what specifically it is trying to accomplish. When that clarity is lacking, support for the organization declines, and the dilemma confronting organizational leaders grows more difficult.

Purpose anchors a nonprofit, allowing it to shape beliefs about the organization and the problem it is trying to solve. This includes simple things like geographic focus and the stakeholders being served (e.g., students, veterans, accountants, etc.). Purpose also encompasses more complex beliefs, like how urgent and worthy of attention the problem is and its significance for a particular group of stakeholders (e.g., issues that are important to accountants are likely less important to veterans). How well a nonprofit defines and conveys its purpose can significantly shape opinions about how impactful the organization is (or can be in the future). It also influences attitudes about the uniqueness of the nonprofit. For example, how might the missions of two competing hospitals serving the same city differ from one another?

Nonprofits that lack clarity of purpose are ultimately defined by others. This is not good. A nonprofit's "customers" are rarely the same people as those that provide the organization's financial support. The needs of these two stakeholders can sometimes conflict. Entities providing financial support (health insurers, donors, foundations, or governments) have their own objectives, priorities, and beliefs about what change is needed and the best ways to bring about that change. A notable exception to this is membership associations, where the members are both customers and financial supporters.

This can ultimately lead a nonprofit to adopt the aims and beliefs of its financial supporters. In this way, it can lose control of its destiny. For example, an organization without a clearly defined purpose may reimagine itself with each grant, morphing from one funder's purpose to another as it accepts funding contingent on each funder's goals. In another example, a nonprofit health system may adopt the priorities of health insurers (including government insurers like Medicare and Medicaid) even when they believe the insurer's priorities aren't the right ones for their local community. Nonprofits with a clear, carefully considered purpose are better positioned to frame the relationship with their financial supporters in a healthy way.

Clearly defining and conveying your purpose creates a solid foundation for shaping the organization and its future. A lack of clarity results in a nonprofit whose reason for existence is muddled. Organizations that find themselves in this existential crisis grow reliant on revenue streams that don't advance their mission, resulting in confused and disheartened employees and a loss of stakeholder trust. Ironically, this sometimes means losing the support of the very funders whose priorities were adopted. Too many nonprofits find themselves in this situation.

So, how do you ensure clarity? What is it that you are trying to transform, change, innovate, or bring to an end? Be specific. Why exactly is that important? How likely are you to succeed? There are many questions to ask about your nonprofit's purpose.

- Is the cause clear and compelling?
- Is there too much of a focus on the problem and not enough on the solution?
- How captivating is your solution?
- Is there some elegance to it, perhaps in its simplicity?
- Do people without specialized knowledge need to work hard to understand why your nonprofit is amazing?
- Is it easy to find and convey interesting and inspiring stories of your nonprofit's impact?
- Is your purpose highly congruent with the values or aspirations of a particular segment of the population?

The most successful nonprofit leaders inspire a broad group of stakeholders to embrace, support, and work together toward the organization's goals. It is important to note that *you are only a leader when others follow your lead.* No amount of charisma will help if you lack conviction about what you're trying to accomplish and why. It becomes a significant problem when you're trying to accomplish something different from other leaders in your organization or different from the mission stated on your website and endorsed by the board. Leaders with less than crystal clear missions invite all kinds of trouble.

There are many decision paths that result in a nonprofit having an unclear purpose. Perhaps executives didn't want to limit the organization's growth or limit access to particular grant streams or other revenue. Maybe there is disagreement between board members or between executives and the board. A lack of clarity as to the mission could also be a legacy problem— "That's always been our mission." Whatever the cause, defining your nonprofit's purpose is not the place to accept mediocrity.

To be clear, I'm not just talking about eloquent mission statements on websites.[1] I'm talking about the real you. Why do your staff and volunteers come to work? The motivations, aspirations, and common understanding of an organization are a reflection of the organization's leaders and what they are trying to accomplish. Capturing the imagination of your employees, funders, and stakeholders starts with the foundational truth about why your nonprofit exists and what you are trying to accomplish.

Most nonprofits need to simplify their message. They should get rid of platitudes or inspirational words that cloud the intent of the organization. We're going for ease of understanding and simplicity here.

Intent is essential to clarity. It is the essence of the nonprofit's desired impact, whether that's on people's lives or on the environment, etc. A nonprofit without clear intentions may still have a general sense of the direction it is heading in and why. Over time, however, this lack of clarity will lead to mediocre messaging and inconsistent strategic decisions.

A nonprofit with crystal clear intentions not only has exceptional clarity about what it is trying to accomplish but also understands what it is *not* trying to do. Concrete strategic intent allows organizational leaders to be decisive, consistent, and relevant. That consistency translates into better messaging and promotes the development of a brand identity that differentiates the nonprofit and attracts support over time.

---

1. The eloquent words you choose for that mission may be due for a refresh. See Erica Barnhart's excellent short essay on the topic for inspiration. Erica Barnhart. "Great Mission. Bad Statement." Stanford Social Innovation Review. 2016. https://ssir.org/articles/entry/great_mission._bad_statement#

How healthy is your nonprofit's purpose?

How easy is it for you to answer these questions about your organization?

- What are you trying to accomplish? (This is your purpose or mission.)
- Why does your organization exist? (This is the reasoning behind your purpose.)
- Who are you trying to engage or help? (This helps communicate your purpose.)
- What does success look like? (Defining your vision of success helps people understand and embrace your purpose.)
- How well do internal and external stakeholders understand your mission? (Consider whether you have a definitional issue or a marketing problem.)

If that was a simple exercise and you are confident that all the right stakeholders understand your mission, congratulations! If not, welcome to the club of nonprofits that could benefit from working on clarifying and better communicating their organizational mission and purpose.

Note the subtle difference between *what you are trying to accomplish* and *why you exist*. They sound like they are the same question, but they aren't. Your nonprofit exists because there's a problem that needs solving. Your organization's purpose (i.e., what you are trying to accomplish) is based on a *belief* about what the best solution is to that problem. "Best" may mean most researched, most cost-effective, most politically acceptable, or any other flavor of most feasible. "Best" is also usually based on organizational attributes: geographic focus, finances, expertise, or a legacy of working on the problem in a particular way. Your beliefs about the best solution to the problem are intertwined with your beliefs about your nonprofit's strengths and the constraints it faces. This demands that you convince others that your solution (i.e., the one you are most capable of delivering) is the best solution to the problem. It is healthy for nonprofit leaders to test the assumptions behind that logic periodically and assess whether there are alternate solutions that the organization could rise to deliver (e.g., perhaps through partnering with others).

For nonprofits, convincing others is both a marketing strategy and a solution unto itself. You may try to convince donors of the need to support your organization, policymakers of the need for policy change, or end-clients of the need to change behaviors. Whatever the goal, nearly all nonprofits should include education as a component of their purpose. Whether that education is meant to spur advocacy, attract financial support, or change someone's behavior, most nonprofits need to continue to refine their story and increase their marketing budgets. Clarity of purpose leads into the story of *why* that purpose is important. You exist for a reason. Help people understand what it is, why it is important, what you are doing about it (how that's unique), and what you want your audience to do about it.

One sign that things may not be entirely copacetic when it comes to clarity of purpose is if you hesitated on the question of what success looks like. Explicitly defining what success looks like for your organization requires you to walk down the path of reasoning from why you exist to how your organization creates and delivers value. Table 2.1 lays out what I call the "Wow Model of Clarity."

WHY + HOW = THE WOW MODEL OF CLARITY

	5 QUESTIONS	NOTES	EXAMPLES
WHY — 1	Why do you exist?	Focus on the "why"—the problem that needs solving.	• Homeless in our city • Plastic waste in our oceans • Wildfire risk to our community • Access to quality healthcare
2	Who are you focused on informing or educating?	"Who" should you be targeting?	• Policy makers • Donors or members • End-clients • The public
3	What do you hope to accomplish?	What action are you trying to stimulate?	• Policy change • Engagement / financial support • Provide relief and hope • Raise awareness / behavior change
4	What direct actions are you taking?	How are you addressing the problem directly?	• Train, teach, and equip • Deliver care or services • Deliver food, shelter, or goods • Deliver tech solution
HOW — 5	What indirect actions are you taking?	How are you addressing the problem through others?	• Support others through grants • Convey a better vision of the future • Advocate and empower • Make it easier to do the right thing

Table 2.1 The Wow Model of Clarity

Connecting actions to aims allows you to be explicit about goals and to assess whether they are the best actions to further your aims. Once those connections are clearer, revisiting what success might look like becomes much easier.

The "right" mission

The next question to explore is whether your organization has the "right" mission. Just because a mission is well-defined and understood doesn't mean it's the best mission for your organization. Determining whether you have defined and adopted the right mission can be challenging. Okay, honestly, it's probably more like a hornet's nest that you'd prefer *not* to be tossed in your direction. Generally, nonprofit organizations are invested in justifying the status quo rather than embarking on a journey to reimagine the organization and refine its purpose.

Deciding to change your nonprofit's purpose is daunting. Focusing an unfocused organization on a refined purpose is a very difficult endeavor, requiring courage, decisiveness, clarity of reasoning, and transparency with stakeholders. This is why many nonprofits choose to accept a legacy mission that isn't perfect despite the high costs of doing so.

Engaging in a dialogue about purpose with employees, board members, and other stakeholders can uncover crucial misunderstandings and areas where additional specificity could thrust the organization forward. Additional criteria, other than legacy, should inform your choice of purpose. Table 2.2 provides a list of attributes to spark your thinking about ways to refine your organization's purpose and make it more compelling.

The "Right" Nonprofit Purpose...

Offers clear possibility of positive impact	Creates an emotional connection with funders	Is specific, yet can scale with growth
Attracts talent and inspires employees	Serves to differentiate from other organizations	Fosters collaboration and partnership
Is easy to understand and intrinsically motivating	Drives strategy and organizational alignment	Supports creation of a compelling brand

Table 2.2 Nonprofit Purpose

The relationship between organization size and purpose

Consider two nonprofit organizations with quite different missions: one is focused on climate change, and the other on supporting teachers and students in the local school district. They are tackling problems with different scopes and perceived urgency. They also vary in how their mission connects to and is relevant to stakeholders.

You may know the teachers or the families of students helped in your community by the education-focused nonprofit. You may also become aware of a pressing need in the current school year, creating a sense of relevance and connection to the organization's mission. Compare that to the massive, slow-moving problem of climate change. Personal relevance is more difficult to define, even if you or a family member were impacted by flooding attributed to climate change, for example. The connection between the environmental nonprofit's work and your life is indirect. For the climate change nonprofit, the mechanism of change is slow and complicated; there is a lot of uncertainty, and creating a personal connection to that change is difficult.

Most small nonprofit organizations (remember, 92% have an annual budget under $1 million),[2] have narrowly defined missions. This translates into smaller audiences of people who share the organization's interests. Think about the nonprofit focused on the local school district. There is a small, focused pool of potential donors (though donor turnover is probably high as families move into and out of the district). Personal connection to the nonprofit's mission is high in many households in the community, so the payoff for outreach to that community for support is also going to be high. However, there's a problem confronting small nonprofits with narrowly defined missions:

- There is an ever-present threat to their survival. This forces leaders to repeatedly sacrifice mission impact for financial stability.
- Small nonprofits struggle to put aside enough resources for administering the organization (accounting, HR, IT, marketing, legal support, and grant writing). Because they can't afford these

---

2. National Council of Nonprofits. Data available at
https://www.councilofnonprofits.org/about-us.

things, they are typically done in a piecemeal way, often by consultants, and only when absolutely necessary.

These two issues create inefficiencies, hamper the small nonprofit's ability to have the impact they desire, and significantly limit their growth opportunities. Throughout this book, I'll offer lots of strategic advice to help small nonprofits overcome these debilitating challenges.

When examining its organizational purpose, the small educational nonprofit might consider ways to broaden its purpose while maintaining the advantage of dedication to the local community. This would expand the pool of potential volunteers and donors, while simultaneously offering the possibility of spreading administrative costs across a wider set of activities, making the organization more efficient. In large organizations, bureaucracy leads to inefficiency; in small organizations, necessity does.

Consider ways to broaden the organization's purpose without diluting it. Perhaps you could expand into adjoining school districts, fund community-level art or music education, improve local parks, or support youth sports or library activities for children. All of these are possible solutions to maximize impact while promoting organizational health and longevity.

Now, let's go back to the nonprofit focused on climate change. Hopefully, they've adopted a focused purpose given the sheer magnitude of the problem and the overwhelming political and economic inertia associated with it. What kinds of purpose-related challenges might they face?

First and foremost is the perceived likelihood of success. We'll discuss *mechanisms of change* in the chapters on developing and executing strategy. But here, in terms of purpose, the issue is simply whether there is a wide enough group of employees, funders, and others that believe success is not only possible but probable.

For organizations tackling large, complicated problems, the most compelling purpose conveys three ideas:

1. *Focus.* The problem the organization is working on is narrowly and explicitly defined.
2. *Innovation.* The organization believes progress is feasible through a fresh approach to the problem.
3. *Scale.* The organization is committed to developing the scale and leverage necessary to address the problem.

How can the climate change nonprofit convey those ideas through its purpose?

Focus. Define the problem the organization is focused on narrowly and explicitly. Efforts to address complex, unyielding, and hard-to-understand problems feel futile—not what you're looking for when you are trying to inspire support and hope for the future. If the problem is still complex, then prioritize education and communication strategies to make the problem easier to understand for internal and external stakeholders. Organizations that are laser-focused on solving clearly defined problems are more likely to garner the support needed to succeed.

Innovation. Incorporate an element of innovation into the mission to enable market disruption, leading to a paradigm change in what's possible or how an issue is viewed. Sometimes, innovation can empower a whole new class of stakeholders through access to information, novel tools, or making it easier to do the right thing. Organizations that embed the promise of innovation into their purpose convey confidence that they can develop and implement a new change mechanism. That confidence translates into a feeling of feasibility and excitement for what may now be possible.

Scale. Demonstrate that part of the mission includes developing the scale and/or leverage necessary to attack the problem that's been defined. People understand that leverage is required to move big rocks. If an organization's size and resources feel misaligned to the scope of the problem, it needs to focus on growth or other strategies that create additional leverage. Acknowledging the need for scale and leverage should be part of how most organizations tackling tough problems describe their purpose. Growing, innovating, or partnering to increase leverage instills confidence that the nonprofit will ultimately be successful.

FUTURE LEADERS

Nonprofit organizations exist for reasons other than to make money. This is why a nonprofit's mission and its specific goals need to be well-defined. Moreover, the tax treatment of a nonprofit is derived from its purpose. While the activities of most nonprofits are tax exempt, some are not. A homeowners' association (HOA) is an interesting example of a nonprofit that may not be tax exempt.

The purpose of an HOA is not to make money but rather to maintain common areas, enhance the community, improve property values, and govern a neighborhood according to its bylaws. Some HOAs are designated nonprofit organizations, but their activities cannot be characterized as benefiting the public if only the owners or residents benefit. To be tax-exempt, the HOA's activities must benefit a broader community. An example would be maintaining a public park within the neighborhood. If an HOA engages in activities that result in taxable income, it is required to file a tax return as a corporation.

Most nonprofits are tax-exempt because they provide charitable, educational, religious, or scientific services that contribute to the "public good."[3] Tax-exempt nonprofits satisfy a need for certain public goods that are unfulfilled by the government. Were it not for nonprofits, federal, state, and local governments would have to perform some of those functions. In return for their contribution to the public good, these nonprofits are largely exempt from paying federal and state income taxes, and usually property taxes. Donations to them are also typically tax deductible, which further reduces government revenues (more information can be found in the Appendix at the back of this book).

When partnering with nonprofits to deliver public goods, the government benefits by only partially covering the expense of delivering those goods (when the nonprofit has other sources of funding). This is another justification for the favorable tax treatment. However, all nonprofits are subject to taxes on income that is unrelated to their tax-exempt purpose—this is called unrelated business income or UBI. Additionally, while most nonprofits are tax exempt, many have for-profit subsidiaries that are subject to income taxes.

In return for the significant tax advantages provided to nonprofits, the expectation is that they will deliver meaningful value to society. What exactly that means is up for debate. What constitutes a public good is rather fuzzy, and the government doesn't go to any great lengths to mon-

---

3. Public goods can generally be defined as commodities or services that broadly benefit members of society. Examples include national defense, infrastructure, public schools and universities, law enforcement, and firefighting services. See the Appendix for more information.

itor and measure what benefits individual tax-exempt organizations provide to society.[4] For example, a nonprofit hospital may provide charity care to low-income patients, lead community health improvement efforts, and conduct medical training and research. Among healthcare delivery organizations, these are referred to as *community benefit* requirements. These requirements are not well-defined, not easily measured, and not closely monitored by the Internal Revenue Service (IRS). As a result, some hospitals and health systems fall short of delivering societal value commensurate with their tax status.[5]

As a future nonprofit leader, you may be inspired by the mission and leaders of your organization, or you may be disheartened because the mission is lackluster or because you feel the leaders have lost their way. If you're concerned that the organization is not living up to its potential, give voice to those concerns. The path to becoming a purpose-driven leader starts with courage. Take the first step by being brave enough to politely and constructively point out what you believe needs to change to give your organization greater clarity of purpose and ensure that its day-to-day activities are more purpose-driven.

EXECUTIVES & MANAGERS

Part of your job is to motivate and inspire your workforce. Clarifying your purpose is an excellent way to do that. If you are unclear about what your

---

4. U.S. Government Accountability Office (2020). "Tax Administration: Opportunities Exist to Improve Oversight of Hospitals' Tax-Exempt Status. GAO-20-679." U.S. Government Accountability Office. Oct 19, 2020. https://www.gao.gov/products/gao-20-679
5. As I write this book, we are in the midst of a global crisis that has pushed health systems around the world to their limit. In the U.S., the COVID-19 pandemic has repeatedly tested the resilience of our hospital system and the thousands of dedicated men and women who work in it. After the last few years, policymakers and the general public should have a better appreciation for the importance of public health infrastructure, safety-net hospitals, surge capacity in things like N95 masks and ventilators, and emergency preparedness. These are vital public goods deserving of investment, accountability, and oversight. Building this capacity into our local communities sure feels like a community benefit to me.

nonprofit is trying to accomplish, be assured that the people around you are confused as well.

This may sound obvious, but it is common for teams to work at cross-purposes, especially in large nonprofits. Are the aspirations of the leaders in your organization aligned to the same overarching goal? How clearly defined is your organization's purpose, and how often do you convey the connection between intermediate objectives and that overarching purpose? People are inspired when they believe in the intrinsic value of an organization and when they see a clear connection between their day-to-day work and progress toward that organization's mission.

Too many nonprofit leaders take this for granted. They are busy with urgent demands on their time (preparing for the next board meeting, negotiating a contract, meeting with new partners, reviewing finances or benefits, conducting performance appraisals, etc.). The most successful nonprofit leaders make time to reinforce the connection between the tasks, priorities, and intermediate objectives of their team and the organization's overarching purpose.

When employees look to you for guidance, usually what they are looking for is a connection to purpose. The more often you provide that clarity, the more motivated and effective they'll be. I'm sure you already know that an inspired workforce is happier, more creative, and more productive. When you strengthen the connection to purpose it also encourages a sense of belonging. It's a worthy investment of your time to achieve these aims. Show genuine appreciation for the work of individuals and teams in your organization and continually reinforce how their work connects to the larger purpose. If *you* don't know how it connects, then you either have a purpose problem (unclear aims) or a tasking problem (someone is tasking people to work on things that are not mission-aligned). Both require intervention.

Purpose and branding

Besides strengthening internal identity, your mission provides the foundation of your brand.[6] Part of "clarity of purpose" is creating a brand

---

6. Branding is the process of creating and disseminating a name, term, design, or symbol that differentiates your nonprofit in the market.

that differentiates your organization. A good nonprofit brand must exude credibility. It should reinforce that your actions have always been aligned with values that you share with your stakeholders. As a nonprofit leader, you should aim to cultivate a recognizable, authentic, and consistent brand that people trust. This includes being transparent about how you use your money, consistent about the promise of your mission and your commitment to it, appreciative of the contributions of collaborators and partners, and open about the challenges your organization faces (including acknowledging missteps).

Executives and managers have a duty to serve as brand ambassadors for their nonprofit. Your goal is to build a brand that motivates stakeholders to take actions that further your mission. Partnering with you, marketing you on their baseball cap, or receiving services from you all represent support for your mission and your brand.

External audiences need to understand your mission, believe it, and want to embrace it. Effective leaders promote their nonprofits to external stakeholders with the objective of increasing brand awareness, building cohesion around solving a problem, and strengthening the reputation of the organization and its purpose.

Over time, you want your brand to feel familiar. You want supporters to connect so strongly with it that it becomes part of their own identity. You want them wearing your logo, sticking it onto their fridges and the bumpers of their cars. You want them to advertise that they care so much about your mission that it has become part of who they are and what they value. They are not only proud to support you; they believe in you, are committed to you, and feel an affinity toward others who support your cause.

Exceptional nonprofit leaders work tirelessly to cultivate a purpose-driven brand in the marketplace. They also seek to improve clarity of purpose and actively use that purpose to strengthen an internal identity. They consider how their organization's purpose will guide leadership and how it promotes focus, innovation, and scale. You'll know you've defined the right purpose when you are confident that it provides the clarity needed to guide your organization, motivate your employees, and inspire your stakeholders. The right purpose provides the path to maximum impact now and long into the future.

TRUSTEES

Great nonprofits are led with a clarity of purpose. As a nonprofit trustee, it is your responsibility to ensure that your nonprofit is led with clear intention. You don't have to define that purpose yourself. In fact, you need to take care not to over-influence it. If you feel any ambiguity about the organization's mission, or if you sense any confusion among stakeholders about the nonprofit's purpose, you need to ask the question. Chances are, if you are confused, so are others.

Ignoring issues with your organization's purpose is a recipe for waste, employee and stakeholder apathy, questionable investments, and spinning wheels. For your organization to be purpose-driven, your mission must be succinct and easily understood. Clarity of purpose promotes organizational focus. That focus drives efficient business development and operations. It encourages targeted investment, drives market awareness of the organization and its goals, and serves to align the organization's actions and employees.

Clarity of purpose allows a "culture of purpose" to take hold within an organization. This helps to attract, retain, and energize talented employees. We'll discuss how to nurture a culture of purpose in Chapter 7, *Shaping Values & Culture*. For now, let's agree that such a culture cannot flourish without clarity of purpose. By instilling focus, driving the development of mature capabilities, and disrupting the way people view a particular issue—clarity increases the chance that your nonprofit delivers real value to society.

We don't need to belabor the point. To borrow a phrase—without clarity of purpose, you're dead in the water.

SUMMARY

- Great nonprofit leaders understand that everything starts with clarity of purpose.
- The tension between mission and fiduciary objectives in a nonprofit is influenced by how clear and widely understood the mission is.
- Purpose anchors a nonprofit, allowing it to shape beliefs about itself and the problem it is trying to solve.
- Nonprofits with a clear, thought-out purpose are better positioned to frame the relationship with financial supporters. When a nonprofit's purpose is unclear, it loses control of its own destiny.
- Most nonprofits need to simplify their message. Eliminate platitudes or words that feel inspirational but cloud the intent of the organization.
- In large organizations, bureaucracy leads to inefficiency; in small organizations, necessity does.
- Strategic clarity allows organizational leaders to be decisive and consistent. Consistency promotes the development of a brand identity that differentiates your nonprofit and attracts support.
- When employees look to you for guidance, what they often need is a connection to purpose. The more you provide that clarity, the more motivated and effective they'll be.
- A compelling purpose conveys three ideas. *Focus*: the problem you're working on is narrowly and explicitly defined; *innovation*: you believe progress is feasible through a fresh approach to the problem; and *scale*: you are committed to developing the scale and leverage necessary to address the problem.
- Clarity of purpose promotes focus that drives efficient business development and operations. It encourages targeted investment, drives market awareness of the organization and its goals, and serves to align the organization's actions and employees.
- Clarity is a prerequisite to delivering meaningful value to society.

3
DEVELOPING STRATEGY

If you don't know where you are going, you'll end up someplace else.

—Baseball catcher and manager YOGI BERRA

L ET'S START WITH a joke you have likely heard before. How do you make God laugh? Tell him about your plans.

This funny idea is based on an old Yiddish proverb, "Mann Tracht, Un Gott Lacht," which means, "Man plans, and God laughs." When nonprofits engage in strategic planning, they are not just trying to predict the future and plan for it. Often, they are also trying to *influence* it. Strategic planning is a necessary exercise, but one that likely elicits a chuckle every now and again.

In the first two chapters of this book, we explored the fiduciary/impact dilemma that confronts nonprofit leaders and discussed the importance of selecting the right purpose for your nonprofit and defining that purpose in the clearest and most compelling way. All that leads us to developing a strategy. A nonprofit's purpose serves as the foundation of its strategy. That strategy delineates the steps the nonprofit plans on taking to advance both its mission and fiduciary objectives. How the organization's leaders value these competing objectives relative to one another shapes the strategy and the priorities therein.

Some strategic plans focus heavily on growing revenues, increasing grant funding, lowering costs, and improving a nonprofit's balance sheet. Others focus on elevating organizational scale and impact, defining the related investment thesis, and demonstrating the affordability of those investments.

All strategic plans benefit from mission clarity. Embracing a concise, coherent, and intelligible organizational purpose is a prerequisite to strategic planning. It is through strategy that you turn implicit ideas about the future and your organizational aspirations into explicit plans, milestones, and actions.

Your market shapes your strategy

Nonprofits work in markets with varied levels of predictability. This context influences how you should approach planning. Those working in relatively stable and predictable environments should focus their planning on differentiation and growth within those environments. The purpose of the plan is to set a course to build and sustain competitive advantage. This usually involves considerations like how to improve organizational efficiency, how to increase the value of offerings, and how to improve perceived value through marketing. Professional associations are a good example of organizations in this kind of environment.

On the other hand, nonprofits working in dynamic and unpredictable environments should focus their planning on agility and adaptability, as advantages are usually short-lived. The purpose of the plan is to set a course to promote innovation and influence. This usually involves considerations like how to experiment iteratively to find new solutions to old or emerging problems, how to change perspectives about the problem itself, or how to collaborate with others to influence the market (for example, through policy change). Nonprofits focused on emerging environmental or humanitarian challenges are good examples of organizations in this kind of environment.

Most nonprofits fall somewhere between these two extremes. That is, some aspects of their market are slow to change and predictable, while others are highly dynamic and require agility. Healthcare delivery organizations are a good example of this. Emerging diseases, medical knowledge, and payment models are always changing. However, medical practice, local competitive pressures, and the regulatory environment are slow to change. These nonprofits should approach planning in a manner that is aligned with the various market pressures and opportunities they face. In some areas, differentiation and growth strategies are called for. In others, agility and adaptation should be the focus.

Why plan?

The amount of actual planning that a nonprofit does varies by organization and the personal tastes of its leaders and trustees. Strategic planning is the process of contemplating, writing, and communicating your strategy. While this may sound obvious, it's worth remembering that when strategy exists only in the minds of a few organizational leaders, it seldom flourishes. The benefits of a strategic plan are realized when that plan *aligns the intentions of your workforce* and *provides consistency to your investments.* Even the best-run nonprofits usually have room to improve along these two dimensions.

Other benefits really depend on the questions you are attempting to answer with the plan. Perhaps you believe that the societal problem your nonprofit is focused on will get worse without urgent action by your organization and its partners. Perhaps you believe that additional financial flexibility will be needed to weather an anticipated storm or to change the organization in some major way. Whatever the precipitating event, strategic planning is your opportunity to improve the probability of organizational success.

FUTURE LEADERS

If you are given the opportunity to take part in strategic planning, give it everything you've got. Strategic planning is an attempt to exert control over the organization's destiny. If you have a hand in that, chances are it will also influence your own destiny. This chapter provides many useful tools and lines of inquiry. Use them to help your nonprofit succeed.

Given the importance of strategy, it's not surprising that there are numerous academic books, business books, and websites offering models, frameworks, and tools to help tackle strategic planning. Interestingly, the most mature and popular strategic planning resources are almost exclusively focused on the needs of for-profit businesses. They emphasize things like pricing, competition, product differentiation, and profit margins. While these aims are not irrelevant to nonprofits, they can be secondary considerations, and so these tools can encourage a focus on the wrong priorities. Let's explore seven commonly available strategic planning frameworks before walking through the approach I recommend for nonprofits. If your current job includes the word "strategy," it is probably worthwhile exploring these models further. They include lots of useful concepts and ways to frame organizational problems. Perhaps one of them will meet a specific need within your nonprofit.

SWOT Analysis. This is the most widely used strategy framework. It breaks down your analysis of the nonprofit into four themes. *Strengths*: what your organization does well; *weaknesses*: what you struggle with and should probably address; *opportunities*: things outside your organization that present new possibilities; and *threats*: things outside your organization that are emerging and may cause damage, like new competitors or regulatory changes.

SOAR Analysis. This is similar to SWOT but less widely used—though perhaps more applicable to nonprofits. *Strengths*: what your organization does well, and what you have to build on; *opportunities*: things inside and outside your company that present new possibilities; *aspirations*: what you value, and what your employees dream about accomplishing; and, *results*: what your goals are (how you will know you are making progress).

Ansoff Matrix. This is another two-by-two strategy/risk matrix.[1] It explores the relative attractiveness of four growth strategies, based on how new or existing markets and the products/services in those markets intersect. *Market penetration*: (the least risky strategy) refers to growing the market share of current offerings in existing markets using branding, marketing, or pricing strategies. *Market development*: is finding or creating new markets for an existing offering (e.g., positioning an existing product to meet different needs). *Offering development*: introducing new products/services to an existing market (usually riskier due to the research and development costs of creating new products/services). *Diversification*: which involves simultaneously entering a new market and introducing new products or services into that market (the riskiest strategy).

Balanced Scorecard / Strategy Map. This is a structured approach to strategic management across (you guessed it) four dimensions. However, it's less of a strategy development tool and more of a mechanism to track strategy implementation. While there are variations to serve different industries, the "balanced" concept is typically about expanding the definition of success beyond the company's bottom line. Here are the four dimensions that are typically balanced. *Financial*: the most important measures of financial success. *Customer*: what customers and stakeholders believe is most important. *Internal process*: what the organization must excel at. *Learning and growth*: where new knowledge or innovation can create value for the organization.

Blue Ocean. This framework focuses on value innovation and marketing strategy. The metaphor of the blue ocean refers to market space

---

1. Igor Ansoff also coined the term: "paralysis by analysis."

that is not yet explored. You can think of existing market spaces as red, shark-infested waters where competitors drive down profits. Blue Ocean is premised on finding ways out of those shark-infested waters. This is similar to Ansoff's *market development* idea. It's a fun idea, but one that's largely focused on profit-maximizing. Its relevance to nonprofits is more about clarifying purpose than developing strategy.

Porter's Five Forces. This framework is used to assess the competitive environment and an organization's place within it. The five forces are as follows. *Competition*: the number and quality of competitors. *New entrants*: the barriers to entry that new competitors face. (Warren Buffet refers to this as the moat around the castle.) *Suppliers*: the bargaining power of suppliers and the ease with which they can drive up costs. For nonprofits that deliver services, this includes the bargaining power of sub-contractors and partners. *Customers*: the bargaining power of customers, how much leverage they have, and how costly it is to find new customers. *Substitutes*: the availability and relative attractiveness of near substitutes to the organization's offerings.

PEST / PESTLE Analysis. This useful framework is used to consider the environment around an organization. The external factors considered are as follows. *Political*: factors related to government intervention; *economic*: factors related to the economy; *social*: factors related to cultural and demographic trends; and, *technological*: factors related to technology that differentiates the organization, lowers its costs, or provide barriers to entry. You can also add *legal* factors (laws that impact how the organization operates, its costs, and the demand for its offerings) and *environmental* factors (ecological and environmental considerations like climate change). A good way to remember the acronym PESTLE is as a tool you can use to crush the competition (as in mortar and pestle).

Strategic planning models are helpful in two ways: they help the person or team working on strategy to think through various considerations, and they help to structure the reasoning that is communicated to trustees, employees, and other stakeholders. The process is about turning implicit ideas or concerns into a plan of action that is reasoned and explicit. I borrow ideas from some of these models in the tailored approach to nonprofit strategic planning that I describe in the rest of this chapter.

How to tackle strategy development

Imagine your executive director just asked you to deliver a strategic plan during the board's fall retreat. You've got four months to pull this off. You sort of knew this was coming, but that doesn't make it any easier. You've got a ton on your plate already, and you're feeling seriously overworked. If only you hadn't just bought plane tickets for that big family vacation. However, it does sound exciting to show off your amazing strategic insights and remarkable business acumen to the trustees and other organizational leaders. A smile spreads over your face as you imagine a standing ovation at the end of your presentation.

Let's tackle exactly how to develop the best strategy for your nonprofit. Whether you work for a large or small organization, the first consideration is how many people to pull together to work on strategy. It's been my experience that strategy is best *developed* by small groups and *vetted* by larger ones. Developing a strategy is an exercise in focus. The more people involved, the more difficult the journey. However, iterative vetting with larger and larger groups is necessary to gain buy-in. To achieve that buy-in, the strategy's authors must encourage honest dialogue and critical feedback. They must embrace the idea that the pursuit of strategic clarity and employee commitment are vital to organizational success. The best leaders know when it is time to set aside their pride of authorship and their finely honed skills of persuasion and genuinely embrace feedback.

Who develops the strategy should be based on the personal strengths of different team members rather than their titles. There are plenty of people working in nonprofits whose titles give the false impression that they carry some unique strategic insight. Pick your team wisely based on who you feel is most likely to contribute real value. You can pursue buy-in from other key players later. Before you start planning, answer a few overarching questions:

- Does the organization have a "clarity of purpose" issue? If so, resolve (see Chapter 2).

- Is the organization facing an existential threat that overshadows all other issues? If so, you are not planning a strategy; you are putting together a risk mitigation plan.
- Does the organization operate in a particularly dynamic environment? If so, adopt an iterative style of planning that will foster agility. This means developing a planning framework and putting a process in place to verify assumptions and update elements of the plan regularly.

Success in strategy development can be boiled down to two things:

- *choosing the right objectives*, and
- *selecting the right actions to support those objectives.*

Everything else is done to support those two aims. Sounds simple, right? Knowing which objectives are the right ones for your organization and which actions will most effectively advance those objectives is where the "strategy" part comes in.

Choosing the right objectives

A nonprofit's strategy will usually include both internal and external objectives. Internal objectives seek to solve a problem internal to the organization. For example, improving the efficiency of operations, hiring and developing more effective leaders, modernizing accounting practices, reducing supply costs, or introducing initiatives to improve diversity, equity, and inclusion (DEI). External objectives seek to solve a problem outside the organization. For example, improving the organization's brand, growing its market share or influence, developing new strategic partnerships, or extending the nonprofit's impact.

Let's start with internal objectives. There are a few common ways of thinking about how to "get your house in order." You could identify objectives through *strengths-based analysis,* which is all about identifying your organization's strengths and doubling down on them. For example, you could decide to hire more experts in the thing you are already an expert in, or you could invest in a training program focused on developing your best leaders.

DEVELOPING STRATEGY 57

You could also identify objectives through *weakness-based analysis,* which is about identifying and mitigating your biggest problems. For example, you could decide to address outdated technology or inefficient internal processes.

A third way to think about internal objectives is like strengths-based analysis but focused on assessing exactly how you differ from competitors. *Differentiation-based analysis* defines what makes you unique, so you can invest in that. Alternatively, you can identify a *desired* differentiator and develop an investment strategy for that. I call these "aspirational differentiators," and they are a good way for nonprofits to influence their place in the market. Most nonprofits would benefit from identifying aspirational differentiators and focusing their strategic plans on exploiting them. Carving out a path to distinction is usually a worthwhile endeavor. Some nonprofits might not have a differentiation problem. For example, you may be the only professional association focused on a particular profession or the only community organization supporting the local community.

External objectives are those that respond to the market or the problem your nonprofit is trying to solve. These include things like aligning with funder priorities, responding to opportunities or threats in the competitive landscape, and influencing policy or being influenced by it. External objectives also include promoting innovation or technological change (things that make tackling the problem easier), and responding to changes in the prevalence, size, or urgency of the problem you're focused on (reasons to sound the alarm). Focused market research is typically necessary to create a set of well-defined external objectives.

Once you have a short list of robust objectives, a good follow-up is to ask yourself whether the objectives make sense as a whole.

- Are they unifying, or might they create tension in your organization?
- Are there too many? You are trying to focus your organization on strategic imperatives. Having fifteen objectives will dilute the desired effect.
- How likely is it that other leaders in the organization will agree that your list represents the strategic imperatives for the

nonprofit? Depending on your answer, you may need to invest considerable time in developing your rationale.

Logic models

If you're struggling to choose objectives, logic models can help you explicitly describe the relationship between various things and the assumptions you are making as you refine your thinking on what's most important for your organization. They can help you to clarify objectives, build understanding, and promote consensus. There are a few models and methodologies to choose from. Borrow whatever elements are most helpful to your strategic planning.

One example of a logic model is the *driver diagram*. Driver diagrams have been used extensively in healthcare quality improvement efforts and in some public health interventions. Although their use outside those fields seems limited, I believe these models can be useful to nonprofit leaders choosing strategic objectives.

A driver diagram can be used to work backward from a nonprofit's overall purpose to the steps necessary to accomplish it. By framing the purpose as a problem and breaking that problem into its component parts (i.e., the drivers of the problem), a theory of change emerges. This becomes a high-level outline of how the nonprofit might tackle different components of a problem to accomplish its overall goal.

By breaking the problem into smaller components, driver diagrams answer the question: how do we get there? They can help you identify the right objectives to focus on by putting them in the context of your organization's purpose and in the context of one another. By more explicitly describing the overall aim and exploring the primary and secondary drivers behind it, a better understanding of intermediate objectives and viable paths to accomplishing them is possible.

Example of a driver diagram

Suppose you formed a nonprofit with the sole purpose of improving the curb appeal of a house in your neighborhood. With one and a half million nonprofits in the U.S., perhaps there is one with such an audacious and selfless goal. Probably not, but it's fun to imagine.

Using a driver diagram template, you'd start by concisely stating your overall aim—in this case, improving the home's curb appeal. Then you'd ask yourself (or your team of "helpful" neighbors): what's wrong with this home? Why does its curb appeal need to be improved? Let's say one item on your short list is landscaping. The landscaping of this house is overgrown, not attractive, and needs to be improved. That is a primary driver of why the home's curb appeal isn't great.

Drilling down deeper, you say, "Okay, what *exactly* is wrong with this landscaping?" You and your friendly neighbors come up with a long list, and with some back and forth, you're able to whittle it down to a few things: the bushes are overgrown, the lawn is weedy with dead spots, and everything is green or brown. These are your secondary drivers. It is because of these things that the landscaping looks bad, and that bad landscaping is dragging down the home's overall curb appeal.

Once you've identified primary and secondary drivers, take a break. You've earned it! The next day, with fresh eyes, check your drivers to make sure they still make sense and that nothing glaring is missing. Then, brainstorm ideas to address the secondary drivers and refine these "change ideas" until you are confident that they represent a viable approach to tackling them. When you are done, your driver diagram might look something like Figure 3.1.

Doing this exercise can help you think through each objective and how they come together to move the organization, its financial health, and its impact forward. You might choose to complete a couple of driver diagrams. For example, one could be focused on financial health aims and one on mission aims. Remember to compare them to assess whether any of the drivers or change ideas might interact with each other. For example, you might not want to pursue a new strategic partnership at the same time you are aggressively targeting that same organization's employees or revenue streams.

Driver diagrams can be very helpful in assessing and choosing the right objectives to focus on. They can also help you communicate those objectives and break them into relatively small-scale actions that are easier to understand, implement, and measure. This organized logic model approach allows leaders to envision a path to organizational success, and better assess the feasibility of achieving desired outcomes.

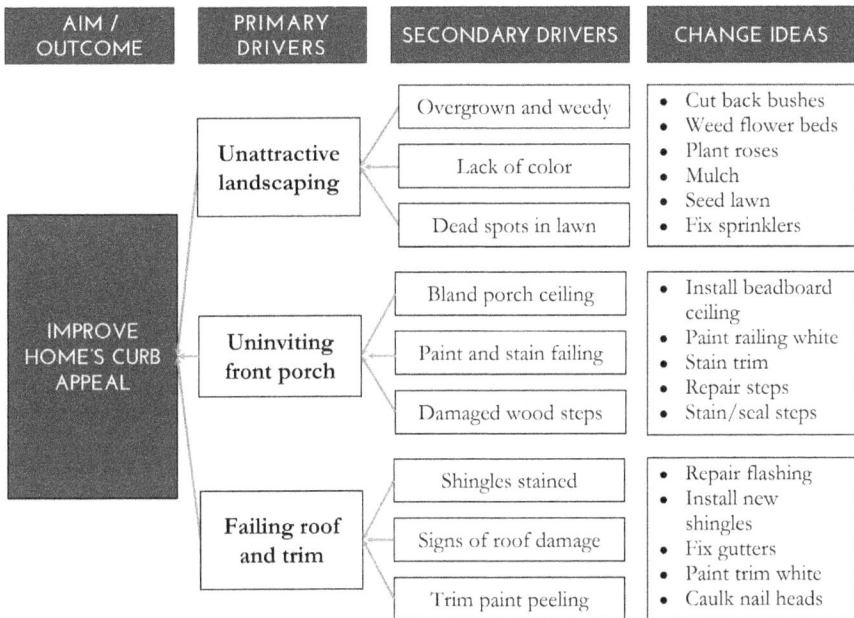

AIM / OUTCOME	PRIMARY DRIVERS	SECONDARY DRIVERS	CHANGE IDEAS
IMPROVE HOME'S CURB APPEAL	Unattractive landscaping	Overgrown and weedy Lack of color Dead spots in lawn	• Cut back bushes • Weed flower beds • Plant roses • Mulch • Seed lawn • Fix sprinklers
	Uninviting front porch	Bland porch ceiling Paint and stain failing Damaged wood steps	• Install beadboard ceiling • Paint railing white • Stain trim • Repair steps • Stain/seal steps
	Failing roof and trim	Shingles stained Signs of roof damage Trim paint peeling	• Repair flashing • Install new shingles • Fix gutters • Paint trim white • Caulk nail heads

Figure 3.1 An Example Driver Diagram

Selecting the right actions to support your objectives

Once you've chosen some vital objectives for your organization to rally around, you'll also have some initial ideas about the actions needed to make progress on those objectives. For example, if you completed a driver diagram, you've already written down potential change ideas or actions for each of the secondary drivers of your overall aim. One important consideration is whether the actions you are recommending are supportive of the current environment and business model or whether they are focused on pivoting the organization toward a new or different environment or business model.

The *Now, Near, Far Framework* (Figure 3.2) is a tool developed by the auto industry to plan for disruptive changes in the demand for transportation (e.g., for autonomous and electric vehicles). This framework has also been adopted by some healthcare-related companies as they plan for significant changes in the demand for certain types of healthcare services due to changing demographics and payment models. The premise of this framework is to envision a future state and the role your nonprofit might

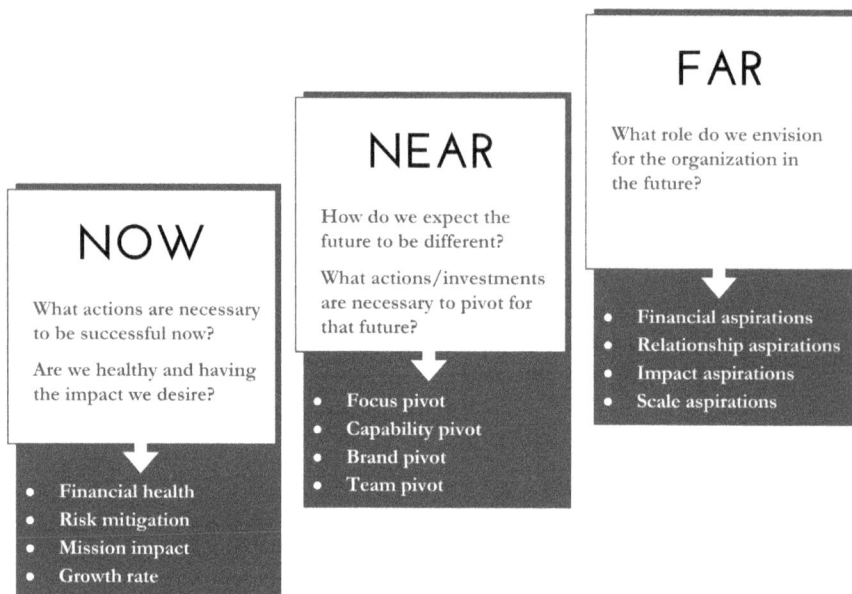

Figure 3.2 The Now, Near, Far Framework

play in that future so you can identify a phased approach to pivoting the organization to be ready for that future.

While this framework was conceived to help large organizations facing disruptive changes to their industry, it is just as useful to nonprofits thinking through strategic priorities. The framework encourages consideration of five questions:

1. What actions are necessary to be successful now?
2. How do we expect the future to be different?
3. What role do we envision for the organization in that future?
4. What actions and investments are necessary to pivot the organization for the future?
5. How should those actions be phased between the now, near, and far timeframes?

Let's imagine you run a community pantry in a town with rapidly changing demographics and food insecurities. In the "now" you need to take actions that best support your current clientele. You must also plan for the "near," where you may need to source and stock more culturally appropriate foods, for example, or recruit more non-English speaking volunteers. Maybe the issue is a growing number of homebound seniors, and you need to add capacity to make home deliveries.

Now imagine the future. Perhaps there is a risk that the community becomes a food desert (one with limited access to affordable, nutritious food). If that happens, how might your organization need to change the role it serves in your community? Maybe your "far" scenario is about broadening your mission to offer low-cost, fresh food. What kinds of challenges do you anticipate in making that pivot? How might building stronger partnerships with other community organizations, churches, or government help? Is there a regional farmers' market you could collaborate with? Are you able to process payments? What about payments through government programs? If you decide to engage in a multi-year pivot, what phasing makes sense to secure funding, build new partnerships, develop new capacities, and brand your organization differently?

The Now, Near, Far Framework helps you to consider these questions and develop an action plan. Because the future is uncertain, this can also be thought of as "contingency" planning—assessing the likelihood of various future scenarios and planning near-term actions that best position the nonprofit for those futures.

Another tool to help you choose the right actions to realize your objectives is the *SMART* criteria for goals. Why am I talking about goals instead of actions? Because during the planning stage, it is critical to make sure each action you recommend is constructed to accomplish a specific goal. Figure 3.3 tailors the SMART criteria to the needs of nonprofit organizations.[2]

Nonprofits will also want to ensure that their goals promote *inclusion* and *equity* (discussed in Chapter 7). Reflect on whether your plans may have unintentional disparate impacts on your employees or those outside your organization. Mitigating those impacts or drafting goals that incorporate a specific inclusion or equity component demonstrates care and foresight. In recent years, the acronym SMARTIE has been adopted to

---

2. Originally described in Doran, G. T. (1981). "There's a S.M.A.R.T. Way to Write Management's Goals and Objectives." Management Review, 70, 35-36. However, his criteria were: specific, measurable, assignable, realistic, and time-related.

S **Specific:** The goal of the action is clear, concise, and easy to explain.

M **Measurable**: The action results in measurable progress and milestones (you may need to use proxy metrics).

A **Attainable:** The action is feasible; the goal can be achieved; it is not impossible to accomplish.

R **Relevant:** The goal lines up with an objective, which is aligned with the nonprofit's mission or financial health.

T **Time-Bound:** The action has a clearly defined timeline, so it is known when milestones will be achieved.

Figure 3.3 SMART Criteria for Nonprofits

reflect this additional emphasis. When choosing goals and actions for your strategic plan, consider whether they can be defined more effectively using the SMARTIE criteria.

There is a lot of emphasis among nonprofits (and among those who fund them) on making measurable progress. While there's nothing wrong with that sentiment, a word of caution is in order. Progress against some objectives is hard to measure, and so we rely on proxy metrics (things that are easier to track and count that we believe are associated with the goals we have). However, sometimes proxy metrics distract us from making progress on the actual goal.

For example, perhaps your nonprofit has a goal of increasing brand awareness and the proxy metric you are using is tracking the number of publications by your employees or those that mention your organization. A year goes by, and your team is proud of the large number of publications listed in the progress report. However, brand awareness among the constituencies that matter most to your organization doesn't seem to have changed. The proxy metric motivated lots of employee activity around generating publications; but that activity wasn't targeted closely enough to the actual goal the nonprofit needed to accomplish. So, when selecting proxy metrics, consider how closely they align to your goals, how clearly they need to be specified, and what behaviors they'll ultimately motivate. We'll discuss this in much more detail in Chapter 5.

It has also been my experience that many leaders are overly optimistic in their assessment of the attainability of certain outcomes. Even when outcomes are ultimately attainable, they nearly always end up costing more time and money than anticipated. My advice is to pay particular attention to how realistic your assumptions are when you outline a proposed course of action. Said another way, don't be unnecessarily naïve.

Documenting an investment thesis

All strategic plans contemplate an investment of time and/or resources. Even if your plan is focused on cost savings, you need an investment thesis to make the case for the investment of time and resources in pursuit of those goals. There are a few ways to approach this.

First, we should ask ourselves why organizations make investments. If you are trying to convince other leaders and board members to endorse a set of strategic investments, what kinds of returns might they provide? Do they offer the promise of revenue growth, improved financial security, increased organizational leverage, cost savings, risk mitigation, employee retention, productivity gains, or broader mission impact? Do they offer some other tangible or intangible benefits? How long until those benefits are realized? How long do you believe the benefits will last?

Strategic investments can have both financial and non-financial returns. The timeline, caveats, and assumptions behind those returns are important to adequately understand return on investment (ROI). So are the estimates of cost. I encourage teams engaging in strategic planning to first dream big and not get bogged down by affordability concerns. Once you've chosen the best objectives and actions to pursue and have defined the rationale behind them, then consider cost feasibility and strategies to reduce or phase-in investment costs.

Be wary of letting your enthusiasm for a particular strategic course cause you to underestimate its costs. Clearly understanding investment requirements and realistic costs is central to long-term success. Hiding those requirements and costs early in the process is a mistake. If affordability is truly a problem, defining the right path forward and accurately estimating its costs allows you to create a mandate. Your nonprofit can choose to tackle that mandate through a fundraising campaign, cost-cutting in other areas of the organization, obtaining financing, or by phasing the strategic actions over a longer time horizon. The accuracy and clarity you provide will help everyone in your organization rally around the best course of action.

Elements of effective strategic plans

The fiduciary/impact dilemma introduced in Chapter 1 is, of course, pertinent to the development of your nonprofit's strategy. As your strategy takes shape, it should be assessed through the lens of how balanced it is across the competing objectives of mission impact and financial health. However, it doesn't necessarily need to be balanced if your organization is already out of balance and your strategy is meant, in part, to address that.

Effective strategic plans clearly define objectives, provide a rationale, outline measures of success, and recommend specific actions. Table 3.1 provides a few high-level examples of these plan elements across a set of example categories (the intent here is only to illustrate concepts).

If you are asked to participate in strategic planning, where the objectives have already been defined, you should probe the rationale behind those objectives to make sure you understand why they were selected. If you're involved in defining success measures and recommending actions, you can use a driver diagram, the Now, Near, Far Framework, or the SMARTIE criteria to organize your thoughts. No matter what your role is in developing strategy, this is the time to engage honestly and show the love and care you have for the organization, its mission, and its future.

Many nonprofits are like rudderless sailboats adrift on the ocean. They lack clarity of purpose, display little evidence of strategy, and struggle to stay afloat. If this describes your organization, it probably makes sense to put on a life jacket and ask some tough questions of the captain.

Category	Objective	Rationale	Success Measures	Recommended Action
Funding Strategies	Diversify portfolio of funders.	Concentration among too few funders presents risk.	25% increase in funders by the end of year two.	Dedicate staff time to pursuing relationships and grants with new funders.
People Strategies	Improve the retention of employees of diverse backgrounds.	A diverse workforce better equips the organization to effectively carry out its mission.	30% reduction in voluntary departures by employees.	Leverage diversity, equity, and inclusion committee to recruit racially diverse employees into the leadership development program.
Communication Strategies	Improve image in the community.	Donations have fallen after negative news story.	Improved survey results, positive news stories, and increased donation levels.	Elevate brand by hosting community picnic and demonstrate commitment to mission by partnering with housing authority.
Growth Strategies	Broaden the organization's impact from a community to a region.	A regional focus will increase efficiency of our operations and extend our impact.	Financial metrics and evidence of expansion into surrounding communities.	Differentiate nonprofit from its competitors through outreach and marketing.

Table 3.1 Strategic Plan Elements

EXECUTIVES & MANAGERS

As an executive or other organizational leader, developing, vetting, endorsing, and communicating the organization's strategy typically falls on you. You likely already have lots on your plate and may struggle to find the time to do this right. Formalizing plans also makes you accountable for executing those plans and can restrict your ability to respond to the market. How constraining will that plan be when your ideas about what's best for the organization change? Be up-front with your colleagues and board about the need to balance strategic planning with other priorities and to maintain the ability to react to a changing environment. A hastily completed and ill-defined strategic plan pulled together "just in time" for the next board meeting is a disservice to your organization.

Strategic planning is about focusing the organization on the most important strategic imperatives. Sometimes, nonprofit executives lose sight of this while trying to gain the endorsement of the board and the buy-in of other colleagues. If you find yourself looking at a list of seven or more strategic imperatives, you're losing the battle to focus the organization (and sacrificing all the benefits that come with focus). While there will undoubtedly be differing opinions about what's most important for the organization's future, the effort to drive consensus toward two to four key objectives will pay high dividends. If there are too many, do not allow the process to move forward. Discuss phasing and pushing certain objectives to be revisited in out-years as part of your negotiation. Also, resist redefining objectives to become umbrella terms that cover loosely related sub-objectives. This isn't the time to lose clarity.

To focus your strategy in the right areas, pull together a small focus group of your best people early in the process to explore the strategic imperatives questions (see Table 3.2 below). Which area or two (no more than three) present the biggest challenges to your nonprofit? Use these imperatives to frame the goals of the person and the team leading your strategic planning. Also, use them to gain buy-in from board members on the reasoning behind the planning effort. For example, "We are facing a strategic imperative to improve our organization's reach and must focus our attention there."

10 Strategic Imperatives for Nonprofits

1	Clarity	Is it absolutely clear to our leaders, employees, and trustees why our organization exists and what we are trying to accomplish?
2	Focus	Are all our employees and investments of resources aligned and focused on the right things?
3	Scale	Is our organization's size aligned to the scope of the problem we are trying to address? Do we have sufficient leverage?
4	Resources	Do we have the resources necessary to execute our mission? Is our balance sheet healthy enough to weather a storm and carry us through the next decade?
5	Cost	Are our operational and overhead costs appropriately sized? Do we need to increase our efficiency?
6	Reach	Are we reaching our intended audiences of clients, funders, volunteers, partners, and other stakeholders?
7	Brand	Is our brand clear, well-understood, and valued in the market?
8	Morale	Are the majority of our employees happy, motivated, and retained?
9	Innovation	Have we created the time and space necessary for our best and brightest to innovate?
10	Impact	Are the efforts of our team and those of our partners having the desired effect? Are we achieving our mission? Do we need to increase our effectiveness?

Table 3.2 Strategic Imperatives

TRUSTEES

How active and substantive a role you play in developing a strategy for your nonprofit is up to you. It's expected that you will ultimately endorse and support the plan, but how involved in its development should you be? Boards can cause a lot of organizational damage by engaging in strategy development in the wrong ways. Even when key board members have extensive domain knowledge and relevant market experience, they should resist the urge to over-influence strategy development.

Strategy works best when the day-to-day leaders of a nonprofit develop it with a passion for the promise it represents. Trustees can encourage that passion, help those leaders refine their vision for the future, relay their own experiences, and point out potential blind spots. They can also (and should) hold executives accountable for balancing consistency and agility after a strategic plan has been endorsed as some nonprofit execs suffer from a form of attention deficit disorder when it comes to maintaining organizational focus. However, trustees should resist allowing their own interests and aspirations to directly influence the nonprofit's strategic objectives in substantive ways.

I recognize that this advice is contrary to common guidance and practice among many of today's nonprofits. A good trustee readily acknowledges the limits of their knowledge and those of the management team. They should ask probative questions, offer insights from their own experience, and then allow the organization's leaders to lead. The perspectives of trustees carry significant weight, given their role in executive compensation and performance reviews. But even the best trustees can only have a rudimentary understanding of employee culture and the aspirations, differentiating competencies, and challenges the organization confronts daily. Trust and empower your leaders to develop the best strategy for the organization.

Of course, this doesn't mean taking a hands-off approach. Besides probing the financial assumptions behind the plan, trustees should examine the following lines of reasoning to ensure that the strategy will move the mission forward.

1. *Clarity.* How easy is it for every employee, trustee, and stakeholder to understand the strategic objective and how we intend to accomplish it? Have we separated an easy-to-understand component of a complex problem and defined a compelling mechanism of change?
2. *Point of intervention.* Where in the lifecycle of the issue does our strategy focus? Why is this the most effective point for our organization to intervene? Are there revenue or grant funding issues that have influenced our choices?

3. *Scope and leverage.* Will our strategy sufficiently increase the scope and leverage of the organization? Are we assuming an impact level that is beyond the reach of our scope and leverage?

4. *Longevity of impact.* Does the strategy seem likely to create change that will last? Can it be adjusted to improve the stickiness of our impact or to catalyze change in a way that motivates others?

5. *Mechanism of impact.* Does the strategy explicitly define the mechanism of impact that the nonprofit is targeting? What are the barriers? How likely is success?

Let's explore the "mechanism of impact." What mechanisms of impact come to mind for your organization? Are you satisfying an unmet need for a product or service like delivering food after a disaster or providing healthcare to the poor? Are you delivering a paradigm-changing technology that empowers people or makes it easier for people to "do the right thing" (e.g., clean energy technology, public health information systems, or a platform supporting social impact investing)? Are you working to change hearts and minds about a particular problem like mental health advocacy or reducing reliance on single-use plastics?

Three common mechanisms of impact for nonprofit organizations are *satisfying unmet needs, developing innovative solutions to intransigent problems*, and *convincing people that they want something else altogether.* Systemic change can theoretically be accomplished using any of the three, but scale and leverage typically limit the reach of nonprofits satisfying unmet needs by delivering goods and services. These needs could possibly be met for a singular issue if Bill Gates, Alice Walton, and Warren Buffett worked together to solve that issue, or if the Federal Government implemented a large, new national program. But for most of us, scale presents a formidable challenge.

Emotional or intellectual appeals can change policy, clinical practice, organizational investment, personal behavior, or attitudes about a social justice issue. Unfortunately, the phrase *changing hearts and minds* is a euphemism associated with failed military campaigns (Vietnam, Afghanistan, etc.). This is a shame because one of the most powerful levers of societal change is public opinion, and the phrase *changing hearts and minds* conveys that those opinions have both emotional and intellectual underpinnings. Nonprofits focused on this mechanism of change have the potential to create real leverage and significant impact through a well-thought-out communications strategy. As a trustee, you can help them achieve this by asking the right questions about strategic intent.

I believe that the best nonprofit trustees are those who inspire introspection and dialogue through probative questions about the organization's strategy and strategic intent. Look beyond the charisma of your friendly executive director (ED) or chief executive officer (CEO) and ask the tough questions. That's why you're on the board.

SUMMARY

- A nonprofit's purpose serves as the foundation of its strategy.
- It is through strategy that you turn implicit ideas about the future and your organizational aspirations into explicit plans, milestones, and actions.
- Nonprofits working in relatively stable and predictable environments should focus their planning on differentiation and growth within those environments. Nonprofits working in more dynamic and unpredictable environments should focus their planning on innovation and agility, as advantages are usually short-lived.
- Strategic plans help to align the intentions of your workforce and provide consistency to your investments. Even the best-run nonprofits usually have room to improve along these two dimensions.
- Planning models are helpful in two ways: they help the team developing the strategy to think through various considerations, and they help structure the reasoning provided to trustees, employees, and other stakeholders.
- Strategy is best developed by small groups and vetted by larger ones. Strategy development is an exercise in focus. The more people involved, the more difficult the journey.
- Strategy development is about two things: choosing the right objectives and selecting the right actions to support those objectives. Knowing which objectives are the right ones for your organization and which actions will most effectively advance those objectives is where the "strategy" part comes in.
- As your strategy takes shape, you should assess it through the lens of how balanced it is across the competing objectives of mission impact and financial health.
- When presented with a strategic plan, trustees should probe financial assumptions and ensure that the strategy will advance the mission. The latter is done by probing clarity, point of

intervention, scope and leverage, longevity of impact, and mechanism of impact.

- Three common mechanisms of impact for nonprofit organizations are satisfying unmet needs, developing innovative solutions to stubborn problems, and convincing people that they want something else altogether.

4

EXECUTING STRATEGY

Real change, enduring change, happens one step at a time.

—U.S. Supreme Court justice RUTH BADER GINSBURG

THIS CHAPTER IS about how you—as a nonprofit leader—can help your organization successfully execute its strategy. In fact, all the remaining chapters of this book are about strategy execution to some degree. Let's start this journey with an old Moroccan proverb that applies to strategy execution: "While the camel driver has his plans, the camel has plans of his own."

This proverb reminds us that trying to control everything is futile, particularly those things you can merely influence. Strategy execution is about directing your energies and those of your team toward the things that are under your control and most important to your success. Yes, you can influence things outside of your control with a little creativity (and you should, at times), but spending all your time fighting the camel will distract you from your map, keep you from noticing approaching marauders, and leave you lost and penniless in the desert!

The fiduciary/impact dilemma is a major source of friction when executing strategy. For example, determining how much your nonprofit should spend to execute its current strategy is a recurring question. The desire to expend resources today is tied to how excited the organization's leaders are about the strategy and its perceived likelihood of success. If your organization is particularly enamored with the prospects of your new strategy, it may even decide to take out a loan to implement it.

Alternatively, if you're more focused on financial health and some board members or executives aren't completely sold on the strategy, they may decide to underinvest in execution. Unfortunately, this usually becomes a self-fulfilling prophecy that begins with, "We're not sure this strategy is going to work, so we're going to approve one-tenth of the funding you were seeking." After you can't accomplish a miracle with that low level of funding, they'll explain how they knew it was a questionable strategy all along. If you have more than a few years of experience in the nonprofit sector, you will have encountered this scenario or something similar.

Financial constraints play a significant role in strategy execution for most nonprofits. Very few nonprofits have the resources to achieve meaningful system-level change on their own. While a nonprofit may have the domain or methodological expertise necessary for success, they are usually beholden to others for resources. Financial considerations almost always play a major role in deciding the scope and speed of strategy execution. They also limit the amount of innovation and risk-taking that nonprofits undertake, which impacts the sector as a whole.

Large funders of nonprofit activities (governments, health insurers, and large philanthropic organizations) have the resources to effectively pursue and accomplish system-level change. These funders can be accessed by creating focused investment strategies that follow a consistent and coherent plan. A plan that carefully integrates the activities of multiple nonprofits and other stakeholders can be quite compelling.

Too often, large funders make suboptimal investment decisions that don't capitalize on their leverage to create change. For example, they may spread resources across too many issues or change their focus too often. They might invest without a well-thought-out theory of change or favor specific organizations or people (limiting the impact of those who could be more effective). Maybe they just don't specify clear enough objectives for their investments or perhaps they specify too many. In other cases, it could be that the funder doesn't adequately appreciate the interdependent nature of the problem they are trying to solve. Like any of us, government bureaucrats, insurance directors, and successful philanthropists can also be naïve at times.

Melinda French Gates summarized these issues well in her 2021 *The Giving Pledge* letter, "…it's important for philanthropists to set ambitious goals and measure our progress against those goals. I've learned, however, that it's equally important to place trust in the people and organizations we partner with and let them define success on their own terms. Philanthropists are generally more helpful to the world when we're standing behind a movement rather than trying to lead our own."[1]

While this book is intended for the leaders of nonprofit organizations, I will offer a little general advice for funders. Think of your investments as a focused, interdependent portfolio meant to bring about a very specific change. Be very clear about that desired outcome. Seek multiple per-

---

1. Melinda French Gates. "Pledge Letter." The Giving Pledge. © 2024
https://givingpledge.org/pledger?pledgerId=428

spectives on your theory of change and investment strategy, including those of nonprofits who may share your goals. Truly partner with those you fund. Leverage their knowledge, experience, creativity, relationships, and passion in pursuit of your common goal. And most importantly, hold yourself and your peers accountable for the design and execution of that focused strategy. Your interdependent investments should combine to create clear advances that persist beyond your support. If additional investment is necessary to sustain these advances, it is your responsibility to fully understand that before launching a program of funding. The community of government and philanthropic funders doesn't typically hold itself to high enough standards. I believe they should do more to design and monitor the execution of their program investments. If you work for one of these organizations, take pride in differentiating yourself in this way. You have a vitally important role—own it.

Pursuing efficiency in execution

As most nonprofits face financial constraints, it is essential that they are focused in their endeavors and efficient in their execution. As discussed in Chapter 2, a nonprofit with exceptional clarity about what it is trying to accomplish is an organization where the leaders can be decisive and consistent in their pursuits. That healthy focus allows a culture to develop where the efficiency of execution can be considered and improved. Said another way, the pursuit of efficiency gets lost in organizations that are constantly shifting pursuits and rethinking objectives. In a financially constrained environment, this is a recipe for repeated failure.

Assuming you have clarity about your organization's purpose (Chapter 2) and have developed a set of carefully considered strategic intentions (Chapter 3), the question becomes how best to realize those intentions. That is, how shall we execute our strategy in pursuit of simultaneously maximizing our impact and financial health? Those two objectives imply that we are efficient and effective, that we leverage the power of marketing and relationships, and that we are successful in our business development pursuits (i.e., that we can obtain the funding necessary to execute our strategy).

To untangle these objectives, I've dedicated Chapter 6 to the topic of business development. I did this for two primary reasons: the topic is complex and deserving of a dedicated chapter, and nonprofits sometimes get so distracted by business development that they lose sight of making progress in all other strategic imperatives.

Regardless of what the finance committee of your board may say, your organizational purpose is *not* business development. While business development may be one of your strategic objectives, it cannot and should not be the sole or even primary strategic objective of a nonprofit. Business development is merely a means to an end. Organizations that lose sight of that fact may lose the dedication of their employees and partners. This impairs their brand over time as others in the market begin to question the organization's integrity and purpose.

The execution pyramid

Figure 4.1 provides the three key enablers of strategic execution. If you do these three things well, your organization will become more efficient and effective in executing your strategy. While business development isn't explicitly captured here, it is worth noting that all three enablers also position your nonprofit for business development success.

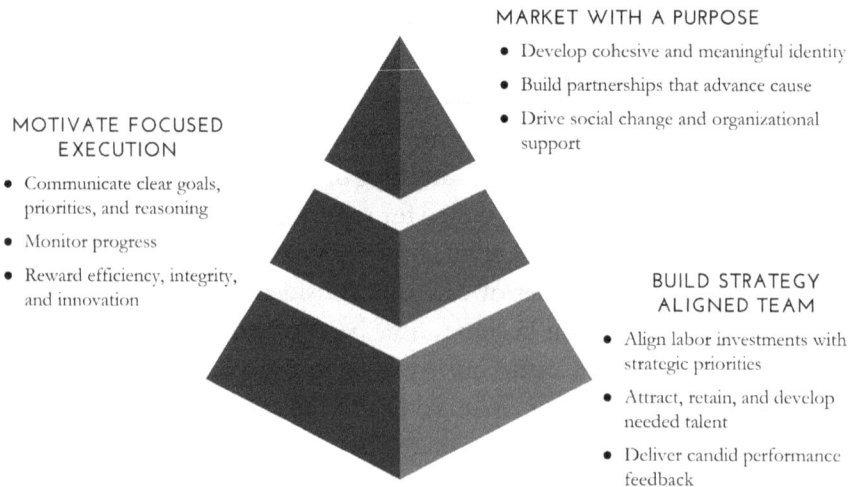

MARKET WITH A PURPOSE
- Develop cohesive and meaningful identity
- Build partnerships that advance cause
- Drive social change and organizational support

MOTIVATE FOCUSED EXECUTION
- Communicate clear goals, priorities, and reasoning
- Monitor progress
- Reward efficiency, integrity, and innovation

BUILD STRATEGY ALIGNED TEAM
- Align labor investments with strategic priorities
- Attract, retain, and develop needed talent
- Deliver candid performance feedback

Figure 4.1 The Execution Pyramid

As you can see, the strategic execution of mission pursuits comes down to three factors that nonprofit leaders must focus on: building a strategy-aligned team, motivating focused execution by that team, and marketing the organization with purpose. Of course, there are additional success factors described throughout this book. However, when it comes to executing strategy, these are the main things that enable success.

Building a strategy-aligned team

Building a strategy-aligned team requires a candid approach regarding the fit of your current team to your strategic objectives. Assessing that fit is seldom straightforward. Nonprofit leaders have colleagues and employees that they like and admire. Perhaps an employee has been particularly loyal to the organization, making significant contributions to executing a previous strategy, or maybe they are central to the organization's social fabric. The question is not whether the employee is capable, friendly, or even particularly loyal—the question is how well their skills and motivations align with the organization's current strategic objectives.

A related problem arises when a nonprofit has an abundance of employees with a certain skill. Even though that skill may be aligned with the new strategy, the organization may find that they have too many resources of a particular type, draining funding they need to invest in other labor resources. Remember, you are not leading a jobs program; you are leading a purpose-driven organization.

Building a strategy-aligned team requires shrewd leadership. Assess the fit of your current team, make any changes necessary, and move forward by aligning new labor investments with elements of your strategy. This not only includes attracting new talent but also retaining and developing the talent you have. The best nonprofit leaders work tirelessly to build an army of change agents—people inspired to work together to realize the organization's vision. After you've built a team aligned to your strategic objectives, ensure that performance feedback is delivered in the context of those objectives. This will reinforce awareness of the strategy and demonstrate where each employee fits in. That creates the opportunity for candid discussion between manager and employee about skills gaps and the rationale behind strategic goals. Ultimately, it also helps to clarify expectations about the future.[2]

Motivating focused execution

The team you build serves as the foundation of your strategy execution efforts. Motivating that team is the next job of the nonprofit leader. Depending on your role, you may be focused on strategy development and reliant on others for execution. Even if you are in a more operational role and "own" the responsibility for strategy execution, chances are that you'll still rely heavily on various teams or other managers. A leader's job is to inspire those teams, prioritize their work, identify and mitigate risks, align resources, engage with them to course-correct or revisit aspects of the strategy, and create an environment that encourages team members to rise to their potential. You motivate focused execution by clearly conveying and reinforcing priorities and the reasoning behind them. That last part is especially important. Reasoning helps employees connect to your strategic vision. Finally, monitor progress (Chapter 5) and clearly reward efficiency, integrity, and innovation as your team successfully executes the strategy.

Marketing with purpose

The third enabler is marketing with purpose. This may seem out of place, but I am referring to the nonprofit leader's responsibility to continually share their vision of strategic success. This requires the development of a cohesive and meaningful organizational identity to align and motivate your teams and partners. Nonprofit marketing for an external audience is about building partnerships with others who share your goals and growing organizational support among funders and other stakeholders. For many nonprofits, it is also about marketing to drive social change. Examples include awareness campaigns, attempts to pressure policymakers, change business behaviors, influence health behaviors, or other constituency-focused engagement strategies. Marketing is only useful to nonprofits with clarity of purpose and firm strategic intentions. In organizations lacking those attributes, marketing typically results in wasted effort and a muddled brand. Said another way, you need to know who you are, why you exist, and what you are trying to accomplish before

---

2. Additional thoughts on building a strategy-aligned team can be found in Chapters 7 and 8.

embarking on marketing efforts to get others to support you. Marketing will show up again in Chapters 5 and 6.

FUTURE LEADERS

The Pareto principle states that 80% of consequences come from 20% of the causes. Put another way, 80% of the organization's progress comes from the efforts of 20% of the people—and you want to be in that 20%. Ensure you are being effective by letting your actions be guided by clear, meaningful priorities. As discussed previously, prioritization may be the most important job of a nonprofit leader, as it motivates focused execution. I'm talking about the importance of prioritizing your own time *and* that of your colleagues (through the delivery of clear expectations). Most executives and managers I've met over my career seem to get this wrong to some extent. For much of my career, I did as well.

Let's start with something you may already be familiar with (or should be): the Eisenhower Matrix. Popularized by Stephen Covey in his bestselling book *The 7 Habits of Highly Effective People*, this matrix builds off an idea that first appeared in one of Eisenhower's speeches (yes, *that* Eisenhower). The premise is that problems or tasks have two key attributes: how important they are and how urgently they need to be addressed. Unfortunately, humans are most likely to prioritize tasks that *feel* urgent (those with a deadline, for example) over tasks that *feel less* urgent, regardless of their relative importance. In other words, we put off working on the most important stuff in favor of being distracted by the "urgent" stuff. Figure 4.2 is my take on the matrix, with some examples.

Now let's dig a little deeper. Ask yourself *why* a particular task is important and *who* it is important to. Is it important because it develops your personal brand with the executive team or board or because it contributes to the financial health of the organization? What's driving the urgency? Is the deadline coming from outside the organization or is it internally driven and more open to negotiation?

Every task comes with an opportunity cost. Great leaders maintain an awareness of this fact throughout their careers. The problem of opportunity cost grows exponentially when teams of dedicated people are working on the wrong things. This problem is made worse by executives and

	NOT URGENT	URGENT
IMPORTANT	Tasks with unclear deadlines that are still integral to your goals. **Examples:** contacting a partner whose performance is lacking, mentoring a key team member, or researching the priorities of a potential funder. **Add to your to-do/schedule**	Tasks with clear deadlines and major consequences associated with inaction. **Examples:** reviewing a draft grant proposal, lobbying a politician before a key policy vote, or reviewing your Form 990 before submission. **Do today**
NOT IMPORTANT	Tasks that don't have significant consequences associated with inaction. **Examples:** things you are doing that are distracting—self-destructive behaviors, engaging in the company rumor mill, scrolling social media posts, etc. **Stop wasting your time**	Tasks with clear deadlines but only minor consequences associated with inaction (i.e., not integral to your strategy). **Examples:** low-value tasks with artificial, internal deadlines and tasks that can be effectively accomplished by someone else. **Delegate or renegotiate**

Figure 4.2 The Eisenhower Matrix

managers who introduce false urgency into the mix. It is relatively common to come across nonprofit executives who unknowingly cause organizational harm by the overuse of artificial deadlines. A steady stream of "urgent projects" results in an ineffective organization that seems to chase its own tail.

"A drowning man is not troubled by the rain." This Persian adage might help you to keep things in perspective and focus your energies on the vitally important. As you grow in your career, have the courage to negotiate deadlines and the assignment of tasks that interfere with more important deliverables. When people are stretched too thin, their performance goes down across the board (including on the most important things they are working on). Remember this when *you* task others. Be sure to have candid conversations about competing priorities.

A key aspect of strategy execution is communication—with your colleagues, partners, funders, board, etc.—that will refine their understanding of your accomplishments, aspirations, and plans. I've seen excellent ideas fail because of lack of buy-in and truly brilliant people held back by their less than stellar communication skills. I've also seen mediocre ideas and leaders celebrated, largely because of savvy communication.

One piece of salient advice I can offer is the importance of being responsive. Too many bright, capable people focus only on being responsive up the management chain (i.e., to requests from their boss). If you want to be a leader, then act like one. When you are unresponsive or respond to a long, thoughtful email with a terse answer, it sends the message that you do not value the thoughts and efforts of the people around you. This is a terrible message to send. If you don't have the time to deliver a thoughtful answer immediately, then *that* becomes the answer you deliver (along with a commitment to when you *can* reply more thoughtfully). View communication with colleagues as a mechanism of building your brand within the organization. When it comes time to consider you for a leadership role, how you are perceived by your peers is a notable part of the calculation. It's not necessarily about being liked. It's about being admired and respected.

Effective communication has three attributes. It is *efficient*, it is *clear*, and it is *compelling*. Leaders in all stages of their career should continually strive to improve these three aspects of their written and verbal communication.

Efficient. The communicator is cognizant of the time being invested by an audience and shows respect for that audience by being judicious with their time. In real terms, this means creating presentations that don't meander aimlessly, anticipating questions and having thoughtful answers ready, and avoiding unnecessarily detailed written communications.

Clear. The objectives of the communication have been carefully considered and the message itself (whether written or verbal) has been well thought out. Avoid the approach to verbal communication used by *The Office's* Michael Scott: "Sometimes I'll start a sentence, and I don't even know where it's going. I just hope I find it along the way." No one wants to follow you on that journey unless they are watching you on TV and looking for a laugh.

Compelling. The communication has a hook or is insightful in a way that engages your audience and makes your message memorable. Take the time to find aspects of your subject that are relatable, humorous, impactful, or particularly perceptive. I still remember the hook used in compelling presentations I attended fifteen or twenty years ago. A good hook goes a long way to relax the presenter, engage the audience, and help them to absorb the message.

Tips to help you improve your emails and presentations

- *Be concise in your written communication.* A concise narrative is easier to comprehend and retain. A memorable list of bullets is more impactful than a ten-paragraph email. If you need to write the ten paragraphs out first, do so, but don't fall into the trap of trying to show off how smart you are or how considered your opinion is by sending the unedited version.
- *Email communications should be respectful, direct, and action-oriented.* If you email your boss, include a proposed course of action in response to the issue you are raising. If you email a peer, re-read your note to ensure that the tone can't be misinterpreted. If you email about a sensitive topic, remember that emails persist and are discoverable during legal proceedings.
- *Keep slides simple and don't rely on them to convey the entire presentation.* Slides with lots of information on them are challenging to present, and you will lose your audience's attention. A common mistake is trying to make a slide deck acceptable as both a read-ahead and a presentation. *Do not do this!* You will disappoint everyone. Focus on including what you want your audience to remember. Use concise bullets or graphics with a few keywords or phrases to help you recall major points.
- *Know your purpose.* The purpose of your email/presentation may be to promote dialogue, mentor, convey guidance, request a decision, or foster the retention of important information. All these goals benefit from focused, compelling content. Make sure that is what you are delivering.
- *Don't read your slides to the audience.* If your slides lend themselves to reading, you're doing it wrong, and your audience is reading your slides and ignoring you.

- *Come prepared.* If you don't feel like an expert in the material you are trying to present, then you haven't prepared enough. A lack of preparation zaps your confidence, and that's all your audience will remember about your presentation.
- *Be confident, smile, and project.* You are the expert, and the audience wants to hear from you. Convey excitement for the content. Excitement is contagious—even for the most mundane of topics. Twenty years ago, I sat through a great presentation on healthcare data standards. The presenter's love for the topic turned truly tedious content into a presentation that was interesting and memorable all these years later.
- *Leave room for dialogue.* Conveying too much detail puts you in the awkward position of trying to remember tons of information and stops your audience from engaging in the conversation. Leave secondary considerations for a Q&A at the end. If you feel something is important, but it doesn't fit into the flow of your presentation, think of ways you might bait the audience into asking about it.

EXECUTIVES & MANAGERS

Some senior managers take pride in working long hours, wearing the badge of being "busy," and are stretched too thin for all to see. Others (including yours truly) sometimes overvalue their contributions relative to their peers: "I need to format this presentation because nobody else will do it right," or, "I need to edit the proposal because I'll do it better than the editor we have on our team." Here's the problem with that—many leadership tasks involve creative thinking, and that requires downtime. If you're running from one "urgent" low-value task to another, you aren't allowing yourself the time and space necessary to contribute in the ways only you can. The organization suffers as a result.

While authentically delegating is an important leadership trait, over-delegation can also be a problem. Consider the following example:

At a dinner with trustees, a board member mentions to the CEO that a report on a particular subject "might be interesting." The next day, the CEO asks the COO to take the lead in pulling together the report for the board. He mentions it was raised "on a whim" so she shouldn't spend much effort on it. The COO then meets with two of her VPs and delegates the task of pulling together the first draft of the report to them. The VPs meet with each other to coordinate and make sure they understand what is being asked of them. Each VP delegates aspects of the task to members of their team, pulling some team members off a proposal and others off an important project to work on "the board report." This goes on for a while, with the VPs meeting to review early drafts of the report, questioning the accuracy of certain assumptions made in the data collection, etc. As the report works its way back up the chain, the VPs ask for changes to it, as does the COO, and finally the CEO. Once the report on the potentially interesting topic is deemed to be mature enough to share with the board, the CEO puts it on the agenda of the board meeting. Months go by and the report is finally presented in the read-ahead materials. A friendly discussion ensues during the board meeting. No decisions are made, or actions taken because of the discussion. The trustee who originally asked for the report doesn't recall raising the question, but everybody is happy with the discussion and thanks the management team for the interesting report.

Does this example sound familiar to you? These kinds of inefficiencies are particularly pervasive in nonprofits. Boards exist to serve nonprofits, not the other way around. Trustees need to carefully consider the purpose of tasking that originates with them. It needs to be action-oriented and/or serve a clear governance function. CEOs need to be comfortable questioning the purpose of tasking that originates with trustees and must act in a manner that protects the organization from wasteful exercises. In fact, everyone in a well-managed nonprofit should be trained, and even conditioned, to ask what the specific purpose or goal of a task is and when it should be completed. They should be ready to have candid conversations about other priorities, opportunity costs, and the relative importance of competing requests. It is amazing how a few people can create wave upon wave of ineffective tasking, distracting larger and larger portions of the workforce. It's even more amazing that senior executives sometimes mistake these people for being valuable contributors (people who "get a lot done").

In the most effective organizations, honest dialogue about the relative importance of various activities and pursuits is pervasive. Just imagine how much untapped potential exists in the people in your organization who are distracted by low-to-no-value activities.

Creating opportunities for all employees to rise to their potential and contribute in the most meaningful ways is a hallmark of good leadership. To do this, you must constantly find and eliminate low-value activities. Every pursuit should be viewed through the lens of opportunity cost. In an overly polite work environment, there's not enough candid dialogue about what employees are forgoing to work on the latest low-value task.

Tasks also grow in importance along the delegation chain. Leaders like to think that delegation is an "efficiency engine" because you are (theoretically) moving tasks to the least costly resource able to effectively complete them. However, as a task moves down the delegation chain, its importance moves up ("I need to bow out of the client meeting to work on a report for *the board*"). Often, the level of effort required to complete the task also goes up because of its perceived importance, uncertainty around the specific goals of the task, and just the lack of experience of the team ultimately responsible for completing it. Delegation is only efficient in organizations with a healthy culture of communication, where the person being delegated to is comfortable questioning the purpose, importance, form, and opportunity cost associated with new tasking. It's your job to create that culture.

Many well-intentioned nonprofit leaders make the mistake of overtasking their top performers with the belief they can squeeze even more productivity from them. While the risk of burnout is real, the bigger risk is simply stifling the creativity and innovation of these high-potential employees. People who are running from one urgent task to another don't have the mental energy and time to consider the more complex challenges facing the organization. A good leadership tip is to focus your energies on continually expanding your pool of top performers. Ask yourself what others on the team need to contribute at higher levels? Often, all they need is your confidence.

Another way for executives and managers to maximize effectiveness is to think about the labor mix of the organization. We tend to think of roles relative to organizational functions or needs and set salaries based on market data we obtain for those roles. While there is nothing inherently wrong with this approach, it leaves one wondering whether we are maximizing the strategic value of our labor expenses. Of course, different roles carry different types and levels of strategic potential. However, there is something to be said for considering the overall portfolio of labor *investments* and working to maximize its strategic return.

I've noticed that the strategic value realized per dollar of salary expended tends to follow a typical pattern. At the lower end of compensation, the strategic value per dollar of salary is relatively high. Yes, I said strategic value. While this may seem counterintuitive, it becomes clearer when you consider labor as a system of resources working together to accomplish all the tasks needed for the nonprofit's success. Every hour of activity that is accomplished by a lower-paid resource frees up more expensive resources to work closer to their potential.

Suboptimal labor mixes cost nonprofits dearly. This is especially pronounced in small organizations. Consider the hourly cost of two employees performing a relatively menial task like formatting a presentation. If the task can be accomplished by someone making $40,000 (about $20 an hour) but is instead being done by a senior executive making $160,000 (about $80 an hour), the organization is paying four times too much! One caveat is that senior managers and executives tend to work over forty hours a week, which drives down their effective hourly rate (this is referred to as "uncompensated overtime"). However, it is quite unlikely that the senior manager in this scenario is working 160 hours a week, which is what would be required to drive down the effective rate to be comparable to the $40,000 employee.[3]

Moving up the compensation scale, the strategic value realized per dollar of salary does some interesting things. At the lowest compensation levels, the effect described in the previous example *drives up* the strategic value of employees. Most nonprofit organizations are awash with daily operational tasks that should be accomplished at the lowest cost possible.

---

3. Tip: since there are a little over two thousand working hours in a year, it is easy to estimate the hourly cost of any salary. Just divide the salary by two and drop the thousands, e.g., someone making $100,000 per year makes around $50 per hour.

These aren't particularly strategic tasks, so the opportunity cost of distracting higher-paid employees with them is a drain on the organization. Therefore, the strategic return on hiring more employees at the lower end of the salary range tends to be positive. Of course, you may need to grow the size of your nonprofit to afford this efficiency.

A different strategic value consideration comes into play as we move further up the compensation scale, beyond people with commonly available skills and toward those with differentiated and unique talents. You should expect one person making $150,000 to deliver more strategic value than two people who make $75,000. However, there are often diminishing returns for higher and higher salary premiums (and, at a certain point, they become negative returns). I've seen this play out many times over my career. For example, it isn't too hard to imagine a scenario where three capable people making $200,000 can deliver more strategic value to the organization than one person making $600,000.

If you're a highly paid executive or an orthopedic surgeon, you may take umbrage at what I am about to say. There's a pretty good chance that the highest-paid employees of many nonprofits represent an inefficient use of resources in pursuit of strategic value. Of course, it's possible that these most senior leaders offer highly specialized and rare skills, perhaps in negotiating mergers and acquisitions, setting and executing organizational strategy, or building exceptional teams (or, in the case of surgeons, replacing knees and hips). However, in the context of maximizing the strategic return across the entire portfolio of labor costs, the hard truth is that many nonprofits aren't getting the best return on these most senior investments.

If you're reading this and happen to be one of the highest-paid people in your nonprofit, I hope it inspires you to be more content with your compensation and to challenge yourself to do even more for the organization you love. Ask yourself whether you are consistently delivering more value than two members of the team who make half your salary. If not, what are you going to do about it?

Strategic execution in small nonprofits

As mentioned in Chapter 1, most nonprofits are small and come with a whole host of unique challenges. If you are an executive or manager in a small nonprofit, you are probably already familiar with the workarounds that small organizations must adopt to survive. Here are a few execution tips for small nonprofits.

- *Focus on return on investment (ROI).* Small organizations can accomplish outsized returns with small investments. Demonstrating that your organization is nimble and an excellent steward of the resources you've received will attract new partners and funders. Differentiate yourself by focusing your team and marketing on the ROI of your efforts. Think about ROI broadly—having a compelling mission statement is good, but demonstrating progress toward those mission objectives is ten times more engaging!

- *Maximize the value you extract from volunteers.* Many small nonprofits go to great lengths to attract volunteers and then don't get the most value from them. Approach volunteering like you would recruiting for employees: identify specific jobs and skill sets needed, recruit targeted volunteers, motivate them by setting a clear vision and high expectations, and then manage their activities to ensure that they are contributing at their maximum potential. Don't hesitate to ask your volunteers for their thoughts on additional ways in which they can contribute. Your volunteers believe in the mission—give them the opportunity to deliver the most value they can.

- *Explore models of earned income or larger multi-year grants.* Large multi-year grants and revenue generating programs offer the opportunity to lessen your reliance on small donors while creating scale and leverage. The fiduciary/impact dilemma is more pronounced in small organizations as existential financial concerns are ever-present. Having a more predictable and consistent funding outlook allows your organization to develop a healthier balance between fiduciary and mission tasks. Again, it is useful to consider ROI. How much of your nonprofit's time and energy is spent pursuing funding? Are you confident the organization is receiving the highest possible return on those investments?

- *Consider ways to create more leverage through partnerships or by altering your impact strategies.* Out of necessity, small nonprofits tend to be very practical. Exercises that encourage your team to dream bigger allow them to see their work and goals in new ways. Challenge them to question the sustainability of their impact, to seek new ways to be more efficient, to gain new community supporters, to create a shared vision, and to partner with other nonprofits. Being pragmatic is good. But being pragmatic and strategic at the same time is better.

- *Pay particular attention to your culture.* While the statistics vary, burnout among the executives and employees of small nonprofits is a significant problem. The combination of extremely lean teams, restricted funding sources, and passion for the organization and its mission is a recipe for burnout. Overworked employees grow resentful and less effective over time. This is a complex issue, with many manifestations. Candid dialogue is important to surface these issues. One of the best ways to address them is through reinforcing a collaborative culture where colleagues respect and support one another, responsibility is shared, roles are broad and multifaceted, and leaders authentically delegate.

- *Consider marketing as a critical strategic execution step.* As discussed earlier in this chapter, marketing should foster a cohesive and meaningful identity. It also supports the development of key partnerships that advance your cause and can drive social change and organizational support. Marketing and storytelling prowess are usually quite evident in nonprofits that succeed in growing their balance sheets, influence, and impact. As an executive of a small nonprofit, prioritize developing and delivering your organization's stories so that you can build momentum among supporters and drive the impact you and your board desire.

TRUSTEES

What is the role of the board in helping a nonprofit execute its strategy? Nonprofits differ quite a bit in this regard. Some boards fully entrust execution to the management team and focus solely on monitoring progress. In other organizations, trustees are directly engaged in strategy execution. For example, trustees may be responsible for significant fundraising objectives, or they may be asked to use their network to facilitate key organizational partnerships or identify candidates for leadership positions. In small nonprofits, trustees tend to be more involved in strategy development and can end up providing consultation to the teams executing the strategy.

The right role for trustees in your nonprofit depends on two simple things: the organization's needs, and the unique strengths of the current trustees. Unfortunately, those don't always align. The management team and the board can quickly grow frustrated with each other when that happens. The challenge is that organizational needs are rather dynamic, and the skills, experience, and professional networks of trustees are much slower to change. So, a board that is well-aligned with organizational needs one year may feel much less useful the next year.

There are three basic governance principles that can help mitigate this dynamic challenge.

1. *Shortened board terms and term limits.* Given that organizational needs are likely to be dynamic, it is important to facilitate regular change on boards. The most common term structure for nonprofit boards is two consecutive terms of three years each. While this facilitates rotation, I would argue that three (or four) consecutive terms of two years would be a better model for many nonprofits (see point 3, below). It's also best practice to stagger the terms across trustees so that the nonprofit avoids disruptive changes associated with the departure of multiple trustees at once.

2. *Specific, well-defined position descriptions.* Trustee recruitment should *always* start with a careful review and update of the position description by both the management team and the members of the board development and governance committee. Generic position descriptions that aren't aligned with the organization's upcoming strategic needs are a disservice to everyone involved. Be clear about what expertise is needed and what service trustees are expected to deliver.

3. *A mature assessment and exit strategy for members.* Invariably, nonprofit trustees develop relationships with one another, and their own small group culture. It is common for this culture to value interpersonal relationships above candor. This can result in

retaining trustees who are no longer aligned with organizational needs or those who are too passive, ineffective, or troublesome. Honest assessments of fit and performance should be done annually by a small team made up of the ED or CEO, one other member of the management team, and two or three rotating board members. These respectful evaluations can be supported by an external consultant, if needed, to foster frank dialogue. Trustees should embrace the expectation that a consecutive term will only be approved if they meet certain performance thresholds and fit well with emerging organizational needs. They shouldn't view consecutive terms as inevitable, or even likely. This is why I recommend nonprofits to move to a two-year term, with a limit of three or four consecutive terms.

Implementing more aggressive board refresh policies comes with some trade-offs: increased time needed for recruitment, onboarding, and assessment of trustees as well as the loss of some organizational memory among the board. However, those trade-offs are more than offset by the creation of a healthier board culture, clearer expectations around performance, and a higher likelihood that each trustee will deliver real value to the organization. That is why you're on the board, isn't it?

Another important aspect of the trustee's role in strategy is helping to "clear the decks." By that, I mean removing obstacles from the management team's path that are preventing them from focusing on impactful work. When it comes to executing strategy, there are many reasons that execution cannot produce the desired results. From poor organizational buy-in and alignment to an ineffective leadership team that cannot communicate and coordinate, there are plenty of potential pitfalls. This is one area where nonprofit boards can cause problems by creating distractions from the real work at hand—but it's also an area where they could excel. Once you understand and have endorsed the strategy, it is your job as a trustee to keep the management team focused on executing it.

SUMMARY

- Financial constraints almost always play a major role in deciding the scope and speed of strategy execution. They also limit the amount of innovation and risk-taking that nonprofits undertake.
- Large funders of nonprofit activities have the resources to effectively pursue and accomplish system-level changes. However, few do.
- Government and philanthropic funders should design their investments to create an interdependent portfolio focused on producing clear, achievable, and sustainable change.
- Business development is merely a means to an end; it should not be the strategic focus of your plans. Forgetting this can impair your brand.
- When executing a strategy, focus on building a strategy-aligned team, motivating focused execution by that team, and marketing the organization with purpose. These are the three things that enable success.
- You build a strategy-aligned team by aligning labor investments with strategic priorities, attracting, retaining, and developing needed talent, and delivering candid performance feedback.
- You motivate focused execution by communicating clear goals, priorities, and reasoning, monitoring progress, and rewarding efficiency, integrity, and innovation.
- Prioritization may be the most important job of a nonprofit leader; you cannot motivate focused execution without it.
- You market with a purpose by communicating a cohesive and meaningful identity that aligns and motivates internal teams, promotes partnerships that advance your cause, and drives social change and organizational support.
- Effective communication has three attributes. It is *efficient*, it is *clear*, and it is *compelling*. If you're not a great communicator, surround yourself with others who are.
- Since organizational needs are dynamic, it is important to facilitate change on nonprofit boards. Boards should embrace

THE NONPROFIT DILEMMA

shortened terms and term limits; specific, well-defined position descriptions for trustees; and a mature assessment and exit strategy for members. A healthy board is helpful to strategy execution in many ways.

98   EXECUTING STRATEGY

5

MEASURING & COMMUNICATING IMPACT

However beautiful the strategy, you should occasionally look at the results.

—British statesman Sɪʀ Wɪɴsᴛᴏɴ Cʜᴜʀᴄʜɪʟʟ

L ET'S START WITH an example I learned in a statistics class at the University of Michigan. The professor relayed a memorable story about measurement that I've since determined was based on the writings of Sir Arthur Eddington—an English astronomer, physicist, mathematician, and philosopher. It goes like this...

A young scientist is studying fish off the coast of Spain. He partners with the fishermen in his village so he can measure the length of the fish in their catch each day. Every afternoon, he waits at the dock, eager to see what they've caught in their nets that day. He then carefully measures and records each fish and any interesting attributes that they have: their color, the presence of gills, the number of fins, etc. One day, a fisherman sits with the scientist and looks at the chart on which he is recording his observations. He sees that the scientist has determined that all fish collected have gills and agrees with that finding. He also sees a graph of the number of fish collected by size, which looks reasonable based on his decades of fishing experience. But then he sees a note the scientist has made about the minimum size of fish off the coast of Spain. He asks, "You've determined that fish smaller than three inches don't live in these waters?" The scientist replies, "Not exactly. I suspect that juvenile fish, those smaller than three inches, probably do exist off this coast, but they are uncatchable. Perhaps they are faster than the others?" The fisherman answers, "It would've been easier for you just to examine my net. The size of the fish we catch is determined by the size of the holes. People don't want the little ones."

This parable serves as a reminder that *what* we measure and *how* we go about measuring it can shape the insights we ultimately gain. What is it we hope to gain from measuring the impact of our nonprofit? How do the metrics we've chosen and the methods we've used to gather and analyze the data shape our understanding?

Of course, the fiduciary/impact dilemma is lurking here as well. Time and money spent on measuring and communicating impact leaves less time for producing impact. Therefore, it's essential for these activities to be targeted, efficient, and managed. This means leveraging the same measurement activity and data for multiple audiences and using the story it tells to further your strategic objectives. Understanding your nonprofit's impact and effectively conveying that story is the foundation of employee morale, stakeholder support, collaborative potential, and funder interest in your organization.

Why measure?

Most nonprofit organizations spend significant resources on measuring and communicating their impact. What is it they hope to gain from these activities? Measurement serves many functions and appeals to conscientious leaders for a few different reasons. While measurement is often about accountability, it also assists leaders in making better decisions. Nonprofit leaders benefit from a constant flow of evidence that their actions are improving the organization's financial health and helping them to deliver on the promise of the mission.

Leaders commonly feel overwhelmed by their responsibility to stakeholders they are accountable to. This includes external stakeholders like funders, partners, and clients (i.e., people receiving services). It also includes internal stakeholders like the board and the nonprofit's employees. Besides accountability to stakeholders, nonprofit leaders usually also have potent feelings about their responsibility to their team, their organization's mission, and its future. These responsibilities can feel as though they are in direct conflict with the interests of other stakeholders. For example, the leader's desire to create career progression for key members of their team can conflict with a funder's desire to keep costs as low as possible.

One way to ease the accountability burden is to align as many parties as possible to the same goals and measures. While some interests cannot be fully aligned, many can with a little creativity. In the example above, the employee's interest in being compensated at a higher level conflicts with the funder's desire to keep costs low. Faced with this problem, good leaders find balance by retaining and developing key employees so that they deliver value commensurate with the compensation they desire. This allows them to demonstrate the efficiency and effectiveness gains that come with a stable workforce that has deeper expertise. If your board, employees, funders, and clients can find goals that converge in this way, those are the best places to focus all parties.

Your job is to find common ground across the various stakeholders you are accountable to. In this process, it's helpful to talk about the opportunity cost and resources required to develop and track different sets of metrics. Alignment between stakeholders occurs when they realize they share the same aims. Even so, there are going to be differences in perspective. Take, for example, *accountability to funders* as compared to *accountability to clients* for service-delivery nonprofits. In a for-profit business, the perspective of paying clients holds considerable sway over the organization's priorities—"The customer is always right." Now consider accountability in domestic violence shelters, food banks, hospitals, and other nonprofits where funding is partly or completely separated from clients. In these organizations, accountability to those who control resources (e.g., government or philanthropic funders) is often better developed than accountability to clients. In these cases, funders should emphasize client satisfaction and other preference metrics to strengthen the voice of clients in the nonprofit's decision-making process.

This dynamic is further complicated when clients have a choice of where to receive services. Consider two hospitals: one rural, with no nearby competitors, and one in a city that competes with two other health systems. Which one will be more focused on patient satisfaction? If a nonprofit feels they are competing for clients (i.e., people to help), opportunities may be found by exploring strategic partnerships with those competitors. There's nothing wrong with competition; in fact, it's somewhat of a cultural obsession in America. However, persistent competition between nonprofits serving the same purpose is evidence of a lack of leadership on the part of the boards and executives of both organizations.

The metrics we choose to monitor shed light on our fiduciary/impact values. Measurement is seldom entirely rational. What we choose to measure and even how we measure it reflects what we value, what we believe we can impact, and what we believe can be easily and reliably measured. Of course, those things that are relatively easy to accomplish and measure are not necessarily those that will bring the greatest mission impact.

It is common for nonprofit executives and boards to focus heavily on financial metrics. If 80% of your time is spent discussing fiduciary objectives, then you are implicitly saying that those are more important than mission objectives. Because fiduciary metrics are relatively easy to measure, they tend to be overweighted. This pushes financial metrics to the forefront of board meetings, executive compensation discussions, employee performance reviews, and strategic planning. Imagine how things might be different if your progress toward mission objectives was just as specific, quantitative, and easily measured.

As nonprofits exist for reasons other than to make money, it is incumbent on the leaders of these organizations (i.e., you) to pursue a balanced narrative and approach to measurement that aligns with their values and goals. If the primary goal of your nonprofit is to grow your financial resources, perhaps you should revisit the discussion in Chapter 2 on clarifying purpose.

Measuring impact provides an opportunity to navigate the fiduciary/impact dilemma more deliberately. Through the process of boiling down what you value into metrics, you can explicitly guide the organization toward the fiduciary/impact balance that is most appropriate for your nonprofit. In short, *you are trying to move the board and employees of the organization from valuing what is measured to measuring what is valued.*

Making this transition isn't easy. Focusing on things that are easier to achieve (and measure) satisfies our instinctual desire for simplicity and progress gratification. Our achievement hormone (dopamine) drives us to seek the reward of consistently achieving small goals even when we know, intellectually, that the goals may be misleading. Imagine if I placed a heavy emphasis on page count as my primary measure of progress while writing this book. How might that backfire?

I could make great "progress" by filling numerous pages with complete gibberish. (Hopefully, you don't think that's what I've actually done here.) But how would this scenario likely play out? For a while, my afternoon tea would probably be quite enjoyable as I grew more and more content with my quick "progress." Later, however, I would be in for an unpleasant reality check when my beta readers and editor started providing candid feedback on the poor quality of the manuscript. I would ultimately realize that the progress I thought I had made wasn't progress at all.

Not all misguided measurement efforts result in such a rude awakening. Many times, we don't even notice the folly of our measurement approach. That "achievement high" can cloud our judgment and become addictive. This causes us to over-rationalize the *easy to achieve/easy to measure* path because we so strongly desire interim success. Even smart, well-intentioned nonprofit leaders tend to overweight the importance of easily attained and easily quantified achievements. But these distract the team from working on foundational issues that are more complex or that take years to yield results. The best path to mission impact is often the harder one to follow—the one with fewer mile-markers and signposts along the way. So, the next time you are in a board or employee meeting where everyone is on a dopamine high, having accomplished a milestone, ask yourself whether that milestone was a distraction from harder, higher value pursuits.

The relationship between measuring and communicating

You may wonder why I bundled measuring and communicating impact into the same chapter. The simple truth is that there are really only three reasons for nonprofits to undertake measurement activities, and they all involve communication.

1. The first (and most annoying) reason is to *meet reporting obligations to funders.* They have given you money, and in return, you agreed to report progress against certain milestones (or outcomes). These metrics may have been defined in a request for proposal (RFP) or proposed by you in your response. Either way, they demonstrate the value of the work being funded. Reporting obligations can be "annoying" for three reasons: measurement activity takes time and energy away from the work itself, the goals are often unrealistic (they expect too much, or you overpromised), and one or both parties engage in gaming the results. Because both parties want the effort to *appear* successful, either may engage in activities that dilute the accuracy of the progress being reported. This includes things like moving the goalposts, excluding certain populations, ignoring the impact of exogenous factors like the work of others, or a policy change, or simply discounting trends that were already underway.

2. The second reason is *measurement for internal audiences*. These are measurement activities that are done at the request of the CEO or board or those that are part of financial monitoring or process-improvement initiatives. They are meant to monitor and improve the organization's health in some way. For example, they may be measuring progress on one or more of the strategic imperatives outlined in Table 3.2 in Chapter 3. These measurement activities can become sources of inefficiency if not carefully managed.

3. The third (and underutilized) reason is *measurement to support communicating organizational impact and value*. This is undertaken specifically for the purposes of crafting and telling the nonprofit's story. Many organizations try to get away with repurposing the results from reason one (reporting obligations to funders) to tell their story. This may make sense if you only have one or two grants. But even then, the metrics you negotiate with a funder may not be the *best* way to tell *your* story.

These reasons for undertaking measurement activities all have communication in common—communication to existing funders, communication to employees and board members, and communication to other external stakeholders (the communities you serve, future funders, policymakers, and potential partners). Nonprofit leaders should carefully consider and define their specific communication goals for each audience *before* selecting metrics and investing resources into measurement activities. Finding the best way to convey the story you want to tell each audience should drive what you measure (not the other way around). The story always comes first.

FUTURE LEADERS

There's an important difference between measuring what "is" and setting a goal of what "ought to be." Goodhart's law, eloquently described by retired Cambridge professor Marilyn Strathern, states: "When a measure becomes a target, it ceases to be a good measure."[1] In other words, when a measure becomes a target, our behavior changes. We tend to prioritize achieving that specific target, regardless of the consequences. Think about my page count example. Instead of page count being a metric that I monitored to ensure that the book was the correct length, it became a target. When producing more pages became the primary goal, I lost sight of the real reason I was writing (to provide value to the reader). This same dynamic is happening across countless nonprofits!

Measurement of a nonprofit's health and impact can be manipulated along the way and data can be framed to tell whatever story is most desirable at the time. This presents a problem for those trying to understand what really works and why. It also represents a huge distraction and opportunity cost. Instead of being honest and feeding mediocre performance data back with the intention of steering efforts toward better outcomes, teams become distracted by finding a way to tell the story of success that they want to tell. Most nonprofits engage in this to some extent, and it's a disservice to their mission. There's an adage made popular by John F. Kennedy after the spectacular failure of the Bay of Pigs invasion: "Victory has 100 fathers and defeat is an orphan."[2] While candor is necessary to learn lessons from failure, it is usually elusive.

Funders have an important role to play in solving this problem. By framing the purpose of smaller assessment grants as assessing the viability of competing solutions and capturing lessons about failure, they can reduce the pressure on nonprofits to present success. Instead of feeling like your grant was wasted on a failed intervention, you can see failure as contributing to the evidence base so that everyone will have a better chance at success in the future. Over time, this experimentation should help to pinpoint the most useful approaches to problems.

Part of the challenge of this approach is that success is context specific. What happens to be successful in one community may not work in another. The best way for funders to approach this problem is to develop a well-thought-out set of "success attributes." That is, what characteristics of a problem, a community, a set of stakeholders, or a policy are necessary for

---

1. Strathern, M. (1997). "'Improving ratings': Audit in the British University System." European Review. Volume 5, Issue 3. pp. 305 – 321. https://doi.org/10.1002/(SICI)1234-981X(199707)5:3<305::AID-EURO184>3.0.CO;2-4
2. In an operation planned by the CIA in 1961, Cuban exiles financed and trained by the U.S. Government, invaded Cuba. This attempt to overthrow Castro's administration was defeated in three days.

a particular intervention to work? Again, collecting better data on failed interventions is necessary to develop our understanding and scale the funder's impact.

The importance of embracing failure is widely underappreciated. In the start-up world, the mantra "fail fast, fail often" is used to convey the importance of risk-taking and iteration. To succeed at difficult challenges or to disrupt the way a particular challenge is viewed, an organization must be open to failure and to *learning from its mistakes*. It's that last part that is usually missed by both funders and nonprofits. Learning from your mistakes requires you to acknowledge them, embrace them, and see them as the great opportunities they are to collect information about why you weren't successful.

Negative findings are especially valuable because they force us to critically review our thinking and try to understand "what went wrong." However, poor outcomes and adverse events are grossly underreported in academic literature and in reports to nonprofit boards. For most of my career, I've imagined creating a *Journal of Failed Interventions and Unpublishable Results*. As a society, we are learning too few lessons from organizational failures because of an overwhelming desire to appear successful. We've been taught that, with a little ingenuity and hard work, anything is possible. So, failure implies that we didn't work hard enough or weren't clever enough. While there may be some truth to that, there is also a lot of truth in the idea of failing fast and often. Many hardworking, insightful people engage in efforts that just don't produce the desired results. Understanding "why" is something we seldom take the time to explore and document. If we can become better at that, we "lift all boats." Humility and introspection are underappreciated virtues.

Determining what to measure

So, with all that said, what the heck should you measure? As I stated previously, the story comes first.

- *Why* are you planning to undertake a measurement activity? "Someone told me to" is not an acceptable answer.
- *Who* is the audience, and *what* story do you hope to tell with the data you capture and analyze?

Assuming that the audience is one of those discussed in the beginning of this chapter, there are only three general areas of inquiry. You could measure the *structural* health of the organization, the consistency, appropriateness, and efficiency of *processes* the organization employs, or the *outcomes* of the organization's work. These three areas of inquiry (structure, process, outcome) are adapted from a common framework used to assess healthcare quality that was first described by a University of Michigan professor in the 1960s and later in his seminal book in 1980.[3] You can frame this in terms of the story you are trying to tell—is the story about *where* you work (structure), *how* you work (process), or *why* you work (outcome)?

Structure

The health of a nonprofit's structure refers to how well its organizational characteristics support its ability to align around and achieve its strategic goals. These characteristics include the nonprofit's balance sheet, staffing, clarity of mission, the integrity of the board and leadership, its propensity to collaborate with others, etc. In effect, these are the prerequisites to success. They provide the context and operating environment that makes the mission possible. I find it helpful to think of structure as *where we work*. Consider the characteristics of where you work. What are some of your organization's structural strengths and what are some of its structural weaknesses?

Process

The consistency, appropriateness, and efficiency of "processes" refers to those that are internally or externally focused. Internal processes are those that are common to many organizations, regardless of mission (like accounting, finance, HR, IT, contracting, and legal). Externally focused processes are those intended to directly advance the organization's mission (like research, advocacy, interventions, executing grants, and delivering services). It is helpful to think of process metrics as *how we work*. How

---

3. Adapted from Donabedian, A. The Definition of Quality and Approaches to Its Assessment. Vol 1. Explorations in Quality Assessment and Monitoring. Health Administration Press, 1980.

do you and others in your organization work? Are the processes employed consistent, appropriate, and efficient? How can they be improved?

You might have noticed that I didn't ask you to consider whether the processes are *effective*. Your organization's effectiveness is determined by many things. While the structure and processes of your organization contribute to your effectiveness, ultimately that effectiveness is reliant upon the actions of others. As a purpose-driven nonprofit leader, you can exert control over your organization's structural health and the maturity of the processes it employs.[4] However, you can do little more than influence the actions of others outside of your organization (remember the camel?). Your effectiveness may very well depend on the actions of other nonprofits, stakeholders, or policymakers. It may depend on consumer behavior, economic realities, media coverage, or cultural perspectives. Persistent societal problems are persistent for a reason. Separating *process* metrics from *outcome* metrics allows a nonprofit leader to better understand what is within their control and what is outside it. This can help the nonprofit develop new strategies when desired outcomes aren't being achieved.

Outcome

Outcome metrics are the ones that are likely most familiar to you. These are usually required by funders to highlight whether the nonprofit's activities are having the desired impact. For example, these might be metrics that show healthier communities, lower levels of carbon emissions, fewer homeless pets, less plastic in the ocean, less gun violence, higher rates of college attendance, less alcohol and substance abuse, lower rates of suicide, or enhanced resilience to natural disasters, etc. It is helpful to think of outcomes as *why we work*. Consider the story behind why you and others in your organization work. Is the organization's story compelling? Are you making a measurable mission impact?

When we think about outcomes, it is helpful to consider intermediate objectives and ultimate goals. If you completed a driver diagram in Chapter 3, some of your primary and secondary drivers likely describe your intermediate objectives. For example, creating access to goods and services

---

4. There is an entire management discipline focused on process maturity. Here, by "mature process," I simply mean one that is appropriate, consistently applied, and efficient.

is an intermediate objective. It is only when your intended recipient benefits from those goods and services that you achieve your ultimate goal. Another example is policy change. Accomplishing a policy aim is an intermediate objective. Only when that policy results in behavior change do you begin achieving your ultimate goal. Policies that are ignored, misunderstood, circumvented, or poorly executed are reminders that policy change is always an intermediate objective. Many nonprofits struggle with setting their sights clearly on their ultimate goals and seeing intermediate outcomes as only milestones along the path.

So, when you consider what to measure and monitor, you want to think about *where you work* and how the structure of the organization supports your strategic objectives, *how you work* and whether the processes used to accomplish your objectives are mature (appropriate, consistently applied, and efficient), and *why you work*. Are you making measurable progress toward achieving the outcomes promised by your mission? Figure 5.1 provides some examples of evidence to look for when selecting metrics to monitor the structure, process, and outcomes of your organization.

STRUCTURE	PROCESS	OUTCOME
Evidence of structural health:	**Evidence of working smart:**	**Evidence of effectiveness:**
• Effective governance	• Using SMART goals based on logic models	• Mission results being achieved
• Leadership integrity & transparency	• Progress being monitored and discussed	• Growth and financial health
• Clarity of purpose	• Processes documented and repeatable	• Healthy brand
• Consistency of direction	• Process efficiency and failures candidly assessed	• Strong evidence of impact
• Mission-aligned project portfolio (no distractions)	• Employees encouraged to identify process improvements	• Stakeholders reporting progress
• Mission-aligned investments for future	• Feedback regularly obtained from external stakeholders (funders, constituents, partners)	• Lasting impact
• Collaboration & partnership with others		• Scalable impact
• Attracting and retaining the best talent		• Regularly asking how we could do even better
• Healthy culture		• Lesson learned captured

Figure 5.1 Structure, Process, Outcome

EXECUTIVES & MANAGERS

Focusing your measurement activities is a useful way to deliver value to your organization. Organizations can easily get caught up in wasting resources by measuring the wrong things or telling ineffective stories because they didn't consider the audience and goals before settling on an approach. Let's start by discussing a few inconvenient truths.

1. The connection between nonprofit programs and achieving the ultimate goals of those programs is usually tenuous. Attributing outcomes of a program to the actions of a single nonprofit is more often an exercise in marketing than accuracy. Consider what would have happened without the program. What alternate explanations for the observed outcomes exist? How can the impact of the nonprofit's program be isolated from those of its collaborators? Are there any unique environmental factors that limit the ability to scale or replicate the results?

2. Research linking specific interventions to achieved benefits is seldom robust enough to adequately support replication. Reproducing the achievements of an intervention is surprisingly difficult, as most nonprofit interventions are highly context-specific. The ingredient that allowed something to be effective in one case may not be present or even understood until after a second intervention fails.

3. Another area that is difficult for nonprofit leaders to assess candidly is the expected duration of impact. The amount of time an observed change persists *after* an intervention is seldom monitored. In finance, this is called "reversion to the mean," referring to how long a significant deviation in an asset price can persist before retreating to its long-run average. Is your nonprofit engaging in activities that fundamentally change an ecosystem or paradigm such that the result can be expected to last? If not, is such a disruptive strategy feasible through collaboration with others?

4. A final inconvenient truth many nonprofit leaders would prefer to ignore is that when interventions *do* have a verifiable impact, the

full cost of the intervention is typically higher than originally estimated and the duration of the impact is lower. This could mean that an accurate representation of ROI would limit interest in replicating the intervention.

So, with those inconvenient truths in mind, what might "focusing your measurement activities" mean? Think about the stories you are keen to communicate to your employees, your board, your funders, and your external stakeholders. Sure, measurement is sometimes about creating situational awareness and mitigating risks, but there are implied stories there as well. With each story, consider how the data captured through measurement activities will support the narrative. What data is essential to making the story compelling and believable? Focus your team's measurement activities on capturing and analyzing *that* data—and *only* that data.

Nonprofit leaders often make missteps here, focusing their measurement activities on what is easily measured rather than on things that are most relevant to the story they are trying to tell. If we can accurately and relatively easily measure something, we convince ourselves that the metric is a useful proxy for what we really want to know. Recall the SMART criteria discussed in Chapter 3. Overvaluing the importance of what is "measurable" can lead us to undervalue the importance of what is "relevant." By basing our thinking on the story we hope to tell, we are more likely to focus our measurement activities on those metrics that are most pertinent to it.

Take, for example, the problem of attributing an outcome to your intervention (the first inconvenient truth). If part of the story you want to relay involves making the case that the observed outcome is directly attributable to your intervention, then you want to ensure your measurement activities focus on gathering data that makes that case. Of course, this would involve collecting baseline data and post-intervention data. It would also involve collecting data on plausible alternative explanations for the observed outcome (possibly resulting in evidence to exclude them). For example, this might involve capturing data in an adjacent community that is *not* benefiting from your intervention. Attributing positive outcomes directly to the activities of your nonprofit is a tricky endeavor, but that's usually the story you are trying to tell.

Unfortunately, funders rarely provide sufficient funding to execute a robust and considered measurement plan. This is why I separated measurement in "support of communicating organizational impact and value" from measurement to "meet reporting obligations to funders" in the introduction to this chapter. Telling the story of your nonprofit's impact and value is too important to relegate to the sparse measurement dollars included in your grant portfolio. As discussed in previous chapters, the more aligned your portfolio is, the easier it is to tell a cohesive story across the different grants you receive. For most nonprofits, investing overhead dollars in the development and communication of their story is essential to long-term success.

It is possible that some nonprofits have a mature enough relationship with a particular funder to make the case for funding that specifically supports the sustainment and expansion of the nonprofit itself. For example, a grant focused on measuring the problem the nonprofit is working on and collecting lessons learned across the nonprofit's entire portfolio of projects. This data would help the nonprofit refine its story and improve its interventions. While the government is an unlikely funder for this project, some enlightened philanthropic organizations may see the intrinsic value of such an endeavor.

Effective nonprofit leaders continually describe *why* the problem they are trying to solve is important and *how* the organization is making progress in pursuit of that mission. Being effective isn't just about doing good work; it's about helping others to develop an appreciation for the problem you are working to solve and for the impact your employees and volunteers are making. The better you can communicate those things, the more support you'll receive from funders and donors, and the stronger your brand will become among partners, stakeholders, and clients.

Another piece of advice I'll offer about communicating impact is particularly relevant to small nonprofits. When I compare the marketing collateral of a large organization with a small one, some common themes emerge. Most large organizations (nonprofit or otherwise) have figured out their story and have "productized" their offerings. They've clearly defined what they can deliver at different price points. Their marketing material is polished, and their solutions are more standardized and sold as if they were individual products. This leads to increased confidence for the buyer (or grantor).

On the other hand, the marketing collateral of small organizations tends to drip with desperation (if they even have collateral). It may contain exaggerations of capabilities or previous engagements. Flexibility, or the customized nature of what the organization offers, tends to be overemphasized. The materials usually feel more aspirational rather than based in fact. There's nothing wrong with positioning your small nonprofit as a partner, willing to do what it takes, etc. However, the more you can refine your story and define what you can commit to delivering, the more confidence you will engender. You don't really need a marketing department; you can do it yourself if you carefully (and honestly) consider how outsiders see your organization and its marketing materials.

As you improve upon the story of your organization and demonstrate your impact, your integrity as a leader and the perceived integrity of your nonprofit increases. A compelling and honest narrative fosters a culture of integrity, motivates employees and volunteers, and demonstrates your effectiveness and authenticity to external audiences. It creates a sense that you have a dream for a better world, are vigorously pursuing that dream, and are making admirable progress. Who doesn't want to be a part of that?

TRUSTEES

This chapter started with a reminder that *what* we measure and *how* we go about measuring it shapes the insights we ultimately gain. We explored how the purpose of measurement is primarily to support the narratives the organization's leaders deliver to its employees, funders, partners, and other stakeholders. Structure, process, and outcome metrics were also defined, ending with a discussion on the importance of focusing measurement activities on the stories you are eager to share about your nonprofit and the problem(s) it is trying to solve. So, what is your role in all of this as a nonprofit trustee?

1. Help the organization strike the right balance.
2. Keep the organization's leaders honest by asking tough questions.
3. Assist the organization in communicating its emerging story to your network, to board members of potential partner organizations, and to donors.

Let's briefly explore each point.

Striking the right balance is all about encouraging a balanced and appropriate investment in monitoring the organization's structural health (e.g., finances, governance, etc.), process health (assessing the maturity of internal and externally-facing processes), and outcomes (organizational performance and impact). It is unlikely that the executive and management team know exactly how best to achieve the organization's aims. A balanced approach to monitoring can uncover unforeseen risks and help to mitigate them. It can also lead to new insights into program effectiveness and, as discussed throughout this chapter, it can help the organization craft the most compelling and engaging stories for internal and external audiences.

Solving tough problems requires leaders to effectively navigate uncertainty and changing circumstances. As a trustee, one way you promote balance is by encouraging reflection and course correction when necessary. As an organization's understanding of a problem evolves, so does its understanding of the role it could play in addressing the problem. With that evolution comes a refinement of strategic priorities and performance targets. Balance encourages a common understanding of what constitutes "good performance," preventing the organization from embracing an executive's or board member's unrealistic expectations. When nonprofit boards set unrealistic goals, they incentivize management teams to overstate accomplishments and waste time and energy trying to game the system.

Asking tough questions is probably something you're already good at. While you want to avoid micromanaging the executive team and getting the board "wrapped around the axle" on various operational decisions, you're not there to make friends and you need to embrace your oversight role. Don't be a rubber stamp board! Probe for candor and relevance, and advocate for efficiency.

For example, you should resist the propensity of some CEOs to dedicate too many organizational resources to measurement and communication *with the board*. Executive compensation decisions are made by the board. The CEO and other executives are therefore motivated to overspend on measurement and story preparation for board audiences. Remember, as a board member, you have a duty to the organization and not the executive team. Sometimes, what appears to be due diligence is nothing more than window dressing for the board's benefit. If something feels like it was designed to create a favorable impression, it probably was. Press the executive team to clarify their objectives in sharing the information, to be explicit about assumptions and the level of effort required to produce the report, and to be candid about inconvenient truths. They aren't there to serve you, and you aren't there to be entertained.

The final role a trustee has in measuring and communicating impact is *helping to communicate the organization's story*. Having a handful of impact stories beautifully conveyed on your website is not enough. You need to work hard to get your stories in front of target audiences. One of the most important jobs that board members have is helping to communicate the organization's story to their network, to board members of prospective partner organizations, and to donors and other potential funders. Aside from the CEO, trustees are the most influential brand ambassadors the organization has. If you are introverted or you do not have a particularly useful network, look to see how you can complement other board members in this endeavor. Perhaps you are an effective writer and can help refine the organization's written stories, or perhaps you are well-connected to a particular stakeholder group and can help the organization better weave the voice of that group into its story. Whatever your strength, use it to help your nonprofit refine and tell its story. That story can lead to great things.

SUMMARY

- What we choose to measure and even how we measure it reflects what we value, what we believe we can impact, and what we believe can be easily and reliably measured.
- Great leaders move the board and employees of an organization from valuing what is measured to measuring what is valued.
- When considering what to measure, think about *where you work*—how the structure of your organization supports your strategic objectives, *how you work*—whether the processes used to accomplish your objectives are mature, and *why you work*—whether you are making measurable progress toward achieving the outcomes promised by your mission.
- Finding the best way to tell the story you want to convey to each audience should drive what you measure (not the other way around). The story always comes first.
- Too much focus on measurement can lead nonprofits to prioritize the things that are most easily achieved or most easily measured. This can be detrimental to a nonprofit's impact.
- Accountability to those who control resources (i.e., government or philanthropic funders) is usually better developed than accountability to end-clients.
- If 80% of your time is spent discussing financial metrics, then you are implicitly saying that those are more important than mission objectives.
- Attributing observed outcomes of an intervention to the actions of a single nonprofit is more often an exercise in marketing than accuracy.
- When interventions do have a verifiable impact, the full cost of the intervention is typically higher than originally estimated and the duration of the impact is lower. This limits interest in replicating the intervention.
- As you improve upon the story of your organization, you should also candidly address any inconvenient truths that may be

relevant. Doing so increases your integrity as a leader and the perceived integrity of your nonprofit.

- Trustees need to carefully consider what constitutes "good performance." When nonprofit boards set unrealistic goals, they incentivize management teams to overstate accomplishments and waste time and energy trying to game the system.

6

BUSINESS DEVELOPMENT FOR NONPROFITS

You have to be burning with an idea, or a problem, or a wrong that you want to right. If you're not passionate enough from the start, you'll never stick it out.

—Tech visionary STEVE JOBS

B USINESS DEVELOPMENT (BD) is the process of actively working to grow a business and improve its position in the market. This includes efforts to identify new opportunities, develop relationships with funders, increase sales, grow revenues, expand service lines or offerings (either organically or through acquisition), and develop new strategic partnerships.

BD within nonprofits may feel contradictory or even objectionable to some nonprofit employees. As we've discussed, a nonprofit exists to advance its mission, and there is a natural tension between the fiduciary responsibilities and mission responsibilities of nonprofit leaders. The best way to address the need to focus on BD is to frame it as creating *organizational leverage*. Over time, growth and market strength create the leverage needed to have the desired impact. Whether you are trying to influence policy, scale an intervention, or attract the interests of new partners and funders, a growing nonprofit is more likely to be successful than a stagnant one.

Finding focus

The first question is where to focus your BD efforts. The Boston Consulting Group (BCG) growth share matrix is a classic BD decision tool that is widely taught in business schools. For companies with multiple offerings, the matrix helps executives and boards decide which offerings to invest in, which to hold on to, and which ones to divest themselves of. The criteria used to inform these decisions are based on an assessment of market share and market trends. *Market share* is the percentage of total demand for a product or service that a company's offering currently satisfies. *Market trends* indicate whether the overall demand for a product or service is expanding, contracting, or stable.

Imagine you sell cherries at a farmers' market. For simplicity, let's say that the farmers' market is the only source of fresh cherries in your community. Last year, you sold two hundred and fifty pounds of cherries out of a total of one thousand pounds sold at the farmers' market. Therefore, your market share is 25%. If the total weight of cherries sold at the farmers' market was one thousand one hundred pounds three years ago, nine hundred pounds two years ago, and one thousand pounds last year, the market would be considered stable. If a celebrity chef comes to town to shoot a cooking show about how to make the best cherry pie and total demand shoots up to two thousand pounds, that would be a *rapidly expanding market*. When demand falls back down the following year, it will be a *contracting market*. But if a popular restaurant decided to source their cherries locally and drives demand up year after year, then you've got a market that is *consistently expanding*.

Growth share matrix results are plotted on a two-by-two chart, where the x-axis represents low or high market share, and the y-axis represents low or high rates of market growth. Each of the company's current offerings are graphed based on their market share and the dynamics of the market they are in. For example, offerings in a mature, low growth market are referred to as either "cash cows" or "dogs," depending on the company's market share.

Cash cows are offerings where the company has the luxury of a relatively high market share (in a low growth/mature market). This implies pricing power or at least consistent profits and an opportunity to "milk the cash cow" by reinvesting those profits in other, more strategic offerings. In the previous example, if you are the only cherry seller in your local community, you can probably get away with charging a small premium for your cherries and using those extra funds to plant a more strategic crop (one where you expect demand to outpace supply).

Dogs, on the other hand, are offerings that only have a relatively small share of a market that isn't growing that much. They are potential cash traps, tying up money that could be better invested elsewhere in the company. I would add that they also distract company executives and other talent from more important endeavors. In the farmers' market example, imagine you also sell bread but can't compete with the local bakery's booth. If the overall demand for bread has stopped growing or has started shrinking because of changes in consumer tastes, the combination of that trend with your small market share means you should probably stop baking bread and focus your energies elsewhere. Maybe try something unique like cherry cookies?

In less mature markets that are growing more rapidly, things get interesting. These represent opportunities for companies because market leaders have not yet been determined. So, if a company's current offering makes up a sizable portion of a booming market, it is worthy of investment (to maintain or even expand the offering's dominance in the market). BCG refers to these as "stars." A good example would be the solitary kale supplier in our farmers' market during the kale mania of the early 2000s. But how would you maintain your market dominance? Perhaps by growing different varieties or producing large volumes at a low cost. Even then, it seems likely that new entrants to the market would start selling kale and your dominance would be short-lived.

For final consideration are offerings in rapidly growing markets where the company does not yet enjoy a significant share of the market. These offerings may have real potential depending on the ability of the company to differentiate its offerings from those of competitors. Of course, differentiation usually involves significant investment. As a result, these offerings (deemed "question marks" by BCG) require careful monitoring to assess the likelihood that they can become stars. A farmers' market example would be if our cherry grower decided to grow a unique variety of kale at the beginning of the kale boom.

The BCG growth share matrix is a useful tool, though it suffers from oversimplification. While pricing power is implied, the matrix does not consider the relative profitability of different offerings. It also doesn't account for future market trends that may result from the actions of the company or someone else. Examples of these disruptive events include introducing new products or marketing strategies that cause significant shifts in market demand. (Recall the market contraction in our example after the celebrity chef created a temporary boom.) Even so, it is a very useful way of evaluating the relative strength and potential of a company's portfolio of offerings. The takeaway from the BCG tool is that companies should focus their BD investments on the products and services that offer the highest potential payoff. That potential payoff is determined by a combination of market trends and the ability of the company to differentiate its offerings in the market.

A BD focus matrix for nonprofits

With that as a foundation, here's my version, which is better tailored to the needs of the nonprofit sector. Again, the question we are seeking to answer is where best to focus BD efforts. As you can see in Figure 6.1, a nonprofit could compare the revenue potential and mission potential of its various offerings to set business development priorities because, ideally, they should focus their investments on strategies that offer the highest combined revenue/mission potential.

Like the BCG example, revenue potential is determined by market trends (i.e., the interests of funders) and the ability of the company to differentiate itself in the market. But, as we know, maximizing revenue is not a sufficient end goal for nonprofits; they must also maximize mission potential. Mission potential is determined by a strategy's alignment to the mission, its effectiveness, and its reach.

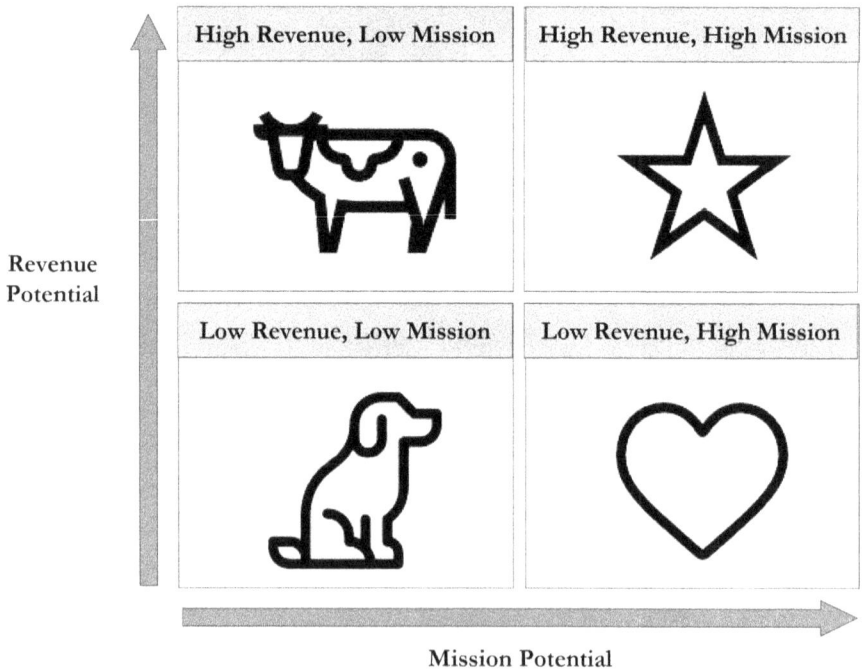

Figure 6.1 BD Focus Matrix for Nonprofits

For simplicity, let's consider a nonprofit with four offerings. One is a "dog"—it has low future revenue potential (for either market trend or market share reasons), and it also has low mission impact potential (it could be ineffective or just not well-aligned with the nonprofit's mission). The second is a "cow"—it has high future revenue potential (perhaps it is highly differentiated in a rapidly expanding market) but only low mission impact potential. While the nonprofit can generate revenue with the offering, it doesn't produce meaningful mission results. The third offering is a "heart"—it has low or even no future revenue potential, but it's something that is squarely aligned with the nonprofit's mission and is believed to be an effective impact strategy. The final offering is a "star"—it's believed to carry both high revenue and mission potential. This is where the planets align between the nonprofit's capabilities, its mission, and the interests of the funder community.

Unfortunately, many nonprofits have only hearts and dogs, and we'll get to their strategy choices in a minute. But this lucky nonprofit has one of each type. What strategic questions might they consider when setting their business development priorities? They might ask whether their dog offering has become a cash trap that threatens the organization's clarity of purpose. They might explore the risks and rewards of siphoning cash away from their cow offering (i.e., "milking it") to fund heart pursuits. They might ponder creative ways to turn their heart offering into a star by attracting others to their cause (including potential donors/funders). Or they might assess the risks to their star offering (e.g., changing funder priorities) and consider what investment will strengthen its growth prospects (in terms of both revenue and mission impact).

What if, like many nonprofits, you are stuck with only hearts and dogs? You probably spend a lot of energy trying to turn those hearts into stars by marketing your organization to donors and talking with foundations. You also probably waste a lot of time on dogs—activities that just aren't going to materially improve your finances or mission impact. This is when having the courage to focus pays off. Consider how you are framing the problem space that your nonprofit focuses on. Are there better ways to differentiate yourself? Consider how your team, solution set, or ideas might differ from others in the market. Is there a more compelling way to position your nonprofit to align with a particular interest in the funding community? Can you approach like-minded nonprofits to see if any strategic partnerships offer opportunities to build new capabilities or alter your positioning in the market? We will discuss that strategy in Chapter 9.

For small organizations, the good news is that winning one large grant can make all the difference. Though, once you win that large grant, you must leverage it to develop your organizational capabilities and strengthen your brand (i.e., story) in the marketplace.

If you have products or services that you've determined to be dogs, then pull together a focus group and brainstorm ways to pivot them into cows (by increasing their revenue potential) or hearts (by increasing their mission potential). Either option is preferable to allowing them to continue as dogs. If you find no compelling pivot strategies, your best bet is to divest them or wind them down. They are distracting to your leadership, your team, and your bank account.

Sometimes, nonprofits pursue lines of business that aren't aligned with the mission, expecting they can serve as a revenue source to fund it. Pursuing these cow strategies can sometimes work (e.g., imagine a hospital that is generating consistent profits from its gift store and cafeteria). However, for most, they also end up distracting leadership, pulling resources away from higher purposes, and diluting the nonprofit's brand in the marketplace. Consider those three factors (distraction, real ROI, and brand effects) when deciding to devote your energies to raising non-mission-aligned cows to milk. If you've got extra pastureland and volunteer farmers, it might still be a good idea.

As you assess your market positioning and begin thinking about where to focus your BD activities, be aware of three traps. We already introduced the idea of a *cash trap*, where too many resources are dedicated to sustaining a line of business that lacks both revenue and mission potential (i.e., dogs). As different perspectives on these activities are drawn out, however, finding clarity can be quite hard. One person's dog is another person's livelihood. The best nonprofit leaders I've known engage in the tough and candid assessment and dialogue necessary to continually focus their organization's limited resources.

We also discussed the merits of pursuing business activities that aren't mission-aligned on the grounds that they may still be lucrative and could help fund the mission. This sometimes works well, but usually they become a *greed trap* where unintended consequences and costs outweigh the mission-financing benefits. This can include the opportunity cost of distracting management from the mission (executives and board members become too focused on profit generation). It can include brand impairment (stakeholders and funders question how "nonprofit" you really are when they see you engaging in endeavors that are strictly profit-oriented). And it causes challenges within the business because of differences in staff motivation and team cultures. Would you want your sole reason for existence to be about financing another team's awe-inspiring mission work? Alternatively, would you want to work in the frugal, mission-focused unit when the employees in the profit generation unit have higher salaries and bonuses?

The final and most common trap is the *heart trap*. Nonprofit leaders must be careful of letting their mission goggles blind them to the organization's business needs. It is easy to be inspired by the passions of employees or board members. However, you must remember that your ability to improve people's lives (or whatever your mission is) is a by-product of the financial health, growth, and reach of your nonprofit. BD success increases your leverage so that your voice will be heard, your advice sought, and your solutions implemented. When you focus all your energies on heart pursuits—to the detriment of the business—you limit your organization's potential. It's good for nonprofit leaders to have a big heart. Just don't lose sight of how business success translates into mission success in the long run.

Nonprofit is a tax designation, not a business model

The matrix introduced in Figure 6.1 might help you evaluate your current market positioning and identify business development options. Eventually, your business development strategy may focus on pursuing revenue from any of a variety of sources: fundraising, charging for services, selling products, or winning philanthropic grants, government grants, or contracts. Whatever the focus, the key is to have strategy guide your BD decisions. This is just as important to nonprofits as it is to for-profit companies. The goal of your BD strategy is the same regardless of the focus of your nonprofit: you want to develop the business in order to grow its impact and improve its financial health over the long run. For a nonprofit, a portfolio of stars and hearts is much better than one with only cows and dogs!

FUTURE LEADERS

Business development is one of the most reliable paths to leadership in any for-profit or nonprofit business. The employees who show care for the future of an organization are the individuals that are eventually given the responsibility for the future of that organization. Given its importance to realizing your goal of becoming a future leader, this section focuses on how you can best support business development activities.

Regardless of your current role, if you desire to be a nonprofit leader, insert yourself into the business development activities and aspirations of the company. I believe it is the single most important thing you can do to position yourself for leadership. I've met hundreds of people who, intentionally or unintentionally, neglected this opportunity to differentiate themselves through business development contributions. Someone that does so intentionally is communicating that they do not want a leadership role in the future (which is absolutely fine as long as it's a conscious choice). Those that do it unintentionally (by focusing all their energies elsewhere) are naïve or lack confidence.

Naïveté and confidence are cousins. Both can be rooted in a lack of experience or knowledge. It's true that people lack confidence for many reasons: introversion, self-image, self-worth, imposter syndrome, childhood trauma, an accent or speech impediment, memory issues, cognitive decline, or simply because they look different from other people in the room. Knowledge and experience can seldom resolve the source of your fear (unless that fear stems from your own recognition of a knowledge gap). However, knowledge and experience can definitely help you develop confidence in spite of your fear. Building confidence will benefit you and the nonprofit organization you care about. With more experience, you'll realize that nearly everyone you meet struggles with some sort of confidence issue—even the people who've accomplished great things and those who appear to be extraordinarily confident. Why not start increasing your confidence by building your business development acumen?

The chapter introduction discussed where to focus business development efforts. Even if you are not currently in a leadership position, you can help your nonprofit make the right decisions in this area. Nonprofit leaders can be out of touch with important market dynamics, such as technological advances, new entrants to the market, shifting cultural attitudes, or viable social media strategies. They can lose sight of the "voice of the customer," in terms of the population the organization serves, or the perspectives of funders or other stakeholders in the market. Nonprofit leaders are also prone to overestimating what differentiates their organization and its specific offerings in the marketplace (it is common to believe you are more unique than you actually are). Any of these weaknesses can lead the organization to focus on the wrong business development priorities.

When you suspect any of these leadership weaknesses, humbly offer your opinion. The decision-makers may not share it; they may have knowledge or experience that you do not, and they may dismiss your perspective. Still, by offering your opinion, you show care for the organization and its future success. Relaying that message is usually more important than winning any specific argument. Unfortunately, some leaders have honed their debate skills more than their listening skills. Avoid engaging in an extended argument with a leader you disagree with. Make your point, provide any supporting evidence you've gathered, and be respectful of the leader's role. The leader's job is challenging, and they may be considering information that is not public or that they can't share. For example, they may know a key employee is dealing with a health issue, an important manager is departing the company, or a strategic partnership is being considered that cannot yet be disclosed. However, it's also possible that the leader's ego is getting in the way of embracing your perspective over their own. Humans are funny, and our internal narratives have a knack for drowning out any contradictory evidence. It may just take a little time for your leader's perspective to catch up to your own. But, staying silent and hoping that this will happen on its own is usually not the best way to help your nonprofit succeed (or to advance your career).

Increasing funding from a specific funder or winning a certain grant are wonderful goals, but they are not what I mean by BD priorities.

- If you are trying to insulate your organization from changes in a single funder's priorities or the potential loss of a favored grant officer, one of your BD priorities should be to diversify your portfolio of funders.

- If you are trying to alter how your organization is perceived, one of your BD priorities may be to develop a brand strategy that better differentiates the organization.
- If you are trying to focus the organization on a star offering, one of your BD priorities may be to develop a scaling strategy and investment plan.

BD priorities are about identifying and capitalizing on strategic opportunities and mitigating future risks to the business. While a nonprofit's BD priorities are unique to the organization, its mission, its financial situation, and its market, there are some common themes that are worth exploring in more detail: marketing, differentiation, and grants.

Marketing

Nonprofits frequently undervalue marketing and underinvest in marketing strategy. Effective marketing can serve as the "tip of the spear" for nonprofits. An effective marketing campaign can pierce through the noise, chatter, and distractions to get the attention of funders, important stakeholders, and potential partners. "Marketing with a purpose" was introduced in Chapter 4. Whether you are marketing to alter the perception of the organization's brand, trying to highlight what differentiates your solution to a societal problem, trying to attract clients to use the services you offer, or supporting a fundraising campaign, explicit goals drive focus, and that's what drives BD results.

I'm not sure why nonprofits discount the importance of marketing. Perhaps it's because they perceive it as having a narrow function—to gain an advantage over competitors and attract customers to your product. Perhaps it's because, in a highly resource-constrained environment, something has to give, and marketing isn't considered critical to mission success. Whatever the reason, marketing tends to be overlooked by nonprofit leaders. We should view marketing and brand development as essential components of nonprofit business development. You are always competing with others for attention, donations, grants, members, patients, supporters, or partners. Whatever your mission, there is competition somewhere, and an effective marketing strategy that differentiates you to a target audience is how you mitigate its effects and accomplish your goals.

Competitive differentiation is essential to the success of any nonprofit, and yet true differentiation, relative to market competitors, can be elusive and hard to define. Often, what we think of as a differentiator is nothing more than an indication of our lack of knowledge about the competitive landscape. As I said, we are seldom as unique as we think we are. Focusing your nonprofit on one particular problem and developing real depth on your team offers differentiation potential. The more your team understands a specific challenge, the better equipped you are to develop, test, and provide novel solutions.

It is important to build a team that includes people with different life experiences and perspectives on the problem you are trying to solve (we'll explore why in Chapter 7). Varied viewpoints are vital to effective solutioning, yet it is also true that you seldom find nonprofits capable of truly differentiating themselves in multiple areas. I recommend you build a diverse team focused on solving one or two problems. That provides the best odds of ultimately differentiating yourself in the market.

Assuming you are focused, have built a capable team, and uncovered some true differentiators, then it's time to get the message out. Whether you do it yourself, contract it out, hire someone to lead your marketing strategy, or can afford an entire department, expect to confront the following five questions.

1. **What is the explicit purpose of marketing your organization?** Some examples are attracting funders or donors, elevating a solution, building brand awareness among clients, attracting volunteers or employees, or building credibility with potential partners or stakeholders.
2. **When you think about the audience you are trying to reach, what attributes can be used to segment that audience into different roles or interests?** Examples include demographic attributes such as age, race, gender, education, ethnicity, religion, or household income, etc. Other possible attributes might be location, history of previous support, political affiliation, membership in other organizations, employment field, social media presence, or certain behavioral characteristics (like engaging in risky or unhealthy behaviors).

3. **Which audience segments make the most sense to target for different purposes?** Casting too wide a net seldom returns positive results. Defining specific personas (representative fictional characters) that you are trying to reach helps you to target your message and communication strategy.
4. **What tailored messages will resonate best with each audience segment?** What, specifically, will they find most relevant and compelling? What call-to-action is most likely to prompt the desired response?
5. **What promotional tactics are most cost-effective in getting your tailored message in front of your target audience segment?** You could consider traditional advertising, social media strategies, outreach campaigns, conferences/galas, newsletters, blogs, or branded products, etc. Cost-effectiveness can only be determined after the fact. Therefore, it makes sense to pilot different tactics before making significant investments.

Differentiation

Differentiation can be a desired outcome of either internal investment or an acquisition. What is it you hope to build or buy that will further differentiate you in the marketplace and set you apart from the competition?

Chapter 3 discussed the importance of defining what makes us unique and investing in that or identifying a *desired* differentiator for the future. I call the latter "aspirational differentiators" to convey the idea that our hopes and dreams are closely tied to our ability to carve out a path to distinction. How we set ourselves apart from others can take many forms. The history of your organization, the strength of your dedication to a specific population or cause, the creativity and diversity of your people, or the innovativeness of your solution are all examples of ways to differentiate yourself.

One differentiator that I am partial to is the *solution orientation* of certain nonprofits (World Central Kitchen is a good example). There are too many problem describers in academia, politics, and the nonprofit sector. Yes, problems need to be sufficiently understood to be solved or to generate the will to solve them. I just think we've got the ratio wrong.

If 80% of nonprofits are describing problems, that's asking a lot of the remaining 20% who are working to solve them. Consider what it would take to transform your organization into a problem solver rather than a problem describer. The more focused you are on finding workable and scalable solutions to a particular problem, the higher the likelihood that you will differentiate yourself from others. Many nonprofits would benefit from identifying aspirational differentiators and focusing their strategic plans on pursuing and exploiting them. Carving out a path to distinction is always a worthwhile endeavor.

Grants

Pursuing grants is an exercise common to many nonprofits along that path to distinction. In the next section, we'll discuss *win themes*—focused takeaways that reinforce why your organization and its solution is better than the competition. This is how you differentiate your proposal. Later, I'll share what I view as the most important win themes that should be answered in *every* proposal. These same themes are also relevant to the pursuit of corporate sponsorships and fundraising. Because executives and managers are typically the ones reviewing proposals before they go out the door, the themes themselves are discussed in their section of this chapter as they provide a good roadmap for part of that review. However, before we get to that, try this exercise to flex your creative muscles:

Take a couple of deep breaths, letting them out slowly. Imagine you are walking in your local grocery store. Your cart has a bum wheel that's mildly annoying. There's music quietly playing in between advertising jingles while you turn down the baking supplies aisle. You walk past flour, sugar, and different flavors of chocolate chips. A warmly dressed elderly woman asks you for help. She can't reach the large can of shortening she needs to bake a pie. You help her and she thanks you, telling you she's making a cherry pie for a party. Her kind eyes remind you of your grandmother. You smile as you continue down the aisle.

You pass by the boxes of cake mix. There are so many flavors and brands to choose from. White, yellow, strawberry, pound, spice, lemon, red velvet, and over a dozen chocolate varieties. Most of the boxes promise a particularly moist outcome, and all contain attractive images of cake. You weren't planning on buying cake, but your mouth is watering in response to the images. You are in a good mood as you continue your shopping.

Think about that shelf of cake boxes. Even though none of the boxes contain icing, all of them (except the pound cake) try to entice buyers with an image of a perfectly iced slice of cake. Most customers make their choice based on that image, along with the flavor. Some may check the price before putting the box in their cart. A few may adjust their choice based on that price. Others make their choice out of brand loyalty, their previous cake baking experiences weighing heavily on the decision. A few may consider the other ingredients needed, as well as dietary restrictions, before making their selection.

The information on a cake box is standardized. An image of a perfectly baked cake is prominently displayed on the front of the box, along with the brand, the type of cake, and some marketing adjectives ("super moist"). The price sticker used to go on the front or top of the box, but it's now relegated to the edge of the shelf directly below. If you fail to note it, you lose your ability to take price into consideration once you've walked away. The sides and back of the box list ingredients, nutritional facts, cooking instructions, and some highlights about the company's history of making the best cakes. The box often includes a number to call if you have questions or complaints. Sometimes, it also contains an advertisement for other products that you might like or need (other cake flavors or perhaps the icing in that attractive picture).

Why does this matter? When you engage in proposal writing, you should imagine that cake box. Regardless of the context and details, you are creating a marketing product. You need to paint a picture of an optimal outcome (the perfect cake)—an outcome that triggers an emotional response from the reviewer. Let your passion for the cause shine through. Don't be afraid to include the icing in your picture. Just because the solicitation or grant officer asks for a dry piece of cake with no icing, doesn't mean that is what you should propose delivering. Contemplate what the "icing" may be and find ways to include it in your vision of the ideal outcome. There are many ways to approach this.

You can propose the icing as an optional task. You can propose in-kind tasks or matching dollars where your organization partners with the funder. Or, underscoring your commitment to the problem, you can outline a plan of partnering with other nonprofits and pursuing complementary funding to realize a more attractive vision. Again, this is part of the overarching benefit of clarity of purpose and organizational focus—your portfolio of work naturally creates connections, efficiencies, and advances in effectiveness.

Painting a compelling vision of what is possible is an excellent way of differentiating yourself. It shows your maturity of thought on the issue and frames you as a partner rather than just a grant recipient. People writing proposals usually spend so much time on the "how," worrying about being responsive to the solicitation, that they forget to adequately relay the "why" and to paint a compelling vision of success. That "why" is what triggers an emotional connection with your reviewer, and that vision is what causes them to salivate.

Keep the cake box in mind when working on other parts of the proposal too. What are the messages you are trying to relay, and how do they fit together in a compelling package? Keep your writing clear and concise, relaying the capabilities of your team (the ingredients), your theory of change and any evidence of effectiveness (nutritional facts), your detailed plan of how you will execute the work (cooking instructions), and your nonprofit's qualifications (history of making the best cakes). Convey a commitment to integrity and quality, and make it clear you are approachable and easy to work with (the number to call if you have questions or complaints). And don't forget to sprinkle in a little advertisement for other products or services that the funder might also like or need!

EXECUTIVES & MANAGERS

The fiduciary/impact dilemma is ubiquitous in business development decisions. How many resources to devote to BD, which efforts to prioritize in BD pursuits, and even the approach to estimating costs for a grant proposal are all imbued with implicit mission impact/financial health values. Consider the BD needs of different nonprofits. Some have an endowment or some other significant and enduring long-term sponsor, like a corporation or university. These organizations have the luxury of worrying less about BD and near-term survival. Other nonprofits have clearly defined a narrow and differentiating purpose and only pursue funding for that. These organizations are ideally situated to balance mission impact with financial health in their decision-making.

Now consider nonprofits with a less clearly defined purpose. Those suffering an identity crisis are easy to spot. Their disjointed pursuit of funding clouds their "why." Nonprofits that aren't clear on what they are trying to accomplish in the world allow their purpose to be defined by what activities funders are interested in supporting. Over time, the purpose of the nonprofit becomes even less clear as its portfolio of funders (and the interests of those funders) change. This can create a crisis of conscience for leadership. It becomes difficult to decide the right path forward. Should the organization continue to pursue the varied sources of funding that it has come to rely on, or should it forgo some funding pursuits to focus its energies on developing needed clarity around its purpose? Of course, forgoing funding implies reigning in organizational costs, and that is seldom easy. Narrowing an organization's focus is a far more challenging endeavor than allowing it to broaden and become unwieldy in the first place. As discussed in Chapter 2, clarity of purpose serves as the foundation of any successful nonprofit. That clarity attracts talent (including great executives and board members). It attracts funders and partners. It enhances efficiency, and it empowers leaders to make decisions with confidence. All these things improve the odds of success in BD pursuits.

Depending on your title and the size of your organization, you may play any number of roles in business development. Here, I am going to assume your role is one of direction, counsel, and review—pointing the team in the right direction, mentoring them, and reviewing their activities and work products. Let's start with direction. By direction, I mean the leader's general role in identifying the north star, clarifying near-term and long-term objectives, engaging when teams have gotten off track, and working to get the entire organization marching in the same direction. Of course, these goals are easier said than done.

BD direction can include helping the team understand why BD is important, explaining the direction in which the nonprofit wants to go and why, and setting grant or sales targets. It can also include clarification around areas of responsibility and accountability, assisting team members in sourcing funding opportunities or potential strategic partners, and helping the team prioritize their time among competing BD tasks.

An important BD leadership role is counseling team members and helping them build their resilience, as failure is frequently encountered in BD pursuits. People and organizations that appear lucky are usually just remarkably adept at turning setbacks into advantages. This is nicely summed up by the Egyptian proverb, "Throw a fortunate man in the Nile and he will come up with a fish in his mouth." If you inquire about an important BD success, you'll most likely be told a heroic story of overcoming multiple setbacks. The more resilient your BD team is, the more creative and successful they will ultimately be.

Reviewing the team's BD activities and work products includes assessing progress against milestones, counseling employees who get off track or who pursue non-aligned activities, and reviewing proposals before they are submitted. Use these reviews as opportunities for coaching and development of your colleagues. The better they understand the reasoning behind your guidance, the better they'll perform in the future. Your nonprofit is always competing for attention and funding. Therefore, you must build a team that can deftly navigate these challenges even when you are distracted by other duties.

Let's look in more detail at *your* role in reviewing responses to grant or contract solicitations. We discussed general approaches to marketing, competitive differentiation, and grant proposals in the *Future Leaders* section of this chapter. Here, we'll focus specifically on how you, as a nonprofit leader, can ensure your organization is putting its best foot forward in response to these funding opportunities. There are three essential components to your review of such work products: responsiveness, cost reasonableness, and win themes.

Responsiveness to a solicitation or grant officer's request is the first thing we think of when we imagine reviewing a proposal. Does the proposal effectively answer all the questions the funder has posed? The easiest way to do this is to build a table of requirements specified in a solicitation and then use that table to evaluate your draft proposal. This will demonstrate that you hear and understand the "voice of the customer." Use what you know about the funder (their priorities, mission, values, etc.) to ensure your team accurately interpreted the various solicitation requirements and the intent behind them. Not all requirements are equal. Inexperienced proposal authors tend to devote far too much narrative to low value, "check-the-box" type requirements. This leaves little room to respond to the real strategic intentions of the funder. A responsive proposal is one where it's easy to determine that all requirements are met and where the most critical requirements have been given the most attention.

The perceived *reasonableness of your costs* varies with the funder. If a solicitation or grant officer doesn't specify the amount of funding that they are making available for a specific activity, try to find evidence of their previous awards. Grant research tools, government contracting databases, news releases from previous awardees, and the funder's website or annual reports are all potential sources of data. When you find historical data, look for ways to compare the scope of previous projects to the scope of the current proposal. If you are still feeling unsure about the funder's perspective on reasonable costs, a good strategy is to structure your response by offering an array of optional tasks. This creates a "cafeteria plan" for your funder so they can pick the tasks and costs that align with the funding they've earmarked for the activity.

Another aspect of cost reasonableness is the funders' perception of various components of your costs. Unfortunately, some funders have developed irrational attitudes about the costs of running a nonprofit and how those costs are covered. The actions these funders take to stretch their dollars—like capping overhead costs at unrealistically low rates—only serve to shift those costs to other funders. This creates a dilemma for the conscientious nonprofit leader. When an underfunded grant is too attractive to pass up because of its unique strategic value to your organization and your cause, what should you do? First off, make sure your true costs are clear to the funder. If they aren't willing to negotiate, then be direct about how much you are able to subsidize the work with funding from other sources or in-kind matching. However, be careful. Committing to delivering products or services at below cost undervalues your team and sets a dangerous precedent that is hard to break out of. Recall the discussion about the nonprofit starvation cycle in Chapter 1.

Losing on price is very demotivating for teams, so part of your job as a leader is to minimize the risk of that happening. The truth is that your costs are likely more flexible than you let on. Yes, you'll incur new variable costs when taking on a new project. However, your fixed costs and step-fixed costs (i.e., those that only change with large increases in activity) likely won't change. Therefore, any additional funding that pays some of those costs can be beneficial, even if it pays less than its fair share. Taking a "loss leader" attitude toward justifying low-margin pursuits can be a wonderfully useful nonprofit strategy. Just be sure it is based on strategy and does not become your status quo approach to BD!

Unfortunately, it's not enough to deliver a responsive proposal at a reasonable cost. You must also differentiate yourself from others who have been able to accomplish that feat too! Here's where *win themes* come in. Win themes apply whether you are pursuing revenues through fundraising, charging for services, selling products, or attempting to win philanthropic grants, government grants, or contracts. In short, a win theme is a focused takeaway about your nonprofit that resonates with your audience and increases their interest in you over the competition. The more you know about the problem, the competitors, and your own organization and its solution(s), the easier it is to devise useful win themes.

Proposal win themes relay a memorable story to the reviewer; one that resonates, inspires, and differentiates you from the competition. They should convey, "We, like you, are dedicated to solving this problem. We share your understanding of the problem and the urgency to address it. We have a compelling track record and exciting capabilities. Here's why we believe we would be an excellent partner." Figure 6.2 provides twelve win-theme questions I've used to review, improve, and win many multi-million-dollar grants. They fall into four themes: why this problem, why our organization, why our solution, and why now.

Why **This** Problem?	1. What are the direct costs of the problem? 2. What are the indirect costs of the problem? 3. How is the problem evolving?
Why **Our** Organization?	4. Why are we better than the competition? 5. What history of impact can we cite? 6. How is our dedication evident?
Why **Our** Solution?	7. How are we capable of solving the problem? 8. What makes our solution unique? 9. Why are we confident in our solution?
Why **Now**?	10. Why is there urgency to the problem? 11. What kind of ROI can we offer now? 12. What costs come with waiting?

Figure 6.2 Win Themes

When reviewing a draft proposal, ask yourself how clearly the answers to these questions come through. What (specifically) is the problem the solicitation is trying to solve? Think broadly about the costs of that problem and how the funder perceives it. (Remember the discussion above about creating an emotional connection with the reviewer?) Consider how strong the narrative is in making the case for why *your* organization. Here's where clarity of focus really pays off. What makes you an excellent partner in this endeavor? Consider the strength of your solution. What makes it unique? Does the narrative showcase your team's creativity and dedication or the previous investments you've made in the solution? Will the reviewer share your confidence in your team and their solution? Finally, consider whether there is an urgency to the problem. What kind of ROI can the funder expect? Like the costs of the problem, ROI should be viewed broadly. What impact can be expected? How sustainable is that impact? What questions will be answered? What lessons learned? Can you offer a higher return because of previous investments, partners, or concurrent activities?

Once you have reviewed a draft proposal for responsiveness, cost reasonableness, and win themes, return it to the primary authors, giving them the opportunity to refine the narrative. In practice, you'll be pressed for time and doing reviews concurrently and in phases as different proposal sections are drafted. Over time, the proposal authors will learn to expect recurring themes in your feedback, so the quality of their work will quickly improve. Together, you and your team will grow progressively more efficient and effective at responding to grant solicitations and other funding opportunities.

There's one final BD role for nonprofit executives and managers, and it's perhaps the most important one. Great nonprofit leaders are adept at identifying and developing strategic relationships with potential funders and other organizations that have aligned interests. Relationship development is vital to positioning the growing nonprofit. Part of your job as a leader is to promote brand awareness among potential major donors and the leaders of philanthropic organizations, government agencies, partner organizations, and corporations.[1] How to do this will differ between leaders, but it is a job that must be done. Whether you network in conference settings, during lunches, rely heavily on social media like LinkedIn, or prefer one-to-one outreach and video or phone conversations, relationship development is essential to BD success.

Many nonprofit leaders shy away from engaging in BD activities that feel too sales-oriented to them. However, it's important that you help tell your organization's story. As with everything else, clarity of purpose makes this much easier. I'll also offer a note of caution that sometimes the people who are most eager to meet with you are just interested in obtaining competitive intelligence about your organization and its capabilities and intentions. Others may want to sell you something. That said, part of your job is getting your story out there and finding others who share your passions (and who may become future employees, partners, funders, or other supporters). Your approach should be dictated by your individual preferences and unique skills. If you believe in your organization's potential, use that to develop the confidence to search for others who will also see that potential. You're not selling them anything. You're giving them the gift of knowing you and the amazing organization you work for.

TRUSTEES

What is the trustee's role in business development? In some nonprofits, trustees have a well-defined fundraising role or even a personal donation commitment. In others, they take on an active but more generalized role, focused on developing relationships or pursuing corporate sponsorships. Yet another scenario is that the trustee's role in BD is more limited, and they focus on ensuring a healthy balance between BD progress and mission activities. It is my belief that *all* nonprofits should have at least some trustees that are capable of, and dedicated to, advancing the organization's BD priorities.

If you have a very well-defined fundraising role, chances are you were recruited to the board based on your ability to raise or donate funds. You don't need my advice about how to go about doing that. Just continue to

---

1. There are two types of corporate BD relationships: those that directly fund the nonprofit's activities (for example, a health insurer funding the delivery of care at a nonprofit hospital) and those that could serve as corporate sponsors (sponsoring an event or program, providing in-kind support, paying for media advertising, facilitating employee volunteering/giving, etc.).

share your passion for the organization with others and take pride in the progress you make in sustaining it and attracting others to the cause.

If you have a less well-defined role but are asked to help with relationship development or corporate sponsorships, I have a few tips to offer:

- **Before reaching out to any third party, coordinate with the leaders of your nonprofit.** Let staff know who you intend to reach out to and why you think they could be helpful. Seek their candid feedback. They may already have a relationship with the organization, or they may feel one is unwarranted for any number of reasons. It's not uncommon for nonprofit staff to waste time on meetings that clearly have no potential out of an ill-placed sense of duty to the board. You are there to serve the organization, not the other way around, so make sure the management team sees value in the relationship you are trying to foster.
- **Relay the right message.** Even when you have the right target, it is easy to send the wrong message. Are you trying to encourage the organization to explore a partnership? Are you trying to position the nonprofit for future funding? Are you implicitly committing the nonprofit to something? Again, coordinate the messaging and discuss the goals of the outreach with the person who best understands how the relationship might benefit the nonprofit.
- **Consider shared values and public relations (PR) impacts.** Does your nonprofit share similar values with a third party that you can highlight and use as reasoning for a relationship? Are there differences in values or interests that should be considered before proceeding? The third party may compete with the nonprofit for resources, or they may have conflicting PR objectives. Be clear-eyed about why the third party may be interested in a relationship. Partnering with nonprofits is a common PR strategy for corporations that profit from perpetuating social problems or those involved in polluting activities, etc.
- **Leverage your outreach to gather intelligence and position the nonprofit for the best possible follow-up.** Yes, getting a meeting on the calendar is a good outcome. A better one is coming away with intel about the third party's objectives and level of interest. This enables the staff doing the follow-up to tell a more compelling

story and better tailor their "ask" to the other organization or person. For example, if you find out that a potential corporate sponsor is interested in improving their branding with a particular demographic, your staff can prepare data about how that demographic is represented in your nonprofit's membership or at its events, etc.

Regardless of how well-defined your BD role is, all nonprofit trustees should help their management team navigate the fiduciary/impact dilemma. This is where business development intersects with organizational development (OD) in nonprofit organizations. Both BD and OD can positively affect financial health, assuming they return more benefit than they cost. Each can also improve a nonprofit's mission impact (though again, cost-effectiveness is a factor). Business development is predominantly *outward facing*. BD efforts seek to improve an organization's position in the market (and hence its financial health). As discussed previously, your position in the market heavily influences your potential for mission impact. Organizational development on the other hand, is *inward facing*. OD efforts seek to improve the efficiency and effectiveness of operations. OD is also focused on building capacity for organizational change. While this chapter is about BD, the rest of this book is really about OD.

One of the best ways you, as a trustee, can advance BD is by ensuring that the organization evolves in ways that answer the twelve win-theme questions. Instead of viewing win themes as strictly a marketing exercise, see them as questions you ask about the state of OD. What can you do to promote OD that honestly reflects the desired and most compelling answers to those twelve questions? What are the mission impact and financial health implications of that development? Let me illustrate this with an example.

In the Florida Keys, there is a small purpose-driven nonprofit housed in a modest facility right off U.S. Route 1 (also alluringly called the Overseas Highway). The Turtle Hospital is dedicated to the rehabilitation of endangered sea turtles. When my daughter was young, we visited for the first time. To see the turtles, you must take part in a ninety-minute guided educational program. We were a little apprehensive about our young daughter's attention span, but she was just as engaged in the entire experience as we were. We learned about different species of sea turtles, the environmental hazards and diseases they face, and the important research being conducted by hospital staff. We toured the operatory and met many wonderfully engaging humans and turtles. The Turtle Hospital's founder and director, Richie Moretti, was there, with his ponytail and trademark turquoise t-shirt, working alongside his team. Like many tourists, we came for the chance to see sea turtles up close. But we left inspired to be better stewards of the earth and all its amazing creatures.

We've visited the Turtle Hospital several times since then, and we've also visited other sea turtle rescue facilities like the Loggerhead Marinelife Center in Juno Beach, FL. Though it was seeing Richie's humble dedication firsthand, and the commitment of his hardworking team, that inspired us to make monetary donations to the Turtle Hospital over the years. The strength of their dedication to a very narrow cause convinced us that our help was needed and that it would be impactful. We weren't sea turtle advocates when we walked through their doors, but we were by the time we left.

When assessing the state of OD, ask yourself how clear the dedication of your nonprofit is to others. How are the leaders, employees, and actions of your nonprofit inspiring to outsiders? At some point, the organization inspired you to join the board. What was it about the organization that motivated you to commit your time to help? Is that something that should be made clearer and emphasized in the nonprofit's interactions with other stakeholders? What can you do to help the organization inspire others to support it? While the BD role of trustees varies across organizations, I'd bet that the management team of *your* nonprofit would appreciate more BD and OD assistance from you. Just make sure you coordinate with them before acting on your ideas.

SUMMARY

- Business development (BD) is needed to create organizational leverage. Over time, growth and market strength create the leverage needed to have the desired impact.
- Nonprofits should focus BD that offers the highest combined revenue/mission potential. Revenue potential is determined by market trends (e.g., the interests of funders) and the ability of the company to differentiate itself in the market. Mission potential is determined by *alignment*, *effectiveness*, and *reach*.
- The *cash trap* occurs when you dedicate too many resources to sustaining a line of business that lacks both revenue and mission potential. The *greed trap* occurs when you pursue business activities that aren't mission-aligned but which might be lucrative. The *heart trap* occurs when you lose sight of how business success impacts mission success over the long run.
- Often, what we think of as a differentiator just indicates our lack of knowledge about the competitive landscape. We are seldom as unique as we think. A leader's job is to cultivate that which makes the nonprofit truly unique and tell that story through effective marketing.
- There are too many problem describers in academia, politics, and the nonprofit sector. If possible, differentiate your nonprofit by having a solution orientation and becoming a problem solver instead.
- When responding to a grant solicitation, painting a compelling vision of what's possible is an excellent way of differentiating yourself. It shows maturity of thought on the issue and frames you as a partner and not just a grant recipient.
- Nonprofits that aren't crystal clear on what they are trying to accomplish allow their purpose to be defined by what activities funders are interested in supporting.
- A win theme is a focused takeaway about your nonprofit that resonates with your audience and increases their interest in you over the competition. Example win-theme topics include *why*

this problem, why our organization, why our solution, and *why now.*

- Become adept at identifying and developing strategic relationships with potential funders and other organizations that have aligned interests. Promote brand awareness among potential major donors and the leaders of philanthropic organizations, government agencies, partner organizations, and corporations.

7

SHAPING VALUES & CULTURE

If they don't give you a seat at the table, bring a folding chair.

—The first African American congresswoman SHIRLEY CHISHOLM

I N THIS CHAPTER, we'll explore the nonprofit leader's role in shaping values and culture. Values and culture have a profound impact on a nonprofit's financial and mission success. Values are the core beliefs and ideals that guide the actions of trustees, executives, and employees. These are intrinsically connected to organizational culture. They influence the collective mindset, attitudes, and behaviors that prevail in the organization. They also reflect desired ethical standards and provide cues to employees as to how they are expected to act. Ideally, values serve as a compass, influencing how employees interact with one another, make decisions, and prioritize objectives. Given that balancing mission and fiduciary objectives is an ongoing challenge in nonprofits, the translation of values into priorities is particularly relevant to sound leadership.

Sometimes, espoused values differ from the actual behaviors and practices within a nonprofit. This may be due to resource constraints, external pressures, communication failures, accountability failures, or simply leadership ambiguity. For instance, an organization might emphasize collaboration as a core value but then have a hierarchical structure that is highly focused on rewarding individual achievements. When this happens, the organization's values lose their ability to shape culture and behavior. Conscientious leaders need to periodically assess how their decisions and policies incentivize behaviors that are aligned with the values they champion. If you champion values that are balanced across fiduciary/impact objectives, are your actions and policies reflective of that balance?

Consistent reinforcement of values strengthens their ability to shape organizational culture. It is not enough for nonprofit leaders to simply proclaim their values; they must consistently demonstrate them through their actions and expectations of others. This includes holding other leaders accountable when their actions do not align with desired behaviors. When values are genuinely embraced, they become a powerful force that shapes the nonprofit's identity—elevating the credibility of the organization and its leaders.

Culture

Organizational culture describes how employee perspectives and behaviors are shaped by unwritten rules, norms, attitudes, and assumptions. Culture impacts how employees perceive, interpret, and respond to various situations. It sets the tone for the work environment and the level of collaboration, innovation, and adaptability of the workforce. Culture is shaped by many factors in addition to values. Examples include leadership style, organizational history, team diversity, hiring and performance appraisal practices, and resource constraints. Culture provides a sense of identity and unity among employees, which can foster a cohesive and consistent approach to work. It can also reinforce and sustain certain values through organizational processes, expectations, shared experiences, and stories that reflect and give meaning to the organization's values over time.

Very small nonprofits may have one overarching culture, while larger ones typically have several subcultures within the same organization. The fiduciary/impact dilemma is present here as well. In larger organizations, different roles or departments tend to be more aligned with one objective or the other. For example, an accounting department that is clearly aligned with fiduciary aims is likely to adopt a subculture that values standardized, efficient processes (which save money). Compare that to a subculture that values innovation and risk-taking (i.e., inefficiency) that might develop in a department on the mission front line. Striking the right balance means imbuing both subcultures with values that may not come naturally given their organizational function. That is, the accountants should be encouraged to be creative in looking for process improvements (which requires expending additional resources), and the frontline team executing the mission should be encouraged to seek efficiency through standardization.

In large nonprofits, it's also common for healthy and unhealthy cultures to coexist in different parts of the organization. A healthy culture fosters collaboration, engagement, and shared values, while an unhealthy culture breeds negativity and dysfunction. It is crucial for all nonprofit leaders to recognize and address the signs of an unhealthy culture whenever and wherever they arise.

A lack of transparency, poor communication, excessive bureaucracy, favoritism, or outright discrimination are all signs of an unhealthy culture.

Other indicators include excessive competition, fear-based decision-making, and resistance to change. Whatever the negative signs, they demand attention. In unhealthy cultures, individual interests quickly replace shared organizational objectives. This toxic environment leads to low employee morale, high turnover, and, ultimately, a decline in mission effectiveness and financial health.

The subcultures within your nonprofit govern your ability to attract and retain essential talent. Positive cultures make that job easier and negative cultures can make it nearly impossible. If you suspect that you have a culture problem in your organization, chances are it is much worse than you think. Negative subcultures have a way of feeding themselves. They can create a vortex that pulls down good people, zaps productivity, and demotivates teams. Job candidates and new hires will quickly recognize the red flags, either in interviews or during their first few weeks on the job. High turnover among recent hires is a solid indicator that you have a culture problem.

Exceptional leaders nurture organizational culture by ensuring that values are consistently communicated, reinforced, and integrated into decision-making. They promote transparency and hold individuals (at all levels) accountable for upholding the organization's values. They encourage employee engagement and ensure thoughtful hiring and promotion practices while supporting continuous learning and development. These actions support a thriving work culture conducive to growth, innovation, and impact. Healthy cultures also embrace diversity, equity, and inclusion (DEI). This creates an environment that fosters trust, collaboration, communication, motivation, and employee satisfaction. Employees feel a sense of belonging, are motivated to do their best, and are resilient when faced with challenges. Their actions and behavior consistently support the nonprofit's goals.

The relationship between values, leadership, and organizational culture can be complicated. The fiduciary/impact dilemma further challenges this relationship in nonprofit organizations. Each of us comes to work each day with our own notion of the correct balance between these objectives. We judge the actions of those around us through the lens of our personal values and beliefs about what should (and should not) guide the decisions of our colleagues.

You work for a nonprofit because you believe in the mission's importance. You also deserve appropriate compensation for your time and that requires a healthy organization. Your daily behavior might be guided by a desire to advance the organization's mission or to improve its financial health. At the same time, you also seek to advance your own interests: seeking higher compensation, increasing your influence within the organization, and enhancing your work-life balance. You can see how all those objectives might not always be fully aligned.

Understanding subcultures

The behavior of a nonprofit's trustees, executives, managers, and staff sends a message about its values. Sometimes, a certain culture or an aspect of culture pervades the entire nonprofit. More typically, there are unique subcultures that shape the beliefs, norms, and behaviors of different groups within the same organization. Because subcultures develop in relatively small groups, they are heavily influenced by individual actors. This means nonprofit leaders can actively shape organizational subcultures by changing the attitudes, beliefs, and behaviors of a handful of people. Let's explore three quick examples.

Subculture example 1

A relatively new environmental health nonprofit is struggling with its legal department. The small department is led by a risk-averse corporate attorney who sees their role as protecting the organization by eliminating all legal risk. Contracts and agreements are approached with hardline tactics and take months to negotiate. This prevents the operations teams from taking on important new projects or engaging in partnerships they view as particularly strategic (and not particularly risky). Over time, this difference in perceived risk causes friction between the legal department and the COO. The subcultures of the two teams evolve in ways that are detrimental to the whole organization. To resolve this problem, the CEO addresses the cultural issue with both leaders. When they can't agree on acceptable levels of risk-taking, one leader is counseled to seek employment elsewhere. After this change, the two groups work closer together, have more respect for one another, and the nonprofit thrives.

Subculture example 2

The executive director (ED) of a small nonprofit in New England is struggling to keep her board focused on governance. One board member, in particular, has trouble staying out of operational details. Board meetings end without action on important decisions, and individual trustees have met with the ED to express their frustration. The culture of the board is suffering. The ED finds the courage to engage in firm, candid dialogue with the trustee about how their actions are preventing the board from being effective. Probing deeper, she explores whether trust has been broken in some way. The trustee and ED agree to meet separately for a while to build their relationship and give the trustee a deeper understanding of the organization's operations. At the end of the next board meeting, the trustees take turns commenting on what a great meeting it was and how they are proud of their accomplishments.

Subculture example 3

A large nonprofit is struggling with internal competition between two departments. The leaders of each department have had similar tenures and see themselves as competing for the attention and praise of the executive team. As a result, one of the two teams develops an unhealthy culture that undervalues the contributions of the other team and avoids collaboration at all costs. To address the problem, the executive director (ED) has both leaders in for a candid discussion. They agree to take steps to improve the situation. The two leaders set up recurring meetings with each other to discuss potential areas of collaboration; they create a focus group of staff from each department to build rapport and identify barriers to collaboration; finally, the ED updates performance objectives for the two leaders to emphasize internal and external collaboration. While some competition between the two leaders persists, they find ways to collaborate, and their teams find that they actually enjoy working with one another.

The outsized influence of individual actors on culture is clear in each of these examples. Nonprofit leaders can guide the subcultures in their organization by working to understand *who* is shaping them. Working with those key actors, the leader can then uncover the underlying issues and take deliberate steps to address them.

While all three examples were negative, the same dynamic applies to positive subcultures. There are likely one or two key employees whose attitudes, values, and actions are primarily responsible for the positive team culture. Unfortunately, it is common for trustees, executives, and managers to underestimate the impact of an individual on team culture. Worse yet, it is common to attribute cultural influence to the wrong person! Sometimes, things only become clear after a team member leaves the organization and a rapid change in culture is observed.

By correctly identifying individual cultural catalysts, leaders can "counsel out" negative influences and retain the positive contributors. Look for ways to elevate the voice of positive influencers within your organization. Instead of relying solely on your own observations (and those of your management team), it is useful to seek the perspective of employees on the team in question directly. Asking, "Which team member do you most admire and why?" or, "What do you think is causing the stress on this team?" can be quite clarifying.

Becoming a great nonprofit leader starts with building and inspiring the team around you. The values you help your team to adopt will guide their actions and strengthen their resolve. Remember, values are shaped by the behaviors you model, the conversations you have, the expectations you set, and the decisions you make. They are also shaped by the attitudes and behaviors you accept in others. The values you and your team embody can differentiate your nonprofit, and that can substantially increase your financial health and mission impact.

FUTURE LEADERS

A common saying is that "culture eats strategy for breakfast," meaning that the best organizational strategy in the world still needs to be executed, and culture dictates the success of that execution. The team implementing the plan has a tremendous impact on whether that plan is successful. Not only does the team have to be capable of delivering results, but they also need to be supported by a healthy culture to reduce the risk of failure and help them bounce back when they encounter failure. Strategy *is* important, but culture is often *more* important. If your nonprofit is led by a brilliant strategist who cannot build healthy teams around them, your organization's story becomes one of repeated disappointments. The environment around any strategy is constantly evolving. Therefore, a healthy and resilient team culture is necessary for success. This culture anticipates and reacts to obstacles, takes advantage of emerging opportunities, and stays focused and motivated after setbacks.

Nonprofit leaders influence the values and culture of their organization in many important ways. Let's start with something obvious but easily overlooked. Personal connections and friendships among employees are the foundation of any organization's culture. If you work with people whom you genuinely like and admire, you are more likely to stay with that employer. You will work hard so as not to let your colleagues down, you will feel proud of the team's accomplishments, and you will be more resilient in the face of challenges. This sense of "we are in this together" is an essential ingredient in effective teams and a healthy culture.

Recognizing this, good leaders create time and space for employees to get to know one another, support each other, and celebrate life events. These leaders know when to engage in these activities and when to give employees the space needed to form bonds. My advice to newly minted leaders has always been to show up, be friendly, socialize with people you do not normally talk to, and then give people the space to talk about you behind your back. Eventually, they will move on to talking about themselves and connecting with one another.

Nonprofit leaders also influence the culture of their organization by promoting focus, innovation, and scale. For instance, an employee's drive to expand an organization's reach (i.e., scale) comes from believing that the organization is needed, its goals are honorable, and its impact unique. Similarly, a leader can promote innovation in their organization by appreciating and encouraging risk-taking, diverse perspectives, creativity, and having a genuine passion for the mission. The relationship between culture and innovation is perhaps the biggest differentiator between mediocre nonprofits and great ones—building an innovative, purpose-driven culture allows your organization to separate itself from the pack and flourish. Too many nonprofits are risk averse.

Building a diverse, equitable, and inclusive culture

Some may narrowly view DEI as a way of advancing career opportunities for BIPOC (Black, Indigenous, and people of color) populations. However, it's a broader concept that has many personal and organizational benefits beyond that. Nonprofit leaders must build high-performing teams that can achieve mission and financial goals. The most effective way to do that is by intentionally building diverse teams, ensuring a fair and just workplace, and encouraging openness, acceptance, and engagement. In the introduction to this chapter, I noted that healthy cultures value diversity, equity, and inclusion. Let's explore how leaders build teams with these attributes.

Diversity is shorthand for teams of people of different backgrounds, ages, genders, races and ethnicities, sexual orientations, religions, abilities/ disabilities, etc. Unfortunately, this never quite happens on its own. It requires deliberate intention in recruitment, hiring, and development practices. Diversity of perspective is a prerequisite to creative problem-solving and innovation. Thus, the diversity of a nonprofit's workforce is a good indicator of the organization's creativity and agility.

Equity is about ensuring that the organization's programs, processes, and managers are fair and impartial—and that success is equally available to all. Equity includes helping managers understand their own *implicit* biases. These attitudes and stereotypes influence our thoughts, reactions, and decisions without our conscious knowledge. Being less receptive to a candidate because the name on their resume is unfamiliar and difficult to pronounce is a good example of an implicit bias. We *all* have implicit biases. Fairness and equity require that we recognize them and acknowledge their influence on our thinking.

Inclusion is primarily about respect. Building a diverse team and placing them in an equitable organization is not enough. Employees need to feel a sense of belonging and that they are integral team members. You make that happen by demonstrating acceptance and respect for all your colleagues and creating an environment that encourages all employees to participate in various decisions and development opportunities. This is harder than it sounds because decisions are usually made by a small subset of employees (i.e., managers and executives), and sometimes, unpopular decisions must be made for the overall health of the organization. Nonprofit leaders must find authentic ways to demonstrate that the organization respects its employees and values their input.

It is easy to see how a lack of diversity can translate into a lack of perspective. If your nonprofit serves people who have been historically underserved, the people who share that lived experience have exclusive knowledge of what will and won't help. If you are solving a complicated and stubborn problem, diverse perspectives increase the creativity of your solutions and, therefore, your odds of success. To attract and retain the best talent, start by creating a thoroughly equitable and inclusive environment. If you want to build a team with equal amounts of empathy and drive, pursue diversity with determination and support the team with authentic development and engagement opportunities open to all.

In many ways, DEI is a useful indicator of the overall health of a nonprofit's culture and values. For example, it can be a problem if a nonprofit's leadership team or board appears largely homogeneous in *any* way. That can be indicative of limitations or bias in thinking, creativity, decision-making, or advancement opportunities. Imagine looking at the leadership of an organization and not seeing anyone like you. It would discourage your hope for the future, wouldn't it? It may also lead you to wonder how far the leadership team or board would go to maintain the status quo. When a group with some authority appears to share a common trait, people outside that group naturally wonder whether that is because of deliberate action (i.e., the trait is required for membership) or inaction (the group has not tried to add members without that trait). Either way, it's not good.

When we think of diversity: age, sex, and race are the attributes we usually think of because they are the most visible. However, good leadership requires a bit more nuance. For that, we should look for diversity in social background and lived experience to better inform our thinking and decisions. People of different ages, sexes, and races can have very similar perspectives when they share other traits (coming from privileged backgrounds, for example). Since diversity of perspective on boards and executive teams is so vital to organizational performance, ensure you are getting diversity of perspective.

Most leaders today recognize the importance of DEI in their work environment. However, DEI-related cultural issues can still go unnoticed and can have far-reaching effects, such as causing staff turnover, reduced productivity, decreased effectiveness, and organizational liability. It's essential for nonprofit leaders to assess and improve DEI-related policies and practices regularly. By advancing the representation and authentic participation of people with different lived experiences, these leaders create teams that are more insightful, resilient, and effective.

The most common way to uncover DEI-related issues is to regularly survey employees in a safe and thoughtful manner. During conversations about DEI, leaders should acknowledge the existence of societal inequities and that there is always room for improvement. For example, if recruitment or promotion practices are biased (or perceived as biased), or a particular group of employees feels disrespected or uncomfortable at work, a leader must act. They can take steps to update HR policies and practices or provide DEI coaching to managers. They can prioritize DEI management principles, such as recognizing bias, acting with transparency, or addressing equality or accessibility concerns. By doing these types of things, nonprofit leaders are building a better organization and team for the future.

As a future leader, you have a role to play here. Inclusivity is about respect, but it is also about communication. Don't be afraid to speak up when a leader in your organization talks about a priority that isn't aligned with core or aspirational values based on your experience with the organization. I'm not suggesting you grandstand in a company meeting to pressure and embarrass the executive, but don't assume that your executive and managers don't need to hear from you. It is easy to assume that the leader has already considered all possibilities in the process of vetting a particular course of action. Yet, there is no harm in asking a simple question in, or right after, the meeting or sending a short email asking for clarity. Your engagement will help you understand the decision-making process while also building your brand with the current leadership team. It may even help that team make a more informed decision. Even if you tend toward introversion, find a way to do this. It is difficult enough to be successful in a nonprofit without the lingering distraction of worrying whether you and the leadership of the organization share the same values. If you have concerns, raise them.

I can think of dozens of times over my career when a gentle nudge from an employee altered my perspective on an issue. I would've made some really silly mistakes without that input. As you move into your own leadership role, remember the power and value of engaging your colleagues. (By the way, "colleague" refers to someone you view as a peer and whose perspective you value. Since you should respect and value the insights of *all* employees, it is helpful to consider *all* employees as colleagues. They, like you, chose to work in a purpose-driven organization, and that alone deserves your respect.) Always do your best to keep an open mind when hearing opinions and perspectives that differ from yours. That's part of what makes a leader outstanding, and it also makes life more interesting and fulfilling!

The importance of resilience

Another thing you can do to contribute positively to your nonprofit's culture is to be a source of resilience within the organization. Resilience is an important part of any healthy organizational culture and a key personality trait found in the best nonprofit leaders. In fact, resilience is helpful in many facets of life; indeed, it's vital to life itself. Allow me to illustrate with a short story.

After many years of saving, my family purchased a vacation home in Naples, Florida. We were drawn to the beauty of the ocean, the joy of tropical gardening, and the amazing breadth of animal life in the area. It was honestly a dream come true. Then Irma came along. Hurricane Irma was the most intense hurricane to strike the continental United States since Katrina in 2005. The eye of the storm passed directly over our new vacation home and a Weather Channel personality did much of his reporting on the storm a few blocks from our house. It was all a bit disheartening.

Luckily, the storm caused only minor damage to our house. Our gardens, trees, and landscaping, on the other hand, were obliterated. The storm had caused so much infrastructure damage that water, power, and sewer systems were offline for many weeks. When we were finally able to travel to Florida, we found lots of devastation, and the cleanup was more than we could handle, though we did as much as we could.

While cleaning away piles of dead brush from around our mailbox, my wife found a short segment of our beloved plumeria. It was really nothing more than a short fat stick, about a foot long. Plumeria (also called frangipani) is a beautiful tree. Its clusters of waxy, fragrant flowers come in a variety of vibrant colors. The flowers themselves have a rotational symmetry, and the petals look as though they were drawn with a spirograph. In Hawaii, they are used to make the floral necklaces known as leis that are presented as gifts to visitors.

The little plumeria stick had been suspended in the dead brush for months, and yet it had the beginnings of roots forming on one end. We discussed its impressive determination to continue growing, and my wife stuck it in a pot of dirt. Months went by and, wouldn't you know it, that stick became a small shrub. We transplanted that shrub, and it has now become a beautiful plumeria tree. Each time that tree blooms, each time it celebrates life with a dazzling display of flowers, I am reminded of the importance of resilience. To borrow a phrase, it's "a happy little tree," and its joy is contagious.

People who want to facilitate a positive change in the world are attracted to purpose-driven work and careers in the nonprofit sector. For many, that altruistic flame slowly diminishes as progress remains elusive. This can be due to poor leadership or a lack of resources; or perhaps the incentives to maintain the status quo are just too strong. Whatever the reason, the goal begins to feel like it will always remain out of reach. Wonderful people, who started out with so much potential, begin to question the sacrifices they are making. This leads to resentment, burnout, and a painful loss of talent from the nonprofit sector.

Many nonprofit organizations are focused on tackling tough problems that can feel overwhelming to their employees. *You* can be a source of resilience in this scenario. Personally connect with those around you in the organization and help them make further connections with other colleagues. These relationships are the connective tissue of resilience. They support, protect, and bolster morale. When you are surrounded by supportive colleagues who enjoy working together, it's harder to become jaded and pessimistic about the future.

A related building block of resilience is gratitude. This isn't a book on mindfulness, so I won't go into all the data on the importance of gratitude. I'll just pass along an observation. Human beings who routinely notice and appreciate the positive aspects of their daily lives, who are grateful for the world around them, and who value and cherish the people they interact with are happier. They are also more resilient when faced with setbacks and sadness. Like my plumeria, they innately know there will be sunny days ahead when they will be able to bask in the sunshine and spread joy to all who pass by.

Another way you can help build resilience among your teams is by contributing to a shared vision. This vision can be about financial growth or organizational impact, but it can also be about how people in the organization treat each other and the values they display in their actions. Passion for a nonprofit's mission and belief in the merits of a team are not only contagious; they also build camaraderie. The work of most nonprofit organizations is hard. The shared values and togetherness of the people who work in these nonprofits is what makes success feasible (and work fun).

We've briefly discussed ways in which future nonprofit leaders can positively influence the culture of the teams around them: demonstrating genuine care for their colleagues, embracing creativity and appropriate risk-taking, seeking out diverse perspectives, advancing equity and inclusion, and encouraging resilience. Each of these behaviors is contagious. When you model the right behaviors, others will emulate you. And, regardless of your title, when others look to you for cues as to how they should behave, you have already become a leader.

EXECUTIVES & MANAGERS

In Chapter 5, we talked about the connection between your integrity as a leader and the perceived integrity of the nonprofit you work for. Your integrity sends both implicit and explicit messages to your team, the board, and even passive observers of your organization. Reading this book is a good indication that you try to act with integrity in all that you do. Otherwise, why bother? So, with that in mind, let's explore your influence on organizational culture.

The leader's influence on culture

Managing a nonprofit can be tricky. Throughout your career, you'll make mistakes. People may misjudge your actions because they don't know the full story. Sometimes, you'll be overly confident and not hear the input of others trying to help you make better decisions. There will also be times when you deflect criticism or feel vulnerable and react defensively. With experience and maturity comes recognition that you are only human, and missteps are to be expected. Hopefully, this translates to how you view the mistakes of those around you. Seeing mistakes as learning opportunities is a great cultural asset that accrues in organizations where the leader leads by example.

A mature leader can have a profound impact on the culture of the organization they lead. Your ability to inspire your workforce, to set clear priorities, to own tough decisions, and to acknowledge mistakes all shape the culture around you. As a leader, everything you do (and even the things you don't do) is scrutinized by your employees. Every interaction contributes to their understanding of what is expected, what is valued, what is tolerated, and what is not. The values you embrace, the expectations you set, and the attitudes and behaviors you accept in others all carry significant weight in shaping your team's culture.

It's common for nonprofit leaders to harm the culture of their organization by failing to fully own decisions. If you are a seasoned leader, you've probably made missteps in this area. I know I have. Taking full responsibility for difficult or unpopular decisions is one of the hardest parts of leadership. However, if it comes too easily, you can be viewed as harsh and uncaring by your employees. I once worked with a brilliant young leader in New York. This was the one thing holding him back. He would oscillate back and forth between owning and harshly delivering unpopular decisions when he wanted to project strength and becoming "simply the messenger" when he wanted to avoid accountability. You could never predict whether he was going to scare the hell out of his team or claim powerlessness and blame the head office.

Fostering a culture of integrity means modeling behavior and coaching other members of your leadership team to model them as well. These behaviors include demonstrating genuine care for your employees, being candid in your dealings with them, and fully owning your responsibilities, decisions, and mistakes. A lot of this comes down to how you communicate with your team. Table 7.1 provides examples of positive modeling in leadership.

Deflecting ownership, avoiding responsibility for mistakes, or trying to portray yourself as separate from the "bad guys" who made an unpopular decision causes problems and undermines respect for the leadership of

Instead Of...	*Try...*
I considered promoting you, but the other members of the management team weren't supportive of the idea.	While you aren't ready to be promoted today, I discussed your solid performance with other members of the management team and want to work with you on a development plan.
I wanted to pay you a higher bonus but was overruled by the executive director.	While I wish I could reward you with more, this bonus is what we can afford today. You have tremendous potential, and we really see you as integral to our future.
If it were up to me, we wouldn't be wasting our time pursuing this strategy.	As part of the team that developed this strategy, I recognize it may need to be refined. We should discuss ways to improve it, but it is ultimately up to you and me to execute it to the best of our abilities.
I think you deserve... but HR won't allow it.	I can't play favorites. Let's talk with HR together to see what flexibility there is in our policy. Part of their job is to make sure all employees are treated fairly and equitably.
I advocated for our employees during the discussion of healthcare coverage, but the benefits committee wouldn't hear it.	Our leaders care about our employees, and the benefits committee discussed what we can and can't afford to do right now. As the organization grows, so will our ability to improve the benefits we offer.
I'm disappointed that your team lost that grant; you should have worked harder to bring that key partner along.	I made a mistake by not recognizing how vital it was to have that partner on our team. Let's sketch out a plan of how we can convince them to partner with us in the future.
We've missed our fundraising targets and have been overspending. What's the matter with you guys, can't you see we're in trouble?	As executive director, the buck stops with me. I'm ultimately responsible and should have intervened earlier. I'm sorry. We'll course correct from here and get back on track. Let's set up a meeting with the team to discuss lessons learned.

Table 7.1 Communicating with Integrity

an organization. How you communicate a decision can be as important as the decision itself.

Whether you are leading on your own or are part of a team, decisions—once made—must be delivered confidently. Don't deflect or provide a rationale that attempts to project you in a positive light. Be honest about your role and help people to understand the objective rationale for decisions that didn't go their way. Over time, this will also help to build leadership maturity among junior members of the team.

It's equally important for leaders to acknowledge their mistakes. Doing so demonstrates that they are accountable for their actions and willing to learn from missteps. This encourages the development of important cultural traits in the organization. Demonstrating that it is acceptable to make mistakes serves as a reminder that everyone is fallible, creating a culture of accountability, learning, and growth.

When leaders admit their errors, they show that setbacks and failures are a natural part of the journey. This encourages a culture of resilience where team members feel comfortable sharing their ideas, even if they are not yet perfect. Showing vulnerability encourages employees to find common ground with leaders. We all make mistakes. It is only the weakest among us whose ego gets in the way of acknowledging those errors in judgment. We've all met those people. Try not to be one of them.

Owning unpopular decisions and acknowledging your mistakes is easier said than done. Each of us has a unique relationship with our colleagues and a desire to be liked by them. But having the courage to make tough decisions and own them shows that you care about your colleagues and your organization. That care inspires both respect and emulation.

The last thing I'd emphasize about your maturity as a leader and its impact on organizational culture is the importance of authentic delegation—tasking someone to do something while conveying confidence in their abilities. Demonstrating faith in those you delegate to means not micromanaging. You can coach or mentor, but you need to give people the space necessary to rise to the challenge and their potential. When you clearly communicate that you expect great things from people, you will be surprised by how often they deliver.

Falling short of expectations should be addressed in the moment, directly, and with care. A second chance may even turn someone into a top performer because they develop a better appreciation for where the

166   SHAPING VALUES & CULTURE

goal actually is and what it takes to get there. Imagine a soccer game. There's quite a difference between kicking the ball in the general direction of the goal and working as a team to navigate the ball across the field, past the defense, past the goalie, and into the net. You're looking to teach people to do the latter. They can't learn how to excel if you don't give them the ball and encourage them to work as a team.

Nonprofit burnout

By authentically delegating, owning tough decisions, and acknowledging your mistakes, you give your team the best chance of developing a healthy and productive culture that promotes resilience. However, burnout is something to watch out for in even the healthiest of work cultures. It can be insidious.

The best nonprofit leaders work tirelessly to build an army of change agents—people inspired to work together to realize the organization's vision. How you go about doing this will vary between organizations and leaders. However, all the effective strategies I can think of require leaders to manage burnout and help their teams see both potential and progress—the potential to facilitate a positive change in the world and the progress the team has made in that quest. Progress may be slow, but by sharing your belief that progress is happening, you inspire confidence in the organization and its potential. Given that any organization is just a collection of people working to accomplish a shared goal, it also means inspiring confidence in your people. Confidence breeds excitement for the future, and that excitement is an excellent antidote to burnout.

Nonprofit leaders also need to be honest with themselves about how susceptible *they are* to burnout. It is easy to feel overworked, underpaid, hamstrung by your board, and disillusioned by the lack of urgency others feel toward the problem you are driven to solve. Leading a nonprofit organization is uniquely challenging, and if you allow resentment to take hold, you aren't doing anyone any favors (including yourself). Nonprofit leaders sometimes need to take measure of their work-life balance, step away to reset, or actively work in other ways to put things into perspective.

There are many strategies you can use to avoid feeling overwhelmed and mentally and emotionally exhausted. Introspection, mindfulness, physical exercise, setting realistic expectations for yourself (regardless of the expectations of others), recognizing and managing life changes, acknowledging competitiveness and jealousy, separating career goals from personal ones, and focusing on what you can control are just a few. What works for you may or may not help your colleagues. Be open to trying different approaches.

In my career, recognizing the beginnings of burnout encouraged me to focus on family time and on working more closely with colleagues who inspired me. This made me feel more connected to the people I most admired and whose values I shared. It also made me feel less isolated in the challenges I faced (even when I couldn't share those challenges). I found that writing down reasonable goals and monitoring progress against them helped quite a bit when I felt others had unrealistic or unattainable expectations of me.

Just like your employees, you need to feel part of a dedicated team and have some level of excitement for the future to avoid getting burned out. Your ability to maintain optimism and drive not only impacts *your* performance but the performance of those around you. When you see signs of burnout in a key member of the team, know that the team's performance is suffering in unseen ways. Your job is to intervene and not look the other way.

Culture-related costs and opportunities

Aside from performance considerations, here's another thing to think about. There is clearly an inverse relationship between culture and labor costs. As culture deteriorates, labor costs go up because you have to pay people more to stick around. Each employee does their own calculation about the relative importance of salary, team culture, advancement opportunities, and mission. A poor team culture puts upward pressure on labor costs as the company tries to retain talent who grow frustrated and begin to imagine greener grass elsewhere. The opposite is also true: an exceptional team culture puts downward pressure on labor costs because employees don't want to leave, even if they can earn a higher salary elsewhere. It's not hard to imagine scenarios, therefore, where improvements to team culture offer both mission impact and financial health potential.

While most of the attention given to organizational culture focuses on the performance implications of exceptionally good (or bad) cultures, most employees work on teams with cultures somewhere in the middle. It can be difficult to harness the energy to move a team's culture from good to phenomenally good. However, there are unique benefits to doing so. An organization (or team) with a phenomenally good culture can attract phenomenally good people. A group of phenomenally good people who work exceptionally well with each other usually accomplish amazing things. If that's your goal (and it should be) then invest your time and energy into continuous cultural improvement.

The role leaders play in shaping organizational values and culture in nonprofits is worthy of an entire book. Good executives help leaders at all levels of their organization understand the importance of culture and their role in shaping it. As we discussed above, becoming a great non-profit leader starts with building and inspiring the team around you. This should be something you regularly reflect on as a conscientious leader. Efforts to improve culture tend to deliver benefits far greater than initially expected. It is vital for you to mentor the team around you to promote continuous cultural improvement. An example of this form of coaching is engaging when another leader is hesitant to address an employee issue that is negatively impacting team culture. By mentoring other leaders on your team, they can become effective catalysts to translate your values and expectations into enduring, organization-wide cultural advantages. This can make all the difference between mediocrity and phenomenal success.

TRUSTEES

Recognizing that organizational culture directly impacts nonprofit per-formance, what is the board's role in the pursuit of continuous cultural improvement? Let's start off with some general advice for nonprofit trustees:

1. **Set clear expectations.** Work with the executive team to articulate desired values and cultural attributes. Establish clear expectations that guide administrative practices and executive decisions. Over time, these will influence the behavior of all employees.
2. **Incorporate cultural goals into strategic planning.** Consider how culture might support the achievement of specific strategic

objectives. Integrate culture-related goals into the nonprofit's strategic plan.

3. **Listen to stakeholders.** Actively engage with non-executive staff, volunteers, partners, funders, beneficiaries, and other stakeholders. Ask open-ended questions to understand their perspective on the cultural strengths and weaknesses of the organization. This feedback can provide valuable insights.

4. **Monitor culture metrics.** Establish metrics to monitor cultural aspects of the organization. Examples include satisfaction surveys, retention rates, DEI metrics, and volunteer feedback. Work with the executive team to identify annual improvement goals.

5. **Enhance board diversity and promote DEI.** Diversify the board to incorporate a variety of perspectives, experiences, and backgrounds. Board diversity itself can promote a more inclusive nonprofit culture. Encouraging a diverse, equitable, and inclusive culture should be a priority for all boards. This means advocating for DEI initiatives, supporting training programs, and ensuring equitable HR policies and practices.

6. **Review HR practices.** Ask the executive team to review human resources policies and practices to ensure they align with the desired values and culture. This includes examining recruitment processes, performance appraisals, training and development opportunities, and employee recognition programs.

7. **Prioritize the cultural fit of new leaders.** When hiring for executive leadership roles, consider culture fit alongside other qualifications. For example, does the new leader align with the existing team on how best to balance mission and fiduciary objectives? When nonprofit boards put cultural misfits into leadership positions, they cause extensive organizational damage. Promoting from within is a good way to mitigate this risk.

Defining organizational values

It's natural to assume that what attracted you to serve the organization (i.e., the mission) means that others in the organization share your values. While it is likely that you share many values with employees and executives, asserting that something is an "organizational value" is more nuanced. Be aware of over-influencing in this area. Your perspective on what the organization values or should value is important but not always accurate.

When boards adopt value statements that don't ring true to the people working in the organization, those values are dismissed and relegated to website platitudes. Similarly, when boards misunderstand the culture of the nonprofit they serve, their decisions can cause great harm. Resist the urge to project your personal beliefs onto the organization you serve and instead authentically seek the perspectives of the people who live the organizational values every day.

Sometimes, nonprofits embrace value statements that aren't reflective of their team and lack meaning for internal or external audiences. It's good to ask, "What are we trying to accomplish by identifying and communicating our values?" Let's explore why an organization might choose to highlight a certain value or guiding principle. Here are a few examples and how they might be interpreted:

- Shape culture and clarify the expectations of current employees ("I'd better act with integrity as this nonprofit values it.")
- Bolster image in the marketplace and enhance public opinion ("This nonprofit is committed to our community.")
- Attract like-minded funders ("We are both dedicated to helping the same underserved population.")
- Attract purpose-driven employees guided by a certain value ("This nonprofit really seems focused on ensuring their actions are evidence-based.")
- Build credibility in the minds of potential partners ("This organization does good work; have we worked with them before?")
- Differentiate the organization ("Wow, this nonprofit genuinely values innovation and they show that in so many ways—what a cool organization!")

Trying to accomplish many goals *simultaneously* leads nonprofits to adopt value statements that are too broad and generalized to have the desired effect. With value statements, *less is more*. Crafting a value statement that is meaningful to your employees, partners, funders, or clients takes work. It is unlikely that you'll arrive at something equally meaning-ful to all audiences. I suggest picking one audience to prioritize. It's been my experience that the impact on employees should be the primary con-sideration for most nonprofits. It is their actions you are most able to affect. They are less likely to view the value statement as a marketing gim-mick and more likely to embrace it and let it influence their behavior.

Consider whether there are values that are truly intrinsic to the non-profit or whether your statement of values is something that is more aspi-rational. Are you trying to convey something unique and true of the organization today, or are you engaging in visioning about the organiza-tion you hope to build in the future? Usually, it's the latter. This typically leads boards and executive teams to develop a half dozen or more values that they hope will guide the organization as it grows. This seldom has the desired effect. I believe you are better off picking two to three central val-ues that can be reinforced in everything you do. Of course, that won't be easy.

The problem is that many innocuous-sounding values will be offered by well-meaning participants in the process, and it's hard to argue against including any specific value. Who doesn't want the organization to con-duct itself with transparency and integrity? To be collaborative, inclusive, innovative, evidence-based, and efficient? Who doesn't want to work in an organization that cares deeply about its employees, shows empathy toward its clients, and is laser-focused on making the world a better place? However, you can't be laser-focused on anything while also being focused on half a dozen other things. The intentions here are all good, but by hav-ing too many values, you dilute their ability to differentiate the organi-zation in the minds of employees and external audiences. Your nonprofit can still be all those things without naming each one as a driving value. Pick the few that are most meaningful to your organization. These carry the greatest promise to guide the organization as it grows.

Additionally, it is useful to focus on the differentiating and motivating aspects of individual values. You are trying to identify the few values that are genuinely unique to your organization's history and culture or central to your mission. This gives those values a real chance at becoming mean-ingful inside your organization and increases the likelihood that people's actions will consistently reflect them. Over time, your nonprofit's story will reinforce and demonstrate its values, turning words on a website into ideas that truly differentiate the organization and its people.

Board culture

You were asked to be a trustee because of your talents and experience. Be honest with yourself, and other trustees, about those skills and knowledge. Sometimes, boards put trustees in the unenviable position of leading activities they are ill-equipped to lead. For example, they may ask someone to lead trustee recruitment when they don't have a relevant personal network or ask someone without executive experience to lead the board's review of the ED's performance. All trustees should be open to the expertise of their colleagues and candid about their own expertise.

Similarly, don't assume a BIPOC board member wants to serve as the board's "conscience" on all matters related to DEI. Just because a trustee belongs to a particular racial or ethnic group does not mean they desire, or are adequately equipped, to guide the organization's thinking on DEI matters. And just because a trustee happens to have insight and expertise on DEI matters, does not mean that is their primary value to the organization! On effective nonprofit boards, *all* trustees contribute as thoughtfully as possible across all matters confronting the organization.

Effective governance, diversity, and perspective are clearly linked on nonprofit boards. Imagine, for a moment, a board composed of people of different ages, sexes, and races. Before we congratulate ourselves on the diverse board we've built, let's consider the impact of other perspectives that may be missing. Ask yourself these questions:

- Do we need the perspective of stakeholders whose behavior we are trying to change? Is the perspective of our patients or clients adequately captured in our decision-making?
- Could our board benefit from more executive or financial expertise?
- Would trustees with different sexual orientations or different educational backgrounds offer a needed perspective?
- How about trustees with disabilities?
- Would governance be improved by adding board members who have lived in poverty, struggled with substance abuse, been victims

of domestic violence, or have other real-world connections to our mission?

Diversity is often about age, sex, and race—but usually, those are just proxies for the perspective we are really searching for.

Governance culture is shaped by all sorts of trustee attributes and social norms that develop over time. The erudite trustees of nonprofits seldom go feral like the young British boys in the novel *Lord of the Flies*, but odd ideas, weird social norms, and unacceptable behaviors can and do develop in the isolation and power of the boardroom. For example, some boards decide that any decision they make must have unanimous support. Any reasonable person can predict the outcome of such folly. Other boards are dominated by the actions of difficult trustees, or struggle with one or two members who monopolize the discussion at every meeting. Some embrace formality and use consent agendas to such an extreme that real dialogue between trustees and executives seldom occurs. Some boards get stuck in analysis paralysis, others are too cautious, and some are too deferential to the expertise of a specific trustee or member of the management team. Some boards are just too enamored with their executive team and do little more than rubber stamp CEO/ED decisions. As one would expect, the trustees on these boards grow further and further removed from understanding and serving the real needs of the organization they govern.

If you are a nonprofit trustee and any of those dynamics sound familiar to you, what should you do? Do you have the courage to voice your concerns and put forth steps the board can take to improve governance culture? If you are serious about delivering value to the nonprofit you serve, begin by being honest with yourself about your board's culture and your role in it. Is the group self-aware enough to know when they need to seek outside counsel? Are members both respectful and comfortable delivering candid criticism of each other? Are you part of the problem? Whatever your assessment, approach the issue as you would any other important consideration. Observe, note your observations and feelings, consider your own role in the problem, research the issue, and draft potential solutions. Then delicately raise the issue with the right parties and put forth potential solutions for group consideration. It's also vital that you remain resolute until adequate progress is made. Allowing an unhealthy governance culture to persist is unacceptable to the conscientious trustee. And you, my friend, are a conscientious trustee!

For the board to be an effective governing body, its members must have the right expertise (auditing, finance, fundraising, relevant domain knowledge, etc.). I believe all nonprofit boards should also include trustees who have experience being nonprofit executives, so the board adequately understands the trade-offs involved in running a nonprofit. But just gathering a group of people with the requisite knowledge and skills isn't enough. It's the group dynamic that dictates effectiveness. That means considering culture when adding new members, planning retreats, and designing board development goals. Governance culture is like organizational culture in one particularly consequential way: a group of phenomenally good trustees who work exceptionally well with each other can accomplish amazing things.

SUMMARY

- The values you and your team embody help to differentiate your nonprofit, and that can substantially increase your mission impact.
- Values that are unique to your nonprofit's history and culture make them meaningful inside your organization and increase the likelihood that your actions will reflect them.
- Culture governs your ability to be effective. You can actively shape culture by changing the attitudes and behaviors of only a handful of people on a team.
- "Culture eats strategy for breakfast." The best strategy in the world still needs to be executed and culture dictates the success of that execution.
- The environment around most any strategy is evolving. A healthy and resilient team culture is necessary to anticipate and react to obstacles, take advantage of emerging opportunities, and stay focused and motivated after setbacks.
- Take on the introspective work of understanding DEI in your organization. By advancing the representation and authentic participation of people with different lived experiences, smart leaders help their nonprofits to be more insightful, resilient, and effective.
- The best nonprofit leaders work tirelessly to build an army of change agents—people inspired to work together to realize the organization's vision.
- Resilience is an important part of a healthy organizational culture. Inspire confidence in your team by reinforcing the progress being made. Confidence breeds excitement for the future, and that excitement is an excellent antidote to burnout.
- When you clearly communicate that you expect great things from people, you will be surprised by how often they deliver.
- There is an inverse relationship between culture and labor costs. As culture deteriorates, labor costs go up because you must pay people more to stick around.

- Nonprofit boards should take an active role in pursuing continuous cultural improvement on the board and in the organization.
- Governance culture is shaped by trustees' attributes and the social norms that develop over time. Conscientious trustees pay attention to this and actively work to improve it.

8

DEALING WITH "BRILLIANT JERKS"
(AND OTHER HR DILEMMAS)

The one thing that doesn't abide by majority rule is a person's conscience.

—Novelist NELLE HARPER LEE

T HIS IS A fun chapter where we'll explore lots of important human resources (HR) topics. As you might expect, the fiduciary/impact dilemma shows up here as well. As a nonprofit leader, you'll develop an internal compass based on the relative financial and mission priorities you have for the organization. You implicitly (and sometimes explicitly) relay those priorities every time you decide who to hire, who to coach, who to praise, and who to promote. Get the balance wrong and the team's perception of you and your values will begin to veer from your actual values. Of course, this impacts their attitudes, behaviors, and priorities.

Early in my career, I received a glowing evaluation from the COO of the nonprofit I was working for; someone who coached his team with care and for whom I'd developed a deep respect. Amid the carefully worded statements about my accomplishments was one brief statement that I didn't understand. Under the heading "growth areas," it said that I "did not suffer fools gladly." I was unfamiliar with the phrase. This was in the 90s, before the internet became the source of all answers to simple queries, so I couldn't just Google it. Instead, I asked about it when we met to discuss my evaluation.

He gently relayed that I could be impatient or intolerant toward people I thought were less intelligent, less hardworking, or whose knowledge didn't seem (to me) to be clearly aligned with the task at hand. He said he felt it was a perception issue. By this, he meant that he believed that I did, in fact, respect my colleagues. I just wasn't showing it. He said, he "just wanted me to be aware of the issue." The more we talked about it, the more I realized that I did indeed have a perception problem that I was completely unaware of until that moment.

I also realized that I was sometimes too quick to dismiss the input and perspective of my colleagues. This included people who had technical expertise far different from my own—those who had PhDs, and those whose work experience exceeded mine by at least a decade. Part of me felt defensive and wanted to argue that he was mistaken. Perhaps "the fools" were just being too sensitive. Perhaps they didn't care as much as I did about the mission. The more reflective part of me wondered why I didn't see value in some of my colleagues. I wanted to understand *exactly* what I had done that made him concerned enough to raise the issue. Was I really missing the true nature of my colleagues' perspectives and abilities? Was I being rude or dismissive? Were my colleagues complaining about me behind my back? Did even my workplace "friends" consider me an arrogant ass?

Receiving that feedback and taking it to heart changed my career trajectory. By that time in my life, I knew I had an introverted and aloof personality. I knew I was more comfortable in front of a computer than going out to lunch with coworkers. And I knew I could be smug and quick with humor (to this day, my wife is fond of calling me "a smart-ass"). What I didn't understand was that I needed to compensate for those personality traits if I wanted to be effective in my career. I needed to regularly seek the input of my coworkers and embrace the fact that their perspectives would improve my own work products and their acceptance of me. While I've always been friendly, I needed to remember that my preference to be introverted sent unintentional signals to those around me. It was hard for them to tell that I liked and respected them. I was both self-conscious and brash (not a great combination). In between bouts of brilliance, I was causing organizational harm, and I wasn't even aware of it.

My deep respect for the COO allowed me to hear and accept his message. Employees need to hear the unvarnished truth from those they admire and respect the most. It can (and should) be delivered with kindness, but also with candor. If you are in a leadership position and have earned the respect of your colleagues, it's your words that carry the most weight. Your candor can inspire people to reflect and grow. Your care will help them overcome their fears and flaws, and it's your coaching that will ultimately allow the organization to benefit from their untapped potential.

Many years later, during an HR-focused retreat, an outside facilitator talked about the organizational harm caused by "brilliant jerks." These were people who had great ideas or made significant contributions but who just couldn't work effectively with others. He encouraged us to identify them and phase them out of the organization because we were significantly underestimating the organizational harm they caused.

By that time, I was a well-respected and accomplished leader of the organization. During the break, I asked the facilitator if I could have a few minutes to share my story. He agreed, and I shared my experience of receiving that confronting feedback with a room full of company leaders. I relayed that early in my career I was well along the path of becoming a "brilliant jerk," and if it wasn't for that nudge by a thoughtful manager, my many accomplishments and the organizational benefits that came with them would not have happened.

Candid dialogue with struggling employees is an essential element of leadership. It's one that too many nonprofit leaders shy away from. This chapter will help prepare you for this challenge and others.

FUTURE LEADERS

Leadership is primarily about two things: setting a strategic course and communicating. A nonprofit leader's communication responsibilities include delivering feedback to employees. Ideally, this is done regularly and not just once a year during performance appraisals. Nonprofits attract kind, thoughtful people who tend to care quite a lot about other people's feelings. When that kindness gets in the way of providing frank feedback, however, the culture suffers, individual development slows, and organizational effectiveness is constrained. As a future leader, realize that there truly is kindness in delivering honest feedback to your colleagues. When done well, your feedback will help them to better see their own strengths and weaknesses, motivate them to grow, and give them confidence that you care about their development.

Delivering timely, effective feedback to employees begins by determining your goal. Are you trying to get the employee to behave more civilly toward their colleagues or to work harder or smarter? Do you want them to take on more responsibility, or do you want them to just leave the organization?

Table 8.1 is a simple two-by-two matrix that helps you to categorize feedback goals based on a combination of a person's ability/potential and their personality (i.e., how kind and team-oriented they are). It is purposely not nuanced to force you to make frank assessments and approach individual messaging with very clear goals. You'll note that it has an overly candid, smart-ass quality to it. That's what *I needed* to help me adopt explicit feedback goals for each of my direct reports.

	NOT KIND / NOT TEAM-ORIENTED	KIND / TEAM-ORIENTED
CAPABLE / INSIGHTFUL	Brilliant Jerk: How do I get them to stop being an ass? 10%	Brilliant Saint: How do I retain them, give them more responsibility, and find more like them? 25%
NOT CAPABLE / INSIGHTFUL	Inept Jerk: How did they get here and how do I get them to go away? 5%	Inept Saint: How do I assess if they are in the right role and can be successfully developed? 60%

Table 8.1 An Exaggerated Personnel Assessment Tool

As you can see, I've used exaggerated categorical labels to represent the extremes of ability and personality. Few human resources (HR) professionals would approve! However, these labels have helped me to be honest about the most salient issue I needed to prioritize and address with each employee. The "brilliant jerk" isn't jerky all the time. The "inept saint" clearly has *some* talents; it's just that they also have clear and painful gaps in their abilities. You get the idea. Also, these are certainly *not* the words you would use to deliver feedback! These are categories that you should use in private to help you embrace real candor; they will kick off the journey toward more direct, individual messaging with explicit goals. If you can pull that off, you will be a better leader.

I believe more than half of nonprofit employees (including managers and executives) and most trustees fall into the "inept saint" category. These are well-meaning, hardworking people who just aren't adequately equipped to be fully successful in their current role (for many reasons). My blunt assessment is that this describes about 60% of nonprofit sector employees. You may disagree with this viewpoint or struggle with its harshness, but take a moment to consider the implications. I'm basically saying two things: there is tremendous untapped potential in the nonprofit workforce, and *you* might not be adequately equipped to be fully successful in your current role, regardless of how kind and team-oriented you are.

I believe there is a high reward for investing in workforce, leadership, and board development. Remember the "saint" part of the definition? The payoff comes because nonprofit staff and volunteers care deeply for their organizations and colleagues. Given that potential, there should be more focus in the sector on creating innovative and engaging development programs tailored to specific nonprofit roles. This is part of the reason I wrote this book.

Even if I'm wrong and the number of "inept saints" is closer to 40%, imagine what could be achieved with further professional development! Future nonprofit leaders could empower thousands of team-oriented nonprofit saints by helping them efficiently and effectively execute their meaningful work. As they say, "knowledge is power." As a future nonprofit leader, don't just concern yourself with your own development—coach your colleagues and advocate for their development.

It's also been my experience that around 25% of people working in or leading nonprofits fall into the "brilliant saint" category. They are friendly, collaborative, hardworking, smart, efficient, effective, and an inspiration to their colleagues. These are the people that make good things happen. They mitigate risks and help the organization avoid pitfalls. Even so, further development will equip them to take on roles of greater consequence (and reduce the chance that they are promoted beyond their abilities). Following the Pareto principle, I assume that 80% of positive nonprofit outcomes can be attributed to the efforts of these people. Let's celebrate the ones we know, analyze what makes them successful, and aspire to be more like them!

Only about 10% of people working in or leading nonprofits fall into the "brilliant jerk" category. While these people may have great ideas, get things done, or even save lives ("brilliant jerks" are a little more common among MDs)—people dislike working with them. Inflated egos, insecurities, attitudes, or prejudices regularly get them into trouble. These individuals can be aloof, manipulative, or even downright mean. Some are alcoholics, others are self-centered—all sorts of unenviable things. But in the end, some rather unhealthy or unpleasant aspect of their personality tarnishes their achievements and impedes the success of the surrounding team. Whether or not it's done with malice, "brilliant jerks" cause a lot of organizational damage that offset the impact of their moments of brilliance. Helping these individuals develop an appreciation for that fact can turn some of them into "brilliant saints." For the others, it just isn't worth it in the long run.

That leaves around 5% of nonprofit staff that have neither the personality nor the talent necessary for any kind of meaningful success ("inept jerks"). The goal is to get these individuals out of your organization as fast as possible!

I should note that when I did analyses of my staff, I always used acronyms in case my notes found themselves in the wrong hands. For example, DP-IS stood for "development priorities for inept saints" and PGA stood for "please go away." Of course, those were not super professional and were developed for my own entertainment (you must make work fun). The point is to be discreet. Respect the privacy and feelings of all staff, and don't lose sight of why you're doing the analysis in the first place. You are teaching *yourself* to have explicit people goals, to embrace candor, and to deliver feedback with a balance of kindness and directness that moves the team and organization forward. There's a saying that's relevant here: "Good advice is often annoying, bad advice never is." If you don't help the people around you to see where and how they need to improve, who will?

A less controversial (and less fun) HR assessment tool is the 9-box (Table 8.2). You may have already come across a 9-box in your career, as they are widely used. The goal is to categorize employees based on current performance and future potential and to use that categorization to decide the best course of action for them. I provide an example below, with my commentary on each of the boxes. These assessments can be completed individually by managers or as a group in a facilitated session. As with most group exercises, candor can be watered down in the group setting and the utility of the tool suffers. It takes just one person in the room to move the exercise from being helpful to being a waste of time.

This tool can be quite useful if those doing the assessing and categorizing really contemplate the drivers of performance and challenge their

	POOR PERFORMANCE	AVERAGE PERFORMANCE	HIGH PERFORMANCE
HIGH POTENTIAL	An enigma, perhaps a "brilliant jerk." Needs candid coaching and a performance improvement plan.	A developing leader and rising star? Or is this just someone we all like? Why are they not consistently realizing their potential?	Currently an effective and consistent leader (star player). Needs a clear path to realize potential.
MODERATE POTENTIAL	Questionable fit and inconsistent player. Needs candid conversation about motivators and a performance improvement plan.	Consistent contributor. Discuss career satisfaction and consider adding responsibilities to further assess potential.\n\nInquire about goals.	Had a great year. Discuss career objectives and consider adding responsibilities to further assess potential.
LIMITED POTENTIAL	Needs to go. Quit making excuses. Causing more organizational harm than you think. Terminate or counsel out ASAP.	Specialist, plateaued professional or someone struggling with motivation? Are we overlooking some important aspect of potential?	Plateaued professional or expert who is unlikely to develop further. Could also be a "brilliant jerk." What exactly is causing us to question their potential?

Table 8.2 The 9-Box Assessment Tool

own assumptions about why a certain employee has more potential than another. Judging performance is subjective. (How well are you really able to separate one team member's contributions from that of others? Are they just superb at claiming responsibility for successes or putting out the fires that they caused?) Look for quantitative performance metrics that take a lot of the subjectivity out of it. Resist judging an employee's performance intuitively if you have evidence to the contrary. Honesty is always the best policy when today's performance falls short of what you believe someone is capable of. It is also the best policy when an employee you're not particularly fond of surprises you by delivering the goods.

When assessing an employee's potential, we are implicitly referring to their display of desired leadership traits: their ability to problem-solve, authentically delegate, manage team stress, and inspire other employees, etc. It is also impacted by how a person makes us *feel*.

- Do they exhibit a strong loyalty to the organization?
- Are they uniquely introspective and humble?
- Is their optimism about the future contagious?
- Are they unusually industrious or conscientious?
- What is it that is making us feel they have great potential?

Keep in mind that some employees are more focused on managing their image than others. Some staff get quite good at "managing up" by only relaying news they think we want to hear. This is how so many "inept saints" get promoted into leadership positions they are ill-equipped to handle. When considering potential, seek the input of others who have a different relationship with the employee. Their perspective is less likely to be the product of a carefully curated experience.

Just because a person makes you feel a certain way, doesn't mean they possess distinctive potential. For example, familiarity and shared experiences promote feelings of comfort and candor. But your comfort with someone doesn't necessarily translate to the comfort of other members on the team. Assessing potential is where unconscious bias shows up in a big way. We are more likely to see potential in those who are like us, with similar backgrounds or life experiences. This is an alarming problem when you think about it. If we primarily see potential in the people who remind us of ourselves, how much potential are we missing?

With the goal of becoming a conscientious leader, challenge yourself to find the potential in those *least* like you. Of course, the first step in doing so is getting to know the people who are least like you. While it may take you out of your comfort zone, it usually ends up being fun and enlightening, and the potential organizational payoff is tremendous.

Assessing performance, recognizing potential, and delivering direct and honest feedback are skills future nonprofit leaders must learn and continue to refine over their careers. These tasks require introspection and courage to execute accurately and equitably. Take the time to consider why you believe certain things about your colleagues and seek the input of others. Be cautious of unconscious bias, confirmation bias (the tendency to favor viewpoints that just reinforce your own), and attribution errors (attributing positive or negative actions/outcomes to the wrong person). As you advance your skills in these areas, you will become better at building and inspiring your team. An added benefit is that you will solidify your position as a "brilliant saint"!

EXECUTIVES & MANAGERS

Since most nonprofits are focused on delivering services instead of goods, the employees of the nonprofit are the source of value creation. Attracting, retaining, inspiring, and developing the right talent is a critical success function. As such, HR plays a strategic role in the well-managed nonprofit. Unfortunately, in many nonprofit organizations, the HR function is understaffed, not led by an especially talented leader, or underestimated in terms of strategic value. If nonprofit EDs and CEOs spent more time sourcing skilled HR leaders and positioning them for success, their organizations would reap the benefits of a talented and engaged workforce driven to deliver more strategic value.

There are plenty of HR-related topics worthy of exploration with nonprofit executives and managers. Here we will focus on answering the following HR-related dilemmas: how to find, acquire, and retain the top talent in your industry, what to do when employees go around their day-to-day manager and directly to you for guidance, and how to recognize and extract value from your most introverted employees.

How to find, acquire, and retain top talent

It is especially hard to find, acquire, and retain talent when your organization lacks the necessary HR foundation. Laying the groundwork includes clearly documenting roles, responsibilities, and competency models (the knowledge and skills needed to successfully carry out a role). It's more important that these be *specific* rather than an exhaustive list of requirements. The ideal length is a two-page role description, including the responsibilities of that role and the competencies required. In small non-profits, you may only need to develop a handful of these. In larger organizations, there might be fifty to a hundred organizational roles that should be accurately defined. Unfortunately, it is common for nonprofit organizations to lack this kind of structured documentation and rely solely on job descriptions written for recruiting purposes.

Role documentation helps candidates understand what the organization is looking for. It also helps the organization's leaders agree on what they are looking for. Documentation can also substantiate labor category slotting on government grants and pricing on philanthropic grants. It helps managers set job expectations and measure performance, while giving employees insight into the skills development necessary for promotion. If you create a template, along with standardized terminology, and involve the right people (i.e., the ones who understand each role), this can be a relatively quick and painless exercise.

With role documentation in place, your attention turns to candidate sourcing. This isn't a book meant for HR professionals, so we'll stay focused on the needs of non-HR managers and executives when sourcing candidates.

What if you aren't seeing the caliber and diversity of candidates desired? Begin by taking a second look at the job description and talk with your recruiter about broadening their approach to sourcing candidates. Consider posting the position in a different way on LinkedIn or on job boards affiliated with targeted programs at different universities (e.g., Historically Black Colleges and Universities, or schools with unique academic programs or student populations). You should also review your online presence. Is there something that is intimidating or scaring candidates away? Enlist the help of current employees in advertising the position by asking them to share their experiences as employees, and to source potential candidates. However, this strategy may backfire if you lack a diverse employee base as your staff are likely to source candidates like themselves.

Keep an open mind when reviewing candidates. Consider what they've accomplished in the context of the opportunities they've had. This idea was wonderfully captured in a line from the TV adaptation of Celeste Ng's *Little Fires Everywhere*. During an impassioned argument between two mothers—a white, upper-middle-class mother asserts that she made better life decisions than the Black single mother she's arguing with. The Black mom responds, "You didn't *make* good choices! You *had* good choices." This succinctly sums up why nonprofit employers should look harder at candidates who have faced adversity or have had fewer notable education and career opportunities.

Candidates are more than a collection of skills. Their character, resilience, and resolve shape how they'll respond to workplace challenges and perform under pressure. You may have an image of your ideal candidate. Let that image evolve as you review applicants who bring a different set of knowledge, maturity, and skills to the table. While filling your organization with Ivy League grads who've benefited from prestigious internships sounds great on paper, in practice it can be a recipe for a myopic organization focused more on itself than the people or the cause it exists to serve. Ultimately, a diverse team will outperform others.

Retaining good talent requires treating your employees with dignity and demonstrating appreciation for their contributions. It also helps tremendously if you have a healthy workplace culture. In Chapter 7, we discussed strategies to improve culture. Here, I want to highlight the value of thinking about your development programs as inclusion and retention tools. The sad truth is that it's easier to retain the least effective employees and harder to retain the most effective ones. It's also easier to retain employees who see people like themselves in leadership roles and harder to retain the ones that don't. Retaining quality employees takes effort. But even small nonprofits can mentor, coach, and develop their teams so that they can retain their top talent.

Addressing employee complaints

When an employee has a problem with their manager, what should you do? You face two competing moral obligations. One to the manager to whom you've "authentically delegated" responsibility, and one to the employee who came seeking help (possibly representing the interests of other employees). Put on your coaching waders, as the water is about to get mucky. This is a situation where even seasoned executives can make errors of judgment.

Let's start off by recognizing that some categories of manager complaints (discrimination, sexual harassment, allegations of fraud, etc.)

should be triaged to HR immediately. By immediately, I mean it's best to not even engage in an initial fact-finding conversation with the employee without HR present. Reassure the employee that the issue will absolutely be treated confidentially but that you need to get HR involved. They have more knowledge of, and experience with, the best way to handle these issues.

Schedule a meeting between you, the employee, and HR to discuss the complaint. Make sure the meeting is marked as private on everyone's calendars. Since you likely know the manager and team in question, participating in at least the first conversation is usually helpful. Be on the lookout for simple misunderstandings and ulterior motives that may be behind the complaint and avoid defending or trying to explain the manager's actions during this initial meeting. Listen. Keep your notes high-level (they may end up being used in a court case), reassure the employee that you are taking the complaint seriously, and genuinely thank them for bringing the issue to your attention.

If you have reservations about the employee's complaint, save those for when you debrief with HR, one-on-one. We all want to believe the best about the people we've given important responsibilities to. Sometimes, these kinds of complaints are without merit or come from a disingenuous place. However, it is important for you to keep an open mind and not jump to any conclusions. Allow your HR professional(s) to do their job.

For all other less serious problems employees have with their manager, the solution is usually one of coaching the employee about ways to raise the issue with their manager and then coaching the manager about hearing critical feedback and being open to course correction. Don't make the mistake of promising to engage directly to resolve the issue based only on the employee's perspective. And don't express agreement with the employee about the manager's shortcomings or development needs, etc. I've made that mistake, and it made things much worse. It's okay to *empathize* with the employee's situation generally, but you should also help the employee seek to understand their manager's perspective. A good outcome is when the employee leaves the meeting having developed even a little empathy for the situation their manager finds themself in.

In healthcare, we use the term *self-limiting* to describe disease processes that go away on their own without intervention (like a cold). Some day-to-day issues that nonprofit leaders face are self-limiting, but this typically isn't one of them. Don't make the mistake of assuming that by letting the employee get things "off their chest" you've resolved the issue. It is more likely that the problem will linger, becoming a source of rumor and distraction for other employees. It's also likely that inaction will ultimately lead to one of the two employees choosing to leave the organization (often the better one).

Make a point of having a candid conversation with the manager and following up with the employee in a week or two. It's important that everyone knows that your organization values feedback and continued development of all employees (including managers). Embrace employees who have the courage to raise issues and demonstrate, through your words and actions, that the organization has zero tolerance for any type of retribution. These ideals need to be reinforced regularly, not just when an issue arises.

In most cases, you should avoid taking direct action and redirect the employee to discuss the concerns with their manager. One of the best things you can do is to provide guidance to the employee about how to raise the issue in a constructive and thoughtful way. Most issues can be resolved with better communication. Newer or terribly busy managers tend to engage in too many *linear* interactions with their direct reports (one-way conversations where they are lecturing or emphasizing directives, etc.). Helping managers and employees to become better communicators pays great dividends over time. Here are ten communication tips that may help:

1. Treat each other as respected colleagues, regardless of role. This includes being respectful of each other's time and competing priorities.
2. Recognize that lived experiences, both within and outside the organization, shape how you construct your messages and how others receive them.
3. Strive to be less manipulative and more genuine. Share similar experiences you've encountered. Be open about challenges you've experienced and things you do not know.
4. Honestly seek input and actively listen when it is offered. Recognize the urge to explain or react defensively, and try your best to control it.

5. Treat others with empathy. We seldom know what else is going on in other people's lives (divorce, health concerns, parenting stress, etc.).

6. Use affirming, validating responses. Respond to colleagues in ways that acknowledge their feelings, experiences, perceptions, and fears.

7. Solve problems, not people. Try your best not to take things personally.

8. Value yourself and your own experiences. Have the confidence to be candid and assertive.

9. Strive for clarity and understanding. What inferences are being made? What facts are agreed upon? What goals do we share? How can we help each other?

10. Make time for dialogue. The better we communicate with one another, the better we understand each other's perspective, and that improves our chances of success.

Introverted employees

"Empty barrels make the most noise" is an idiom that reminds us that people who are the most vocal or who monopolize conversations are often the least informed. Nonprofit organizations can benefit from increasing their understanding and engagement of introverted employees.

People perceived as having leadership potential are often extroverts who find being with other people to be energizing. They're recognized as successful because they contribute the most in meetings, ask insightful questions, and enjoy socializing. They like to present or network at conferences, and many have a good sense of humor and can be the life of the party at company gatherings. Extroverts are hard to miss as they are always making their presence known, demanding your attention and recognition for their contributions.

If you build your organization primarily around the value of your extroverted employees, you are unnecessarily limiting its potential. There are many talented nonprofit employees who find being the center of attention or engaging in social events exhausting. They may be shy, lacking in confidence, or constantly battling anxiety in highly stimulative social environments. Yet, people who keep to themselves or are "quiet" are generally listening more intently, and they usually have deeply considered things to share once you get them in a more comfortable space. These introverts are less likely to demand recognition for their contributions. As a result, their achievements are sometimes misattributed to their extroverted colleagues.

As an introvert, I've felt the sting of others taking credit for my work and ideas. I prefer quiet environments and staying home, I favor written communication over verbal, and I have experienced crippling anxiety many times over my career. Anxiety-inducing activities, for me, include the usual things like making presentations and attending social functions. Though even small things like introducing myself or making small talk with contractors, dentists, or doctors can spur unexpected anxiety.

As I've gotten older, I've learned a few things about the connection between anxiety and introversion. For me, anxiety comes from the unpredictable nature of my ability to verbalize my thoughts. Like a cellular call in rural America, sometimes the connection is crisp and clear, and other times it comes out garbled. Sometimes there is nothing but dead air. I have an idea, raise my hand to share it, and what comes out of my mouth isn't what's in my head, or worse yet, the thought completely vanishes before I have a chance to insert it into the conversation.

My best ideas often arrive after the fact. For example, on the walk back to my office *after* a meeting. As Marti Olsen Laney, the author of *The Introvert Advantage* puts it, "I found my thoughts were like lost airline baggage; they arrived sometime later."[1] There's a reason you're reading my book and not watching my TED talk. Writing allows me to capture and effectively relay my thoughts in a mode that's in sync with their arrival and departure in my brain. [Thanks for embracing my preferred mode of communication.]

Here's something else I've learned about introverted employees. Introversion and introspection are closely related. Introverts tend to be more thoughtful and self-reflective. They make excellent coaches, can be highly creative and strategic problem solvers, and are usually quite honest about their strengths and shortcomings.

---

1. This book is an excellent gift for the introverts in your life: The Introvert Advantage by Marti Olsen Laney (2002). Another great resource is Jenn Granneman's website: Introvert, Dear (www.introvertdear.com).

I've also found introverts are more likely to embrace an abundance mentality. This generally fosters optimism for the future and allows them to celebrate the success of others rather than feel threatened by them. This can make introverts better team members and team builders. They innately (and correctly, in my opinion) believe there are enough resources and successes to share. Contrast that with a scarcity mindset that fosters unnecessary competition and encourages constant self-promotion (a hallmark of some extroverts).

Given that it can be more difficult to extract value from introverted employees, nonprofit leaders should consider how their organizational culture supports or impedes value creation. You may be able to better engage your introverted employees and encourage them to share their perspectives. Perhaps you can create work processes that allow them to contribute more comfortably and in broader ways. For example, imagine you are planning a brainstorming meeting to seek employee input on an important issue for your nonprofit. If you primarily want the input of your most vocal employees, schedule the meeting, and obtain input in real time. I (and I assume countless others) have sat quietly in dozens of company meetings waiting for the vocal group to arrive at what was obvious to me. Sometimes they get there, and sometimes they don't. Either way, it was rare (especially early in my career) that I would offer my perspective. Extroverts usually assume this is about confidence. I wouldn't exactly characterize it that way. I was usually quite confident that my perspective would be helpful to the group. I just didn't want the group's attention to turn to me, didn't want to risk the cellular signal dropping out, and didn't want to allow my colleagues to judge my appearance, be critical of my word choice, or ask follow-up questions that would force further engagement. Basically, engaging felt like a hassle that I'd rather avoid while waiting for others to voice the perspective I had (or one close enough).

If you want to ensure that you are getting input from the whole team, bookend important meetings with requests for written input. Perhaps a week before the meeting, send out a short summary of the topic to be discussed, any read-ahead you'd like the team to review, and a handful of questions for the team to answer before the meeting. Make it clear that answers will be summarized and discussed during the in-person session.

During the meeting, elicit feedback by directly calling on members who are not engaging in the conversation, and encourage people to keep an open mind until the post-meeting input is gathered. Frame post-meeting input as "now that you've heard the perspective of your colleagues and had a couple of days to consider our discussion, what are your thoughts?" If the group meeting produced a couple of potential paths forward, you might include a short survey on the options. It's also helpful to add a question like, "What did we miss?" or, "How can this idea be improved?" This way, you're encouraging introspection by all team members. You're also giving everyone three different points at which to engage (before, during, and after the meeting) and two different ways to engage (written and verbal).

When possible, another strategy is to engage introverts in smaller groups. Many introverts who are observers in a meeting of fifty are amazing contributors in a meeting of five or less. Use break-out groups and other small meeting strategies to give your introverted employees a chance to share their perspectives more comfortably. Again, this works best when employees have time to contemplate the task at hand before engaging. External consultants and meeting facilitators often get this wrong. They come in, share a task, and immediately put people into break-out groups to discuss. The element of surprise doesn't benefit anyone, and it makes the whole experience miserable for your introverted employees.

Introverts be warned that a consistent lack of engagement can be perceived as disdain for your colleagues and their ideas. While that hopefully isn't true, it is definitely a career-limiting message to be sending! It is important that you engage in some manner. For example, send an email with your thoughts after a meeting, or ask a question that might encourage the group to pursue a different line of thought. I've known a few remarkable introverts who have used this strategy to great effect. They would sit quietly listening to the group dialogue and somewhere in the latter part of the meeting they would offer a deceptively simple question that would completely change the course of the dialogue and the meeting's outcome. Now that's efficient engagement!

Other things introverted employees find miserable are icebreakers, team introductions, and most team-building exercises. They're painful for reasons beyond just not wanting to be the center of attention. Many introverts have trouble with word recall in situations they find stressful. This is because of differences in cortisol levels (the stress hormone that makes it harder to focus, recall information, and speak coherently) and other differences in how people's brains work. For instance, introverted people tend to over-activate the part of the brain that notices details and errors, causing them to be hyperaware of the mistakes they are making when communicating.

It seems that the brains of extroverts favor working memory, which is easier to quickly access. Introverts, on the other hand, tend to work more from long-term memory, which makes speech harder because it takes longer to retrieve information from long-term storage. This is why when you ask an introvert who just professed to be an avid reader what their favorite book is, they may be unable to provide an answer and get embarrassed.

However, it's still important for introverted team members to get to know their colleagues and for their colleagues to get to know them. The aim is to plan activities that create some level of comfort and familiarity between the people in the room, so consider how to best engage *all* of your employees. Here are a few more tips:

- Don't make the exercise overly personal (you don't want people to feel they are required to share information they are uncomfortable sharing).
- Give participants a template to fill out so that when it's their turn they have something to help trigger recall.
- Consider letting participants self-identify as introverts or extroverts (it's helpful to know you're not alone, and this can quickly build camaraderie).
- Ask participants to share their greatest strength or something they are particularly proud of (again, you are striving for a feel-good experience).
- Consider whether the team-building goals can be accomplished in break-out groups (introverts will be more comfortable sharing in smaller groups).

With a little planning, you can make these experiences rewarding and fun for all involved, and that will improve comfort and engagement in the rest of the meeting.

Nurture your introverted employees by putting them in situations where their strengths can shine. Be intentional about playing to individual employee strengths and incrementally challenging them to provide opportunities for growth. This, along with your support, creates successful experiences. Success breeds confidence, and confidence allows for safe risk-taking. Exposure to different experiences creates opportunities for self-discovery and builds leadership maturity. This will help your introverted employees realize their leadership potential and deliver greater value to the organization they care about.

TRUSTEES

Let's discuss a few HR-related dilemmas common to nonprofit boards: things like CEO performance assessment, executive compensation and the IRS, and a question that some of you must have had as you read the rest of this chapter—"What if the 'brilliant jerk' is on the board?" But first we need to consider the role of trustees in providing oversight of the overall approach to labor the organization.

Labor costs

Decisions about labor costs are directly tied to our beliefs about the best use of resources and talent. The tension between mission and fiduciary objectives is always in the background of those beliefs.

At a high level, there are really only three categories of labor in a nonprofit:

1. Labor that is directly carrying out the organization's mission.
2. Labor that is primarily concerned with the organization's financial health (e.g., CFO costs, development/fundraising professionals, and grant writers).
3. Labor that is indirectly supporting both of those activities (back-office functions like IT, HR, and ED or CEO costs).

The relative share of labor costs for each category says a lot about your values and the health of your organization. I recommend that every nonprofit board ask for a breakdown of the organization's labor costs into these three buckets. Manager costs should be allocated to the same place as the primary function they oversee, and the analysis should be explicit about where the costs for the most highly compensated employees are allocated. In a small organization, the results can be misleading if a few highly compensated employees are allocated to the wrong pools.

I've not found any reasonable data that would be useful to benchmark these results against. However, I still believe it's an enlightening exercise. The results can be tracked over time and used to validate that the organization is investing its labor dollars in alignment with its strategic and ethical priorities.

Spending too much or too little, in terms of labor, on financial health and back-office functions is indicative of an unhealthy organization. Small organizations (i.e., most nonprofits) tend to spend a greater share of labor dollars on direct mission activities out of necessity. While this can be good to an extent, in the extreme it really constrains the organization's ability to scale, can mean employees are working very inefficiently (with inadequate support), and can expose the organization to some serious risks (fraud, poor legal agreements, data breaches, etc.). One potential solution for small nonprofits is to form a cooperative agreement with other organizations to share the costs of common back-office functions. While this would incur set-up costs, it would likely be more efficient in the long run.

Large nonprofits tend to have the opposite problem, with bloated indirect budgets and executive salaries. It can be useful for trustees to periodically elevate their view of the organization and assess things like the overall mix of labor costs. Here are some other big picture ideas to consider:

- Are you spending significant dollars on a talented executive team who are primarily focused on balance sheet growth? While that can be good, is it your organization's top priority?
- Are you spending beyond your means on employees executing your mission?
- Should the leadership team be more focused on improving financial health?
- Are you underpaying or overpaying key employees?
- Are you spending too large a share of resources on indirect activities? If so, which ones?

While these are all good questions, understanding the overall labor mix across the three categories described earlier is probably more revealing. With that information, you can assess how the organization invests most of its funds and how that may or may not align with strategic priorities. So, start with a simple query about the relative share of labor costs dedicated to mission execution, financial health, and indirect support. The answer to that will guide you as to the next question to ask.

Executive compensation and the rebuttable presumption

Nonprofit boards tend to be quite focused on mitigating risks. An example of this is confirming board practices are within industry standards (i.e., they are acceptable and within the norms of other organizations). As a result, many nonprofit boards expend resources on consultants who provide market data (and supposed benchmarks) on things like executive compensation or employee benefits to ensure the story is clear that they aren't an outlier.

In fact, if you are a nonprofit trustee in the U.S., you are likely familiar with the IRS and their rules for setting nonprofit executive compensation. The *rebuttable presumption*[2] is the government's way of saying they'll presume your executive compensation is reasonable if an authorized body (e.g., the compensation committee of the board) is made up of members who do not have a conflict of interest (i.e., they have no personal interests in the executive's compensation) and that the authorized body bases the compensation on reasonable comparability data (i.e., market data). If you do those things, and adequately document them, the burden shifts to the IRS to prove your compensation plan is unreasonable.[3] That is, they must "develop sufficient contrary evidence to rebut" the data and process used to determine compensation.

In practice, this means boards can pay their executives outrageous sums of money as long as they can find other nonprofits of similar size or com-

---

2. IRS. "Rebuttable Presumption—Intermediate Sanctions." IRS. 2023. https://www.irs.gov/charities-non-profits/charitable-organizations/rebuttable-presumption-intermediate-sanctions

3. The National Council of Nonprofits provides additional detail, guidance, and links to useful templates (https://www.councilofnonprofits.org/tools-resources/executive-compensation).

plexity that are also paying their executives outrageous sums. Basically, it comes down to the ethics and perspective of the trustees on the compensation committee. One person's idea of "outrageous" is another person's "completely reasonable." If the compensation committee is made up of retired for-profit executives, their idea of reasonable compensation is potentially flawed.

Recent law changes add another wrinkle. They impose an excise tax on tax-exempt nonprofits that pay over $1 million in compensation to certain employees (the five highest-compensated employees). The tax rate is 21% of the compensation above $1 million and compensation includes salary, bonuses, and gross income from nonqualified deferred compensation plans (basically, anything that would normally be federally taxable). While this change won't impact most nonprofit organizations, for some larger ones it may put downward pressure on executive pay packages. Some trustees may view this as just another cost of doing business, but some may consider it a reason to reevaluate executive pay philosophy. At the present time, compensation in excess of $1 million is certainly reasonable for leaders of the largest and most complex nonprofits. However, it is likely unnecessary and wasteful for the other 99% of nonprofit organizations.

It's a mistake for nonprofit boards to assume they are in competition with for-profit firms for talent. While some nonprofit executives may switch to for-profit industries late in their careers, most have developed specialized knowledge and a mission drive that works to retain them in the sector. On the other hand, competition with *other nonprofits* for top talent can surely be an issue.

As discussed in Chapter 4, deploying resources at the top end of the pay scale can be inefficient. There are many capable leaders who are more driven to make the world a better place than to seek outsized compensation. You can find and attract these people to your organization simply by focusing on the things discussed in this book: having a compelling and clear purpose, embracing differentiating values that motivate your workforce and supporters, and communicating your organization's impact effectively.

Executive performance assessment

One of the responsibilities of a nonprofit board is to regularly assess the performance of the Executive Director or CEO. There are many resources available to guide this process, so I'll only offer a few thoughts. Nonprofit ED/CEO performance should be judged in a manner that effectively balances the fiduciary/impact dilemma. Because financial health is usually easier to measure, it is overemphasized by many nonprofits. If a leader doubles the revenues of an organization, it's hard to deny they are doing something right!

One way to construct a balanced performance assessment is to revisit the measurement framework discussed in Chapter 5—*structure, process, and outcome*. Leadership effectiveness is a product of the leader focusing on the right issues, knowing or researching the right solutions, and effectively executing those solutions. Said another way, ineffective leaders aren't focusing on the right issues, aren't capable or willing to learn new skills, and/or lack the necessary will and follow-through to fully address the organization's most pressing challenges.

The structure, process, and outcome framework (Figure 5.1) gives nonprofit boards a holistic way of considering what to emphasize in assessing ED/CEO performance. The figure in that chapter provides examples of evidence of structural health, evidence of working smart, and evidence of overall effectiveness. Those examples can serve as a guide for board discussion on what to emphasize in performance assessment and goal setting for the executive. Unfortunately, as shown, even when you get the executive focused on the right issues, their success can be sabotaged by attitudes, abilities, or resolve.

At the beginning of this chapter, feedback goals for four exaggerated employee types were introduced. Take a moment to consider which you'd honestly place your organization's current ED/CEO in.

1. I imagine very few trustees would categorize their organization's leader as an "inept jerk." If you did, please put this book down and take action on those feelings immediately!
2. A few more admirably candid trustees might categorize their organization's leader as a "brilliant jerk." If you did, I would encourage you to discuss that with other trustees and require the

leader to engage in a coaching program focused on improving their people skills.

3. Some trustees may feel their organization's leader is in over their head (i.e., an "inept saint"). If you do, then have a candid discussion with other trustees about whether the leader can be successfully developed on an acceptable timeline. In addition to an outside coach, can one or more trustees also mentor the executive? Can the executive's shortcomings be shored up in the near term by another member of the executive team? I applaud your candor, now own the responsibility of solving the problem you've identified.

4. If you feel your executive is a "brilliant saint," consider why you feel that way.

   - How confident are you that your perspective is accurate?
   - Does the evidence in relation to the structure, process, outcome framework confirm your perspective?
   - Are you sure you are correctly attributing the organization's success to the right person? Does feedback from other trustees, executives, and employees reinforce your perspective? What is the leader's primary motivation (e.g., mission impact, financial health, or their own compensation)?
   - What can you do to raise expectations even further, to develop this leader even more, and to ensure the organization benefits from their continued growth as a leader?

Most trustees would characterize their ED/CEO as a "brilliant saint." Keep in mind that the organization's leader has a lot of control over messaging to the board and credit defaults to them when times are good (they either made the right decision or built the team who did). This also works the other way when the organization struggles. However, struggles can be shielded from the board by talented executives. An executive who is particularly good at redirecting inquisitive trustees tends to be highly regarded. It is the trustee's job not to fall for these shenanigans and ensure they have a firm grasp of both the positive and negative aspects of the executive's performance. Nonprofit executives are only human. I guarantee every one of them has room for development and growth.

When the "brilliant jerk" is on the board

We've all known trustees who make board meetings a chore. If you don't, then perhaps you are just beginning your nonprofit governance journey. There are lots of ways for trustees to make life difficult for others in the boardroom. Here's a short list of things to avoid:

- Coming to meetings ill-prepared (i.e., not reviewing meeting materials in advance).
- Missing meetings and then causing the group to revisit conversations had in your absence.
- Distracting the board by engaging in wandering conversations or other agenda-killing activities.
- Repeatedly multitasking or texting during meetings.

If you are a board chair, one of the most important things you can do is make meetings about decisions and *not* updates. The board's purpose is to help govern the organization. This means helping the organization's leaders to make important decisions. If trustees face information overload at each meeting and time is consumed with staff updates, there's no room for genuine dialogue and decision-making. The board chair and the organization's ED or CEO should work together to plan action-oriented meetings and prioritize what trustees spend their time discussing (consent agendas can be remarkable efficiency builders). Take a few minutes at the end of meetings to discuss how the meeting delivered value to the organization and what could be done in the future to deliver even more value. This isn't about patting yourself on the back; it is about introspection and raising the bar. It is also good for trustees to be reminded that the board exists to serve the organization, not the other way around.

Now, even if you do all those things correctly, at times you'll come across a "brilliant jerk" on a nonprofit board. What now? What is your obligation to the organization and to the other trustees in the room? I'm not referring to board members who professionally and respectfully engage in relevant debate when they disagree with the rest of the board.

These are well-meaning trustees who help to prevent "groupthink" and ensure important decisions are appropriately vetted and discussed. I'm talking about board members who disrespect their colleagues, who are cantankerous and stubborn, and who constantly interrupt and/or repeatedly disrupt the business of the board. Just like in any group of humans, there are people serving on nonprofit boards with all kinds of unhealthy attitudes and personality traits.

What you do about them has a bit to do with your own strengths. If you are confident in your perspective and feel the other trustee respects you, the first step is to meet with them and explicitly call out their behavior. If you feel a different member of the board would be more likely to deliver a message that's "heard" by the offending trustee, then seek their support in addressing the issue. If all else fails, it's the chair's responsibility to discuss the issue with the trustee. Before problems develop, it is good to ensure that the board's bylaws include a quick and efficient mechanism to remove trustees who are delivering little value, are disrupting proceedings, or are making other trustees uncomfortable in meetings. Again, I'm not talking about healthy debate here. I'm talking about remarks that could be interpreted as sexist or racist, trustees who are belligerent, and those who consistently show disrespect for others in meetings. Don't ignore these issues. At a minimum, after three strikes, the chair should ask them to resign, or the board will vote on whether their service will be allowed to continue. To save face, most will just resign and move on to annoy someone else.

SUMMARY

- Nonprofits attract kind, caring people. When that kindness gets in the way of providing candid feedback, the culture suffers, individual development slows, and organizational effectiveness is constrained.
- There is tremendous untapped potential in the nonprofit workforce. Many employees and leaders are not adequately equipped to be fully successful in their current role regardless of how kind and team-oriented they are.
- Take time to teach yourself how to have explicit people goals, and to deliver feedback with a balance of kindness and directness that moves the team and organization forward.
- Delivering honest feedback to your colleagues helps them to see their own strengths and weaknesses, motivates them to grow, and gives them the confidence that you care about their development.
- Assessing potential is where unconscious bias shows up in a big way. We are more likely to see potential in those who are like us, with similar backgrounds or life experiences.
- New or "terribly busy" managers can engage in too many linear interactions with their direct reports. Helping managers and employees to become better communicators will pay great dividends over time.
- Support introverted employees by valuing their strengths. Be intentional about playing to these strengths and incrementally challenging them to give them opportunities to rise to their potential.
- Nonprofit ED/CEO performance should be judged in a manner that effectively balances the fiduciary/impact dilemma. Because financial health is usually easier to measure, it is overemphasized by many nonprofits.
- Spending too much or too little labor on financial health and back-office functions is indicative of an unhealthy organization. It is useful for trustees to periodically take a big picture view of

the organization and assess things like the relative share of labor costs dedicated to mission execution, financial health, and indirect support.

- Remind trustees that the board exists to serve the organization, not the other way around.

9

PARTNERSHIP & COLLABORATION

No one can whistle a symphony. It takes a whole orchestra to play it.

—Theologian HALFORD E. LUCCOCK

In 2019, a small but important nonprofit research institute based in Colorado closed its doors. The reason? Insufficient funding. Unfortunately, the nonprofit dilemma had caught up with them. This little organization had worked tirelessly to connect researchers, educate the public, and "reduce the production and use of chemicals that interfere with healthy hormone function." By all accounts, the organization's founder, the late Dr. Theo Colborn, was a remarkable human being. As a pioneer in the field of research now known as endocrine disruption,[1] Dr. Colborn didn't even complete her PhD studies until the age of fifty-eight. After a career as a pharmacist and sheep farmer, and at the stage of life when many of us are focused on retirement—she was just getting started.

Dr. Colborn quickly became one of the most influential environmental health scientists of the last forty years. She is credited with recognizing that even low concentrations of certain industrial chemicals in the environment can bioaccumulate in wildlife and in humans, causing a host of health problems. She found that synthetic chemicals are concentrated up the food chain. At higher levels, they cause damage to the endocrine system, interfering with the hormones and chemical messaging that control the body's biological processes. The impacts can be particularly devastating during developmental life stages.

Dr. Colborn had to approach her work with collaborative zeal to arrive at these discoveries and convince others of their merits. Cross-disciplinary collaboration was a hallmark of her work and the work of the nonprofit she later founded (The Endocrine Disruption Exchange). The complexity of the scientific questions she sought to answer demanded this type of approach, whether it was the patterns she was trying to uncover, the unconventional associations, the emerging questions, and later, the ability to shape regulation through advocacy. At the 1991 meeting where the term "endocrine disruption" was coined, Colborn had gathered participants from sixteen different disciplines (wildlife biologists, endocrinologists, pharmacists, laboratory scientists, toxicologists, ecologists, anthropologists, etc.). Fostering a coher-

---

1. Colborn, T., Dumanoski, D., and Myers, JP. Our Stolen Future. Are We Threatening Our Fertility, Intelligence and Survival? —A Scientific Detective Story. Penguin Books, 1996.

ent conversation across so many disciplines must have been fascinating but also extremely difficult.

Dr. Colborn's nonprofit was unique in its focus on the exchange of data and ideas between scientists, policymakers, and environmental advocacy organizations. While its closing is a significant loss, Colborn's legacy lives on in regulatory policy and in the public's understanding of the connection between industrial chemicals in the environment and endocrine-related health effects. Equally important, her legacy lives on in the collaborative mindset of a whole new generation of environmental researchers that she inspired. She championed an approach that accelerated scientific discovery, advanced the public's understanding of complex topics, and created the necessary leverage to influence public policy and future environmental regulatory frameworks.

I N THIS CHAPTER, I'll use "collaboration" to refer to largely informal cooperation between organizations and "partnership" to refer to more formal agreements which may involve contractual relationships, structural changes, or a change in oversight. Nonprofit organizations choose to collaborate or partner for many reasons, though they all come down to either furthering the mission or improving financial health and viability. Sound familiar? Yes, the nonprofit dilemma lives here as well.

When a nonprofit's finances don't match its aspirations, it faces recurring challenges. If you work in a small nonprofit, you are likely familiar with some of these challenges: cutting corners, exerting too much effort chasing funding, not having access to the necessary leadership or management talent, and not having the capacity to execute the mission or protect the organization adequately. Many of these issues can be (at least partially) remedied through collaboration or partnership.

Competition for resources stimulates innovation and pushes individual organizations to be more efficient, but it also keeps the nonprofit sector fragmented. When two organizations see themselves as competitors, they are less able to embrace collaborative strategies that would benefit both of them. For all the emphasis American culture puts on the benefits of self-reliance and competition (i.e., that it drives efficiency and innovation), the ideals aren't exactly realized at scale in the nonprofit sector.

Yes, competition drives more money to efficient, impactful, and innovative organizations. However, the nonprofit sector is clearly dominated by organizations of insufficient scale to be effective. The behaviors of these organizations are dictated by the fact that they are competing for scarce resources. Small organizations lead to inefficiencies and duplication of effort. For instance, nonprofits with similar goals pursuing the same grant dollars and often the same clients, administrative expenses replicated many times over, and sacrificing big dreams in the name of remaining independent. This leads to a sector that struggles to achieve its mighty aims.

If we believe that consolidation, collaboration, and partnership would improve the efficiency and effectiveness of the sector, how do we convince individual actors to embrace these strategies? What are the barriers? Of course, working with others is more difficult than working alone. We value independence and self-direction, and partnering with others can compromise our identity and control. It also raises tough questions about who leads, who pays, who to trust, who must change, and who gets credit. Even so, the hard truth is that the problems most nonprofits work on are multifaceted, complicated, and typically larger than any one organization can tackle. So, we come back to the assertion that even with these barriers, nonprofits should collaborate and partner more than they do currently.

FUTURE LEADERS

Developing a clear understanding of *why* nonprofits collaborate or partner with one another equips you to better assess and promote partnership ideas. When nonprofit organizations choose to form relationships with one another, what is the catalyst? If all the reasons come down to either furthering the mission or improving financial health and viability, what are examples of those reasons? Future leaders can differentiate themselves and contribute real value by understanding the factors that drive success and exploring potential relationships with other nonprofits.

Why collaborate?

Nonprofits form relationships with one another with the following motivations (Figure 9.1):

- Complementary reasoning
- Competitive reasoning
- Efficiency reasoning
- Effectiveness reasoning

The broadest reasoning for collaboration is simply that the organizations complement one another in an important way. Perhaps each organization has developed teams with expertise that, when combined, offer the promise of a new and elegant solution. Or perhaps one organization brings needed expertise to another that has the trust and support of a community of stakeholders. Complementary reasoning is easy to understand and defend. We have A, they have B. We believe both A and B are necessary for success. We could develop what they have, but that would take precious time and resources. That approach would delay our ability to have the impact we desire, and it might also be wasteful since we are duplicating something already in existence. When complementary reasoning is used to justify a relationship, it typically has competitive, efficiency, or effectiveness implications.

RELATIONSHIP CATALYSTS

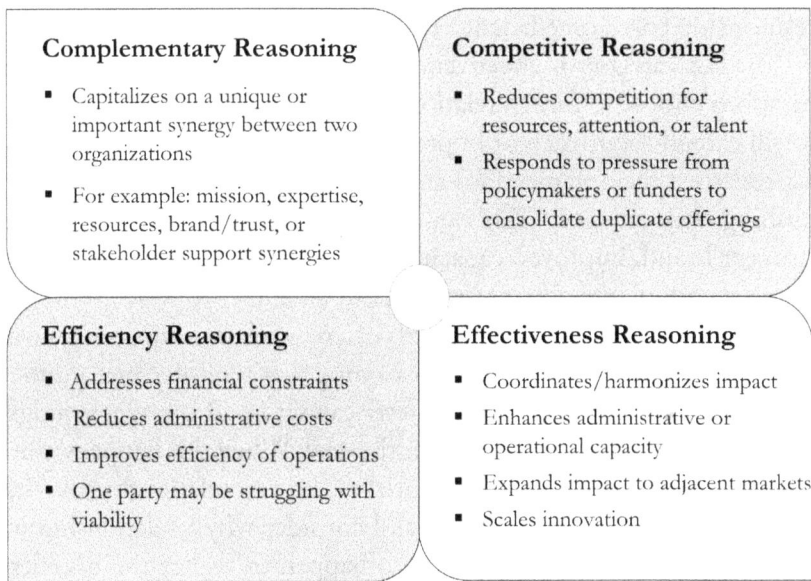

Complementary Reasoning

- Capitalizes on a unique or important synergy between two organizations

- For example: mission, expertise, resources, brand/trust, or stakeholder support synergies

Competitive Reasoning

- Reduces competition for resources, attention, or talent

- Responds to pressure from policymakers or funders to consolidate duplicate offerings

Efficiency Reasoning

- Addresses financial constraints
- Reduces administrative costs
- Improves efficiency of operations
- One party may be struggling with viability

Effectiveness Reasoning

- Coordinates/harmonizes impact
- Enhances administrative or operational capacity
- Expands impact to adjacent markets
- Scales innovation

Figure 9.1 Relationship Catalysts

Competitive reasoning posits that a relationship can reduce the competitive pressures felt by each organization. It may be that their mission and brands are similar enough that they repeatedly find themselves competing for the attention of policymakers, donors, clients, or even talent. The idea behind competitive reasoning is that the two organizations can accomplish more by removing the effort spent competing with one another. This may also be in response to pressure from others. For example, funders who have grown tired of funding two organizations trying to accomplish the same goal but refusing to work together.

Forming a relationship for reasons of efficiency can be out of necessity (e.g., to allow one organization to remain viable). Like competitive reasoning, an efficiency-based relationship can reduce the financial pressures felt by each organization. For example, economies of scale (i.e., the cost advantages enjoyed by larger organizations) that are beyond the reach of many small nonprofits can be realized once a relationship is formed. Or perhaps a reduction in overhead costs will allow more effort to flow to mission activities. Imagine two commuters stuck in traffic on the highway. Ridesharing may not get them to their destination any faster, but at least they are each able to save on fuel costs and environmental impact. That's a relationship based on efficiency reasoning.

The last category is effectiveness reasoning, where two or more organizations choose to form a relationship based primarily on the belief that it will extend their reach or improve their leverage and impact. By working together, the organizations are more likely to be successful in accomplishing their mission. This can be the result of better coordination, a stronger brand, improved capacity, employee development or specialization, expanding into adjacent markets, or an ability to scale innovation.

When contemplating the benefits of a new relationship, those involved usually develop multiple lines of reasoning that reinforce one another. Be aware—as excitement grows, *deal fever* can set in. This is where judgment becomes clouded by enthusiasm for the deal. When this happens, warning signs may be ignored and the potential of the new relationship overstated. In this situation, try to step back and consider why a relationship might present problems and what needs to happen to realize the benefits you envision. The different reasons a relationship makes sense are often related to the same root cause. For example, it may be that a single employee is the source of most of the value you see in an attractive partner. What happens if they decide to leave after you partner with their organization? When quantifying the benefits of a proposed relationship, make sure you understand the path to achieving them and that you aren't describing the same path two or three times over!

The reasons two or more nonprofits should collaborate or partner are not always easy to separate. It's helpful to define the goals of a relationship with these overlapping benefits in mind. As we will discuss later in this chapter, having shared clarity in these relationship goals (along with noting expected challenges) will guide the strategy and equip you to structure the relationship in a way that provides the greatest chance to realize those goals.[2]

EXECUTIVES & MANAGERS

This chapter is about relationships between nonprofit organizations. But before we get into that, let's discuss other common relationships. Collaborations with government entities, philanthropic funders, and academics introduce a whole slew of different issues. We'll discuss each of these briefly (and candidly) so we can set these issues aside and focus on the task at hand.

Relationships with government entities

Relationships with government entities (either as funders or partners) can be challenging for nonprofits. Government entities are rule-bound, which constrains their flexibility and can limit their effectiveness. Unfortunately, it is also common for those working in government roles to be somewhat disconnected from the "truth on the ground," which complicates setting and achieving shared goals. A government partner that is rigid in their view of the problem or unreasonable in their timeline of expected progress quickly moves from being a collaborator to someone that needs to be distracted and kept out of the way. When candor is replaced by perception management (a euphemism for information warfare), it is safe to say the parties are no longer truly collaborating.

Relationships with funders

Similar issues arise in relationships with philanthropic funders. Like government relationships, there is a power differential. Project officers can be

---

2. An enterprising student or researcher should develop a useful logic model of the reasons why nonprofits partner (or not) and the factors that drive success. Such a tool would help leaders better understand the chain of attributes and decisions necessary to achieve desired outcomes.

naïve or rigid in their beliefs, and nonprofit teams are effectively incentivized to exaggerate progress or be less than fully transparent about challenges encountered along the way. Nevertheless, it is more common for honest collaboration to occur between nonprofits and philanthropic funders. While philanthropic organizations can be bureaucratic, they can also be more creative and flexible than government entities. It is common for the staff of philanthropic organizations to have dedicated many years of their careers to a particular problem domain. This means they are more likely to understand and anticipate on the ground issues and share the nonprofit team's passion for success. While similarly equipped people do work in government, the bureaucratic culture focuses on administering a structured process rather than working together to understand and achieve desired outcomes.

Relationships with academics

Speaking of people dedicated to understanding an issue, academics can make excellent nonprofit partners. Though, they too come with unique challenges. Academics can be painfully esoteric, slow, and dithering, and they tend to be better problem describers than problem solvers. It is also relatively common for research motivations to get in the way of efficient project execution. For example, your academic partner might insist that an irrationally long and complicated survey be completed by your clients. Of course, there are exceptions to these generalizations. Some academics are incredibly efficient and revel in the application of their knowledge to solving real-world problems. Some not only offer a wealth of knowledge but also an incredible network of relationships and a passion for change. I'd say the 80/20 rule is a good proxy here for the distribution of useful, effective academic partners. Perhaps that's too harsh, maybe it's 60/40—I'll leave it to you to judge. In the end, finding a really good academic partner is probably worth the hassle.

Action-oriented nonprofits engaging in direct service delivery (i.e., an intervention) can struggle to collaborate efficiently with any (or all) of these kinds of partners. They can find themselves torn between government or philanthropic funders (who may have naïve beliefs about what is attainable and at what pace and cost) and academic partners who overly complicate project design and slow execution. Nonprofit teams bouncing between meetings with funders that seem disconnected from reality and with academics who only want to have esoteric philosophical debates grow frustrated and less receptive to future collaboration. This is unfortunate because effective collaboration with these partners can be enlightening and empowering.

Collaboration between nonprofits

Earlier in this chapter, we explored the reasons that nonprofits decide to pursue relationships with one another. Now let's review the typical forms that those relationships take. Figure 9.2 lists a range of relationship strategies along with comparisons of their relative frequency and level of disruption.

RELATIONSHIP STRATEGIES

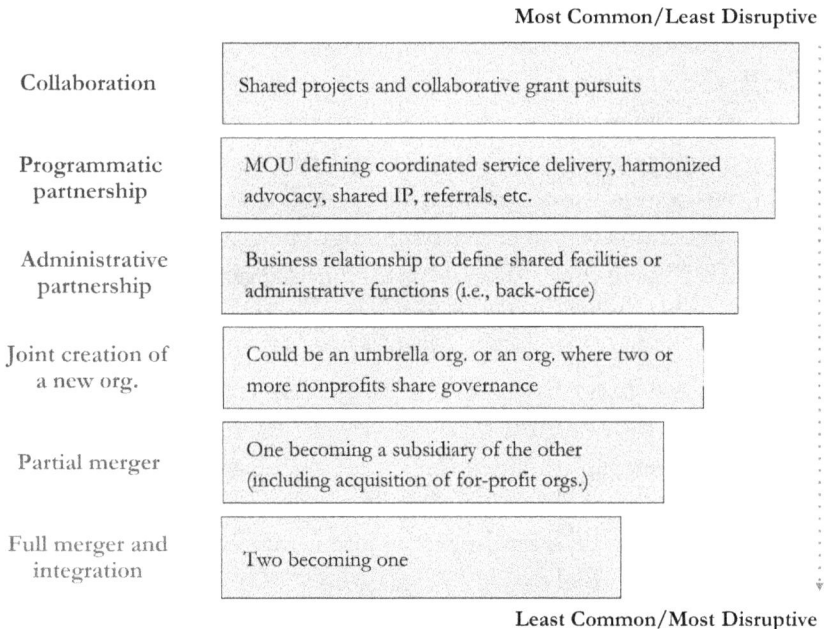

Most Common/Least Disruptive

Collaboration	Shared projects and collaborative grant pursuits
Programmatic partnership	MOU defining coordinated service delivery, harmonized advocacy, shared IP, referrals, etc.
Administrative partnership	Business relationship to define shared facilities or administrative functions (i.e., back-office)
Joint creation of a new org.	Could be an umbrella org. or an org. where two or more nonprofits share governance
Partial merger	One becoming a subsidiary of the other (including acquisition of for-profit orgs.)
Full merger and integration	Two becoming one

Least Common/Most Disruptive

Figure 9.2 Relationship Strategies

The most common way two nonprofits collaborate with one another is in the joint pursuit of grants and cooperation in the execution of projects. If you've spent any time with nonprofits, this is likely a familiar concept.

It is usually based on an assessment that two organizations have complementary expertise, relationships with funders, or stakeholders—which means they increase their odds of success by working together. This form of collaboration is also useful to assess fit and build trust before embarking on more formal relationships.

Relationships, such as *programmatic* or *administrative partnerships*, are more formal and involve contracting for a defined set of services. An example of a programmatic partnership is two nonprofits agreeing to work together in a defined way over multiple projects or grants. Another example is two organizations agreeing to harmonize their messaging around a particular issue and coordinate their advocacy for policy change. There are many examples of programmatic partnerships in the nonprofit sector that have been beneficial to the organizations involved.

Less common are administrative partnerships. Sometimes, two nonprofits can lower their individual overhead costs by agreeing to jointly fund certain administrative activities. There is untapped potential in this type of relationship because administrative functions (e.g., contracting, IT, HR, and accounting) are fairly similar across organizations, and most administrative departments in nonprofits aren't large enough to benefit from economies of scale. Add the risks of being reliant on the expertise of one or two key employees (inherent to a small organization) and you can see why an administrative partnership might be a good alternative.

There are three forms of *structural relationships*: the joint creation of a new organization (i.e., a joint venture), a partial merger (i.e., an acquisition whereby one becomes a subsidiary of the other), and, finally, the full merger and integration of two organizations (i.e., two becoming one). Each of these relationships takes significant planning and effort to execute, and a thorough analysis of mergers and acquisitions (M&A) is beyond the scope of this book. While structural relationships between two nonprofits can be rewarding, they also bring disruption and risks that are more consequential than other relationship forms. Yes, there are benefits to be had, but there are also plenty of horror stories!

Before embarking on a significant structural relationship with another organization, it is prudent to test the waters with less risky pursuits to give the leaders and teams an opportunity to work with one another, build rapport, and assess cultural fit. Too often, nonprofit executives pursue structural relationships without this early form of due diligence. The concept of "diligence" also tends to change after an executive decides that a structural relationship is the desired outcome. Like in a court case, the burden of proof shifts based on the context. *Before* a structural relationship is an explicit goal, the focus is on fit and feasibility (to prove there is real potential to be realized). *Afterward*, the focus inevitably shifts to demonstrating that the risks involved are acceptable (the burden of proof shifts to proving a deal does *not* make sense). The trouble is, once you let the horses out of the barn, it's harder to get the saddle on. Unfortunately, as a result, many structural relationships are entered into without an adequate understanding of their true costs or likelihood of success.

Sometimes, one plus one can equal three, where the combination of brands, resources, and talents equals more than the sum of the parts (i.e., synergy). This is the strategic story executives and boards tell themselves when considering these kinds of deals. However, there is nearly always a power dynamic at play when two organizations form a structural relationship. How likely is it that the two organizations are equally positioned and perfectly complementary? While a positive outcome for both organizations is possible (and hopefully desired by both parties), it is common for some outcomes to feel like a failure to one of the parties involved.

Even when the desired strategic outcomes are realized, success isn't necessarily equally distributed across organizations, departments, projects, or employees. Executives and managers would do well to embrace this reality in their own considerations and in their communications with others. Consolidation is essential to strengthening the nonprofit sector. I'm just noting that it can be quite painful for some of those involved. Going in with your eyes open to the pain points and being committed to transparent discussions during the process increases your odds of a satisfactory outcome.

Success factors

We've discussed: 1) why nonprofits form relationships with one another and 2) the forms those relationships can take. Now let's turn to what executives and managers can do to create the conditions necessary for success.

Collaboration involves two or more parties identifying shared interests and deliberately prioritizing them over narrower individual interests. Overcoming our narrow interests isn't easy. Giving up some element of control, sharing our most coveted ideas, and committing resources all involve some level of risk. Pursuing a relationship requires consideration of that risk and deciding that the potential benefits outweigh it. If we were for-profit leaders, the "benefits" would typically be based on the self-interests of our company—that is, how will the relationship increase our profits?

Nonprofit leaders, on the other hand, are again faced with the fiduciary/impact dilemma. Our decisions are not only guided by our organization's self-interests but also by our mission interests. We must consider how a relationship will benefit our organization *and* how it will benefit our cause. Ultimately, nonprofit leaders should view relationships through this broader lens. Are the risks acceptable given the benefits that accrue to the organization *plus* those that accrue directly to the organization's mission? An example of this trade-off would be giving up grant dollars and control of some aspects of a program in order to improve the quality of services you can deliver through collaboration. Forming a partnership before you pursue the grant might be driven by self-interest (because you feel they increase your odds of winning). Adding a partner after you receive a grant is a clear example of considering mission interests. (By sharing your resources, you expect to improve mission effectiveness.)

Embarking on a relationship is typically a stepwise pursuit. It progresses in a series of distinct stages.

- Researching and assessing the merits of a potential partner.
- Introductory discussions to assess how the two organizations complement one another.
- Determining a course of collaboration that is relatively low risk, allowing you to "kick the tires" and discern the boundary between how the potential partner portrays and promotes themselves versus their actual capabilities and interests. It also allows both parties to begin to assess cultural fit and shared values and goals.
- Progressing to moderately risky partnering efforts. This typically takes the form of defining some future vision and committing to working toward it together. Perhaps you give up some element of control or more formally commit to sharing resources.
- Bumps in the road either weaken or strengthen the partnership. The bumps tend to highlight the distinction between short-term

self-interests and long-term shared interests. How you and your partner react can either instill confidence or erode trust. If things progress positively, working together in this more meaningful way naturally builds a sense of shared identity.

- Over time, trust and confidence grow, which opens the door to taking larger steps together and moving down the relationship strategy chart as detailed in Figure 9.2.

Along this journey, there are things you can do to increase the probability of success and ensure the collaboration lasts long enough to accomplish your goals.[3] The first is to be deliberate and explicit about your goals and your choice of partner. The more complementary the two organizations are, the higher the odds of success. As you begin having conversations with an organization, the more explicit you can be, the better. In fact, throughout the entire relationship, it's what is implied but not explicit that tends to cause trouble. Be clear about why you are seeking to partner, what you bring to the partnership, what you're willing to commit over the long term, and what you expect from your partner. When you begin working together, the clarity and precision of the division of labor (i.e., defining exactly who is going to do what) is particularly important to avoid misunderstandings.

Next, recognize that new relationships typically involve near-term costs and long-term benefits. In the near term, you may feel you're giving up too much or incurring too many costs to fit the new collaborative model. The number of unknowns early in a relationship also makes the risk feel less acceptable. As trust and confidence have not yet blossomed, it's easy to get distracted by excessive "what if" concerns.

Each of us has a different propensity to engage in this kind of thinking—ranging from rational considerations to maintain awareness and mitigate risks to an irrational and unhealthy obsession with conspiratorial concerns. Too many beneficial collaborations have fallen victim to the paranoia of an insecure executive. As in other areas of life, giving your partner the benefit of the doubt is especially important early in the

---

3. Some of these ideas are also explored in Jacob Harold's excellent article: The Collaboration Game: Solving the Puzzle of Nonprofit Partnership. Jacob Harold. "The Collaboration Game: Solving the Puzzle of Nonprofit Partnership." Stanford Social Innovation Review. 2017. https://doi.org/10.48558/Z0QV-MQ13

process of building trust. Having confidence and well-developed aspirations for the future makes it easier for an executive to embrace shared goals and a long-term view. Placing too much emphasis on short-term motivations and contemplating everything that could go wrong will drag you off the path of accomplishing your vision for the future. If you're going to partner, act like a partner.

The third success factor is to reinforce a shared identity. There are many ways that this can be accomplished between two organizations: team building, marketing, sharing data, clearly defining responsibilities, being transparent about challenges, celebrating successes, etc. Jacob Harold refers to this as *designing collective systems,* which are "...formalized systems for knowledge sharing, governance, and external communications."[4]

A shared identity between two organizations builds confidence and positions each side of the partnership to navigate challenges as they arise. A shared identity won't develop on its own, however. You'll have to actively encourage it. It's hard enough to promote a shared identity across two departments within the same organization, much less between two different nonprofits. You need to get leadership together fairly frequently, but you also need to encourage the creation of social connections. People can feel integral to more than one team. They may have one role within your nonprofit and another role in the broader collaborative partnership. I've observed that employees who authentically feel part of more than one team are happier, more productive, and less risk averse. Building a shared identity creates the space needed for this to occur.

TRUSTEES

Collaboration and partnership are strategic tools to build scale, leverage, and reach. These concepts apply to both the work of the nonprofit and its ideas. For example, many nonprofits seek to address a problem by changing how it is perceived by stakeholders, policymakers, funders, or clients. We've discussed these change catalysts before. They seek to do so by shap-

---

4. Jacob Harold. "The Collaboration Game: Solving the Puzzle of Nonprofit Partnership." Stanford Social Innovation Review. 2017. https://doi.org/10.48558/Z0QV-MQ13

ing opinions about the perceived urgency of a problem or the feasibility and relative attractiveness of a certain solution.

Recall the story at the beginning of this chapter. Dr. Colborn was definitely a change catalyst. She had to enlist collaborators from many different disciplines to enrich the story she was trying to tell and to create the advocacy paths necessary to shape policy and public opinion. For most nonprofit organizations, success is highly dependent on stakeholders and often other nonprofits. For this reason, collaborating and partnering are important skills to develop within your nonprofit organization.

Trustees can play multiple roles in facilitating collaboration and partnership. The most straightforward is to connect your nonprofit with the leaders of other nonprofits you know. It is common to expect that you will leverage your network to benefit the organization in this way. However, on behalf of nonprofit employees everywhere—*please ask* before making connections. Board members can create inefficiencies by casting too wide a net and connecting leaders with third parties without coordination.

When you propose a connection, make sure to inquire in a way that elicits a candid response. It doesn't do the organization any good to have managers and executives taking meetings out of a polite obligation to you. Offer the connection, explain why you think it might be beneficial, and ask whether the connection would be appreciated and when the connection should be made. Here are four example responses you might receive:

- "Yes, the connection makes sense, but not right now because we are competing for the same grant."
- "We already have connections with that organization. Let me coordinate with my team to determine the best way to proceed."
- "While I appreciate your motivation, I don't see the strategic value in the connection you propose."
- "Yes, the connection makes sense and is particularly strategic at the moment, thank you!"

There are many reasons a connection may or may not be helpful at a particular moment in time. The trustee's role is to offer connections and perhaps even encourage them. If attending a meeting is really a favor to you, be upfront about it (e.g., you serve as a trustee for another nonprofit, and the meeting was requested by a contact at that organization). This type of ask is fine but be transparent. Meetings where both parties are in attendance out of a sense of obligation to a third party are rarely productive. They're sort of like play dates arranged by well-meaning but misguided parents or grandparents.

Another aspect of your role in collaboration and partnership is to be a balancing force when an executive is displaying signs of deal fever. It's easy to get wrapped up in a rosy vision of the future and exciting to consider the positive aspects of a prospective relationship. Your job is to encourage a candid and balanced assessment. As a member of the board, you can promote consideration of a relationship that offers exciting possibilities, but you also have an obligation to ensure your organization's leaders adequately understand what's required to realize those possibilities. This includes how likely they are to materialize, the full expected costs of the relationship, and the risks that should be mitigated in the structure of any formal relationship.

An important part of your role is to protect the assets of the organization, including protecting the board and leadership team from the distraction of a protracted process. Executives like to portray that they're excellent at multitasking and can handle anything that comes their way. Some executives see themselves as skilled deal brokers and experts in this form of organizational development. While I don't know your executive (and they may have unique skills), it's quite likely that they (and you) underestimate the true costs of these endeavors. The real organizational costs of assessing and implementing anything but the simplest of relationships are partially hidden. Due diligence efforts will uncover additional questions that need to be answered, and there is always an opportunity cost and distraction from other operational and strategic objectives. Therefore, it's important to only pose questions to the executive team that will have a material impact on the decision to proceed.

There are many reasons why a partnership may *not* be a good idea. Everything comes at a cost. There are tangible costs like advisory firms, legal counsel, transaction costs, and assuming debts and future obligations (which may be clouded by the practices employed to account for them). But there are also intangible costs like distracting from other strategic priorities or opportunities to employ capital elsewhere, culture clashes, turf wars between managers/executives, brand dilution issues, and other negative brand effects. Your job is to be clear-eyed about why a partnership either makes sense or doesn't and to understand the true costs and challenges that may arise along the way.

When two nonprofits decide to pursue any of the relationship strategies discussed here, the trustees of each organization have an obligation to ensure that the new relationship advances their organization's mission by:

- expanding the organization's reach;
- enhancing its capabilities and effectiveness;
- increasing efficiency by lowering costs; or
- mitigating some risk that looms in the future.

This requires a clear explanation of how the relationship is aligned with the charitable purpose of *your* organization and demonstrating how that purpose may be furthered by working together. It also means showing why other relationship options don't make as much sense as the chosen path. Why not partner with a different organization or pursue a different relationship strategy (e.g., perhaps you should explore a programmatic partnership before proceeding with an acquisition)?

Once you've decided to proceed with a partnership, there are a few unique governance considerations that apply to structural relationships (e.g., when one nonprofit "acquires" another). A *merger* occurs when two separate organizations combine forces to create a new joint organization. This is relatively rare among nonprofits. *Acquisitions* are far more common and refer to the takeover of one entity by another.

The term "acquisition" can be confusing when it comes to nonprofits. A nonprofit may acquire a for-profit entity (this is more common than you might think). To do this, they conduct due diligence and pay the owners of the for-profit for the assets of the organization. Assets, as used here, is a broad term inclusive of products, real estate, people, intellectual property, brands, client relationships, future revenue streams, etc. However, acquisition is a bit of a misnomer when applied to a nonprofit acquiring another nonprofit. A takeover of one nonprofit by another doesn't involve paying any owners for assets because, by definition, nonprofits do not have owners! This is why I use the term "partial merger" in Figure 9.2. When the boards of two nonprofits agree to a takeover, the rationale is typically based on both business and mission reasons.

For simplicity, let's label the two parties involved as the *surviving* organization and the *acquired* organization. With a merger, you'd have a *new* organization, and two *legacy* organizations. After a transaction is complete, each trustee of the surviving or new organization has a duty to act in the best interests of that organization. That raises the issue of how to protect the interests of acquired or legacy organizations after a transaction. There are a few ways to do this. However, none of them are foolproof.

The first thing that comes to mind for most trustees is representation on the surviving entity's board. One or more trustees of the acquired/legacy entity are named to serve on the surviving entity's board so that they may advocate for decisions that continue to reflect the spirit and intent of the initial agreement. While not a bad idea, this strategy isn't sufficient on its own to protect the interests of an acquired/legacy organization post-transaction.

First off, as mentioned, trustees have a duty to act in the best interests of the surviving entity—even if that means doing something they wouldn't have previously supported. Also, they are likely a minority voice on the board, may resign after a short stint, or could lose influence in other ways as the organization continues to evolve. One way to counteract this situation is to engage the representatives of the acquired/legacy organization in selecting new trustees (e.g., giving them a role on the nominations committee of the board). That way, they can influence the future evolution of the board.

Another way to protect the long-term interests of a legacy or acquired organization post-transaction is by defining investment or sustainment commitments. For example, a commitment could be made as part of the transaction agreement that key programs will be sustained or invested in at certain dollar levels over a period of time. In this scenario, tracking and reporting is necessary, as is setting up a committee to oversee that those commitments are kept. Note that all parties should be wary of tying the hands of the surviving organization too tightly as assumptions about the future are seldom valid for long.

An additional strategy is to protect certain values and interests in the surviving organization's governance documents and structure. Governance documents (bylaws) can be amended to emphasize the importance of the acquired/legacy organization's priorities, allowing their "purpose" to live on in the surviving organization. Additionally, a new committee of the board could be created to shepherd the integration of any legacy program activities adopted. This committee might have members from both organizations and can be given specific authority related to the integration, budgeting, and continuation of certain key program activities. This could be safeguarded in the bylaws by allowing the committee to elect its own members and by requiring a supermajority vote to change the delegated authority.

Ultimately, there's no denying that nonprofits should collaborate and partner more than they currently do. As governments flounder in their attempts to address stubborn societal problems, the need for nonprofit leadership grows. Many of these problems are multifaceted, and most are larger than any one organization can tackle. The nonprofit sector can deliver efficient, effective, and innovative solutions. However, because the nonprofit sector is so fragmented and dominated by small organizations, the path to leadership undeniably involves consolidation in the sector.

When introducing the fiduciary/impact dilemma that all nonprofit leaders face, I argued that only a handful of decisions simultaneously advance an organization's financial health and its impact. Pursuing collaboration and partnership can be one of those decisions. In fact, for most organizations, it may offer the greatest promise of advancing both objectives. Becoming an organization that is adept at collaborating and partnering with other nonprofits is not easy, but it is well worth the effort.

SUMMARY

- Competition for resources stimulates innovation and pushes organizations to be more efficient, but it also serves to keep the nonprofit sector fragmented. Nonprofits should collaborate and partner more than they currently do.
- When two nonprofits see themselves as competitors, they are less able to embrace collaborative strategies that would benefit them both.
- Collaboration raises tough questions about who leads, who pays, who to trust, who must change, and who gets credit. Even so, collaboration is necessary because the problems most nonprofits work on are multifaceted and complicated.
- Nonprofits form relationships for complementary, competitive, efficiency, and effectiveness reasons.
- The most common way two nonprofits collaborate with one another is in the joint pursuit of grants and cooperation in the execution of projects. Less common relationships are programmatic or administrative partnerships, joint creation of a new organization, partial mergers, and full mergers.
- Before embarking on a significant structural relationship with another organization, it's prudent to test the waters with less risky pursuits to give leaders and their teams the opportunity to work with one another.
- Relationships should be guided by a balanced assessment of the impact on each organization's finances and mission.
- Early due diligence is focused on proving the value of a potential partnership. Once an executive declares their intention to pursue a structural relationship, that is presumed to be the correct course of action and the burden of proof shifts to proving a deal does *not* make sense.
- Confidence and well-developed aspirations for the future make it easier for an executive to embrace shared goals and a long-term view. Too much emphasis on short-term motivations will drag you off the path of accomplishing your vision.

- Collaboration and partnership are strategic tools to build scale, leverage, and reach. These concepts apply to both the work of the nonprofit and its ideas.
- Trustees have an obligation to thoroughly understand the financial and mission implications of a proposed relationship. This includes protecting the interests of acquired and/or legacy organizations after a transaction.

10
A CALL TO ACTION

When day comes, we step out of the shade, aflame and unafraid. The new dawn blooms as we free it. For there is always light, if only we're brave enough to see it. If only we're brave enough to be it.

—National Youth Poet Laureate Amanda Gorman

T HANK YOU FOR coming this far on our journey together. This last chapter is going to be a little different, and it starts with a request of you, dear reader. This book is based on the premise that being a good organizational steward while maximizing impact isn't easy. Nonprofit leadership is uniquely challenging because advancing an organization's mission and advancing its financial health are often at odds with one another. *The Nonprofit Dilemma* was written to better equip you for this challenge by delivering ideas, tools, resources, and advice to help you balance these competing objectives. Hopefully, this book has equipped you to be a better nonprofit leader in some way. Now, my only request of you in return is simple: *lead*.

It is my opinion that the nonprofit sector suffers from a dearth of courage. Too many of us prioritize caution and stability over innovation and progress. We prefer the comfort of studying and planning over trying and possibly failing. We tend to overcomplicate and overthink things and allow ourselves to be distracted by chasing the next grant, planning the next fundraising campaign, or preparing for the next board meeting. In countless nonprofit boardrooms, there is a prevailing tendency to prioritize further research at the expense of taking decisive action. Executives waffle and equivocate. Trustees quibble and pontificate. Instead of embracing clarity and accountability, nonprofit board members have a propensity to rationalize and offer praise where it isn't warranted.

Progress is seldom measured in studies and reports; it's measured in action and outcomes. Wallowing in the comfort of excessively risk-averse governance harms nonprofits and their raison d'etre. What good is it to carefully preserve your organization long into the future if it never accomplishes anything meaningful? Boards that encourage bold action and accountability are boards that develop exceptional nonprofit leaders and more effective organizations.

Balancing the desire to make a difference with the desire to maintain one's position and reputation is a struggle for most nonprofit executives. Compensation programs typically prioritize short-term goals over long-term impact. Alienating stakeholders or disappointing board members is an all-too-common fear. Together, these considerations discourage leaders from taking real risks. Some are inclined to equate stability with effectiveness. Others are so prone to inaction that they don't embrace innovation when it is clearly called for. And yet, most are still encouraged and praised for their "leadership."

I ask you to be brave. Acknowledge and overcome your fears. Respectfully call out colleagues when they prefer the safety of reflection and inaction over the gamble of taking action and expending resources. *Action is necessary* to advance the organization and the cause that you care about. Whether you are a future leader, a current manager or executive, or a trustee, have the confidence to dream big, be bold and decisive, embrace risk, and encourage action.

In the introduction, I asked: *What is preventing you from changing the world for the better?* I hope you found something in these pages that helps you to overcome that barrier; something you can take to heart, that makes your job easier, and that inspires you to act. Ultimately, I hope this book helps you to become a better leader—an *exceptional* one, in fact.

Exceptional purpose-driven leaders strive for absolute clarity in their organization's goals and their role in achieving them. Their success comes from defining strategies that set their nonprofit apart—strategies that advance their organization's mission *and* financial health. These leaders use their strategic voice to promote focused execution, honest measurement, and transparency. They are bold and action-oriented. Over time, this allows the compelling story of the nonprofit's impact to emerge. They use this story to develop the business, create organizational leverage, and establish the foundation necessary for long-term success. They build and inspire a team that's diverse and passionate. To nurture that team's culture, they embody key values by consistently communicating, reinforcing, and integrating them into all decisions. They provide honest feedback to colleagues, hold them accountable for their actions, and empower them for success. And finally, to further their organization's impact, they forge effective partnerships and motivate collaborators to action.

I believe *you* can be this leader (if you aren't already). While the fiduciary/impact dilemma presents many challenges, you can be creative, resilient, and driven. As we've explored, fiduciary/impact trade-offs are sometimes easy to discern, and at other times, they require careful consideration to uncover the true impact of a particular decision. Therefore, as you embrace your leadership role, I encourage you to be introspective, thoughtful, and inclusive. These qualities are essential for evaluating your own actions and motivations, determining what's best for your organization, and building high-performing teams. By honing these three attributes, you will undoubtedly evolve into a more effective leader; one whose daily actions reflect an admirable sense of purpose and a commitment to building an insightful, healthy, and innovative nonprofit.

At times, you will fail. Understand that failure is just part of the process of leadership. Dust yourself off and get back to work with even more determination. Your resilience bolsters the morale of those around you, showing them that setbacks are not roadblocks but merely stepping stones toward success. In your journey as a leader, remember that achieving mission success requires resolve and the ability to use failure as a source of wisdom and motivation. Embrace each challenge as an opportunity to learn, adapt, and ultimately emerge as an even stronger and more exceptional nonprofit leader.

There is one vital ingredient to success that we haven't yet discussed. Something some readers will dismiss as corny. Ultimately, the secret to effective nonprofit leadership is love—love for your organization, for your colleagues, and for the people, community, or ideas that your nonprofit serves. Love will motivate and guide your actions, it will bolster your energy and resilience, and it will drive you to work more purposefully and collaboratively. Your integrity as a leader comes from recognizing and embracing that love. It's impossible to be an exceptional nonprofit leader without it. If you do not love your organization, its mission, or working alongside your colleagues, ask yourself what needs to change. Consider whether *you* need to be the agent of change in your organization or whether you need to change organizations altogether. Life is truly short. If you have your heart set on a purpose-driven career, then take whatever action is necessary so that you may lead with love. It is the most fulfilling way to lead your career and your life. Onward and upward, my friend!

APPENDIX:

TYPES OF NONPROFITS IN THE U.S.

T HE TERMS "NONPROFIT" and "not-for-profit" are often used interchangeably. They differentiate between organizations that exist for a
public or charitable purpose (nonprofit) and those that aim to only benefit their members (not-for-profit). Not-for-profit can also be used to
describe the activities and goals of an organization to differentiate it from
similar organizations that pursue a profit. For example, banks are for-
profit financial institutions and credit unions are not-for-profit financial
institutions. Banks conduct their activities with the aim of earning a profit
for the bank's owners, while credit unions reinvest profits back into the
organization for the benefit of the credit union's members.

The distinctions between nonprofit and not-for-profit are not uni-
versally agreed upon, and terminology can vary from one jurisdiction to
another. In practice, however, both nonprofit and not-for-profit organizations share the fundamental characteristic of being mission-driven organizations that exist for some reason other than generating profit for private
individuals or shareholders. Any surplus funds generated must be reinvested into the organization to further the purpose for which it was created.

Nonprofit organizations provide benefits to society that private sector
companies may not. Section 501(c) of the U.S. tax code defines more
than two dozen tax-exempt organization types. These include many kinds
of organizations whose purpose is decidedly *not* profit generation. These
organizations include: cemeteries, fraternal societies, religious organizations, chambers of commerce, labor unions, veterans' organizations, political organizations, recreational clubs, certain insurance organizations, and
many others.

In each of these tax-exempt examples, some earnings may still be subject to the Unrelated Business Income Tax (UBIT). This tax applies to revenues earned by a tax-exempt entity for activities unrelated to its tax-exempt purpose. Additionally, no part of net earnings may be used to benefit individuals who have a close relationship with the organization or exercise significant influence over the organization. This is referred to as "private inurement" (inurement is an old term for benefit). All tax-exempt organizations are subject to inurement rules, which means officers, board members, and key employees are prohibited from using the organization's assets for personal gain.

While many kinds of organizations may be tax-exempt, the rules and regulations that apply to them vary. This is predominantly determined by evaluating who benefits from the organization's activities. Some tax-exempt organizations have a clear public purpose. Others only benefit a specific community, group, or set of members. To illustrate this, let's explore three organization types, their IRS designations, and their unique characteristics.

1. **Organizations with a public purpose: IRS designation 501(c)(3)**

  - *Definition.* Operated *exclusively* for the public good. This includes religious, charitable, scientific, public safety, public health, animal welfare, literary, and educational purposes. These organizations represent the largest category of tax-exempt nonprofits and are the primary audience for this book.
  - *Examples.* Libraries, museums, churches, hospitals, cancer research and support groups, and public charities like the United Way, Feeding America, and the Salvation Army. Also included are private foundations like The Bill and Melinda Gates Foundation, The Ford Foundation, and The Robert Wood Johnson Foundation.
  - *Tax treatment.* Exempt from most federal taxes. Contributions are usually tax-deductible for the donor. Contributions are not subject to federal gift tax. Assets and activities must be dedicated to the defined charitable purpose.
  - *Additional notes*

- Financial and operating information for these organizations must be made public.
- Advocacy and lobbying activities are limited. They can educate politicians on both sides of the aisle to support legislation aligned with their mission. However, lobbying (i.e., attempting to influence legislation) cannot be a substantial part of the organization's activities. Endorsement or critique of specific candidates is also not allowed.
- For most 501(c)(3)s, the board has the power to elect its own members, and bylaws and policies can be easily amended by the board.

2. **Organizations with an advocacy or social welfare purpose: IRS designation 501(c)(4)**

- *Definition.* Operated exclusively for the promotion of social welfare. These organizations are meant to promote the common good and general welfare of a *group* of people.
- *Examples.* Organizations working to advance reproductive or civil rights, civic leagues (e.g., Rotary, Kiwanis, and Lions), social welfare organizations, voluntary fire departments, community associations, veterans' organizations, local employee associations, and advocacy organizations like The National Rifle Association.
- *Tax treatment.* Exempt from most federal taxes. However, contributions are *not* tax-deductible and may be subject to federal gift tax.
- *Additional notes*
  - This broad IRS category is a catch-all for nonprofit organizations that can't be classified under other 501(c) subsections.
  - These organizations do not need to disclose the names of donors to the IRS when filing annual Form 990 returns.

- They are allowed to engage in unlimited lobbying provided that the lobbying is related to the organization's exempt purpose.
- They are prohibited from engaging primarily in political activity (political campaigning), though they are sometimes formed alongside political action committees (PACs) to keep donor identities secret (referred to as "dark money").
- For most 501(c)(4)s, the board has the power to elect its own members and officers.

3. **Organizations with a membership purpose: IRS designation 501(c)(6)**

   - *Definition.* Membership organizations are associations of people with a common business interest. These organizations exist to benefit members of a *specific* group.
   - *Examples.* Business leagues (which are trade or professional associations like the American Dental Association), chambers of commerce, boards of trade, economic development corporations, and real estate boards. There are currently over 70,000 organizations in the U.S. with this IRS designation.
   - *Tax treatment.* Income is exempt from most federal income taxes. Contributions are *not* tax-deductible and may be subject to federal gift tax. However, membership dues are often deductible as a business expense.
   - *Additional notes*
     - They do not need to disclose the names of donors to the IRS when filing annual Form 990 returns.
     - They are allowed to engage in lobbying that is germane to the organization's tax-exempt purpose.
     - Board members and officers are elected by the membership, and terms are usually clearly defined. Board seats can be very competitive.
     - Bylaws and policy changes usually require a membership vote and are thus less frequent than at

other nonprofits. Governing bylaws can also be more formal than in other nonprofits.

These examples are three of the twenty-five tax-exempt organization types defined in section 501(c) of the U.S. tax code. As you can see, there is a lot of variation in U.S. tax-exempt organizations and the regulations that apply to them. *The Nonprofit Dilemma* is primarily concerned with the development of 501(c)(3) leaders, so let's explore the two major types of 501(c)(3) organizations. IRS Section 509(a) classifies 501(c)(3) organizations based on their sources of financial support and their activities. This determines an organization's status as either a *private foundation* or a *public charity*.

Private foundations

Most private foundations have a single source of funding (e.g., a major gift from a family or corporation). These foundations are typically focused on funding the work of public charities rather than delivering charitable programs themselves.

Private foundations are usually "closely governed," meaning the activities, policies, investments, and grant-making decisions of the foundation are controlled by a small group of individuals or even a single family. As such, private foundations are subject to stringent tax rules, including restrictions on self-dealing and minimum payout requirements—though they typically have more control than public charities over how their funds are distributed. As of publication, the ten largest private foundations in the U.S. are:

1. The Bill and Melinda Gates Foundation
2. The Ford Foundation
3. The Getty Foundation
4. The Lilly Endowment
5. The Robert Wood Johnson Foundation
6. The William and Flora Hewlett Foundation
7. The W. K. Kellogg Foundation
8. The Bloomberg Family Foundation
9. The David and Lucile Packard Foundation

10. The Gordon and Betty Moore Foundation

Public charities

Public charities must receive the *majority* of their income from public sources including individuals, foundations, corporations, and government entities. It's important for public charities to track their sources of support annually, maintain accurate records, and ensure that they meet these public support requirements.

Public charities also have more restrictions than private foundations on how their funds are used and must follow strict rules regarding their governance and operations. Here are the various types of public charities organized by purpose:

- *Animal rescue and cruelty prevention.* Organizations that work to rescue and rehabilitate animals in need, promote responsible pet ownership, and advocate for animal welfare. Examples include The Humane Society of the United States, the American Society for the Prevention of Cruelty to Animals, wildlife conservation organizations, and local animal shelters, sanctuaries, and rescues.
- *Child welfare.* Organizations dedicated to promoting the well-being, safety, and development of children and youth. Examples include Boys & Girls Clubs, Children's Advocacy Centers, Court Appointed Special Advocates for Children, Big Brothers Big Sisters of America, The Children's Defense Fund, and family services organizations.
- *Cultural and arts.* Museums, theaters, art galleries, and cultural institutions that promote the arts and cultural activities.
- *Educational.* Schools, colleges, universities, and other educational institutions. They must operate exclusively for educational purposes to qualify for tax-exempt status.
- *Food and nutrition.* Organizations focused on addressing food insecurity, promoting healthy eating habits, advocating for sustainable agriculture, improving maternal and child nutrition, and raising awareness about nutrition-related issues.
- *Healthcare.* Hospitals, medical research institutions, community health centers, hospices, free clinics, mental health and behavioral

health organizations, global health organizations, blood banks, and transplant organizations.

- *Literary.* Organizations focused on the promotion of literature, such as libraries, literary societies, and organizations that support authors and writers.
- *Religious.* Churches, synagogues, mosques, temples, and other religious institutions fall under this category. They are automatically considered tax-exempt under 501(c)(3) without having to apply for recognition.
- *Scientific.* Organizations dedicated to scientific research, development, and education. Organizations dedicated to safeguarding the environment, conserving natural resources, and advocating for policies and practices that promote sustainability are good examples of these kinds of nonprofits.

AFTERWORD

THANK YOU FOR investing your time in reading this book. Those of us driven to make a difference in the world need to support one another. If you found value in these pages, please help me accomplish my mission of delivering value to as many nonprofit leaders as possible by recommending it to your friends and colleagues.

**It would only take five minutes to leave a short comment or review about this book wherever you bought it.

If you bought this book on Amazon, use this QR code to leave a review:

If you bought this book anywhere else, use this QR code to leave a review:

It can be difficult and frustrating to read embedded graphics in e-books, and sometimes you just want to customize a chart or graphic for your own presentation. If you purchased this book and would like an electronic copy of the figures, visit **nonprofitdilemma.com** and use the contact form to request a copy.

Here's a QR code to take you directly to the request form:

You can also read my blog or contact me at **nonprofitdilemma.com**. Feel free to comment on a section of the book, ask a question, or share a dilemma occurring in your nonprofit—I would love to hear from you!

ACKNOWLEDGMENTS

T HE WORLD IS a better place thanks to countless people who dedicate their lives to meaningful work. If you get up every morning and strive to change the world for the better—thank you!

This book would not have been possible without the incredible support I received from my stellar editors Sarah Busby and Lisa MacDonald. Thank you both for being such brilliant writing partners. Thanks to my family for supporting this crazy endeavor. Especially my wife (Shannon) and daughter (Norah) for reviewing and editing multiple early drafts. I'd also like to thank Phillip Gessert for impeccable interior design and formatting, my indexer Sandy Blood (what a great name she has!), my cover designer James Jones (a true artist), and my web developer Rich Radimer (check out his handy work at nonprofitdilemma.com).

I am also indebted to my amazing beta readers for their advice and counsel: Katie Aleck, Beth Beaudin-Seiler, Molly Carmody, Stacy Cook, Carley Kirk, Greg Matthews, Rachelle May-Gentile, Haley McCrary, George Miller, Kristi Mitchell, and Joshua Seidman. I'd also like to thank Dr. Renée Branch Canady for contributing the wonderful foreword (check out her excellent book: *Room at the Table*).

Finally, I'd like to acknowledge the people who've most influenced and shaped my perspective on leadership and ethics: retired police chief Joseph Koren (my wife's late grandfather), the late Carl R. Vann (the Oakland University professor who encouraged me to pursue a purpose-driven career), John R. Griffith (professor emeritus at the University of Michigan School of Public Health, and the father of modern hospital administration), and Linc Smith (a remarkably talented and purpose-driven CEO). These four men were role models, confidants, and mentors. They shared their knowledge freely and held me to a higher standard than I held myself.

INDEX

AUTHOR

D C Armijo is an accomplished executive and award-winning author with over twenty-five years of nonprofit leadership experience. His dedication to purpose-driven work is founded in a childhood marked by poverty and a father's illness. Those early challenges gave him the lifelong gifts of resilience, empathy, and purpose. He believes the nonprofit sector has grown increasingly important in the U.S. because of a decline in governmental effectiveness and floundering public policy. As a result, we need more nonprofit leaders who are driven and equipped to make a difference.

After beginning his career in hospital administration, DC transitioned to working for nonprofits focused on environmental and public health concerns. He has led initiatives in substance abuse, veterans' health, maternal health, nutrition, children's health, and public health technology. He has served in a variety of nonprofit leadership roles including: senior policy analyst, director, SVP, COO, CEO, fellow, and board member. He has mentored executives, led expert panels, chaired board committees, shaped state and federal policies, and written over $100 million in successful grant proposals.

DC has also designed and launched a free clinic, led the strategy and operations of a large nonprofit government contractor, created a leadership development program, divested a for-profit subsidiary, and directed several multi-state federal health programs over his career.

DC has a bachelor's degree in anthropology and health behavior from Oakland University and a master's degree in health services administration from the University of Michigan. He is married and has a college-aged daughter. He spends his time between Michigan and Naples, FL. His blog can be found at **nonprofitdilemma.com**.

www.ingramcontent.com/pod-product-compliance
Lightning Source LLC
Chambersburg PA
CBHW071549210326
41597CB00019B/3178